TEACHING QUEER

Pittsburgh Series in Composition, Literacy, and Culture
David Bartholomae and Jean Ferguson Carr, Editors

TEACHING QUEER

Radical Possibilities for Writing and Knowing

STACEY WAITE

UNIVERSITY OF PITTSBURGH PRESS

Published by the University of Pittsburgh Press, Pittsburgh, Pa., 15260
Copyright © 2017, University of Pittsburgh Press
All rights reserved
Manufactured in the United States of America
Printed on acid-free paper
10 9 8 7 6 5 4 3 2 1

Cataloging-in-Publication data is available from the Library of Congress

ISBN 13: 978-0-8229-6457-5
ISBN 10: 0-8229-6457-0

Cover art: Cy Twombly, *Untitled*, 1966. Oil-based house paint, wax crayon on canvas, 74 ¾ × 78 ¾ in. (190 × 200 cm). © Cy Twombly Foundation.
Cover design by Jordan Wannemacher

For Brie and Max, who are my greatest teachers

CONTENTS

Acknowledgments

ix

Introduction

3

CHAPTER ONE

Becoming the Loon: Queer Masculinities, Queer Pedagogies

27

CHAPTER TWO

Courting Failure

56

CHAPTER THREE

Alternative Orientations

86

CHAPTER FOUR

Becoming Liquid: Queer Interpretations

125

CHAPTER FIVE

Queer (Re)Visions of Composition

167

Works Cited

195

Index

203

ACKNOWLEDGMENTS

I am deeply blessed and actively engaged every day by being a part of a vibrant, dedicated English department and an amazing team of composition faculty at the University of Nebraska–Lincoln. I am so grateful to Rachel Azima, Robert Brooke, Amy Goodburn, June Griffin, Debbie Minter, Rachael Wendler Shah, and Shari Stenberg, whose commitment to teaching and composition is an inspiration to me in my own classrooms and in my own writing. I give my thanks to my department chair, Marco Abel, whose guidance, support, and friendship have made it possible for me to write and publish this book, and I also owe a debt of thanks to my research assistants: Mitch Hobza, Katelyn Hemmeke, Kirby Little, and Wyn Richards.

I also give my gratitude to wonderful friends, family, and colleagues who supported this work in ways they might not even know, especially Grace Bauer, Jan Beatty, Kate Benchoff, Susan Belasco, Jean Bessette, Julie Beaulieu, Mike Bunn, Heather Thompson-Bunn, Joy Castro, Steph Ceraso, Kwame Dawes, Katie Hogan, Gabriel Jesiolowski, Jennifer Lee, Tara Lien, Matt Mason, Beth Matway, Amelia Montes, Jeff Oaks, Wes and Winnie Owen, Dahliani Reynolds, Kayla Sargeson, Timothy Schaffert, Ryan Smith, Pamela VanHaitsma, Annette Vee, Emily Wender, and Brenda Whitney.

Writing a book, of course, involves not just the writing itself. It also involves being surrounded by those who are willing to listen to your doubts, your worries, your crises of faith. Without my closest friends in Lincoln who talk me through all the hard moments of my life, I would not be able to get this many words onto this many pages. Thank you, with all my heart, to Jaime Brunton, Pete Capuano, Jennine Capó Crucet, Lauren Gatti, Emily Kazyak, and Hope Wabuke.

I am honored and thankful to all the journals that have published some of the work in this book and to the journals and presses that have published other work that was foundational to the book. Many thanks, especially, to *Writing on the Edge*, *College Composition and Communication*, *Peitho*, and *Reader: Essays in Reader-Oriented Theory, Criticism, and Pedagogy*. I am grateful to the outstanding mentors and teachers who encouraged me both at the start of my writing career and at the start of this project with their generosity, feedback, and advice, especially Troy Boone, Steve Carr, Lynn Emanuel, Jessica Enoch, Cynthia Hogue, Paul Kameen, Saundra Morris, Karl Patten, Tony Petrosky, Todd Reeser, Mariolina Salvatori, and Jim Seitz.

I owe a great debt to the scholars (many of whom are quoted in this book) who work at the intersections of many disciplines and who gave me the courage to both argue for and enact the form this writing takes. Thank you, especially, to Victor Villanueva, Frankie Condon, Susan Griffin, Mike Rose, Richard Miller, Vershawn Ashanti Young, Kate Bornstein, and Gloria Anzaldúa. Without having read books by these visionary writers, I could not have imagined this book at all. I thank the editors at the University of Pittsburgh Press—David Bartholomae, Jean Ferguson Carr, and Josh Shanholtzer—for their valuable feedback and support as I revised and worked on this project.

With deepest gratitude and love, I thank my family. My parents, Carol and Stefan Krompier, who were my very first teachers and two of the best teachers I have ever known—inside and outside of classrooms. I am grateful to my friends who are family to me, especially Amy Schafer and Brandon Som, as their friendship makes me feel worthy of the responsibility of being a teacher in the first place. Thank you, always, to my partner, Brie, and to our son, Max, who reveal me to myself at every turn. I am so blessed to have a partner whose fierce intelligence and endless grace call me to be the most honest and attentive version of myself.

Finally, I thank every one of my students who arrive in my classes willing to take the risk of showing up in their writing and who challenge me every day to re-imagine and revise my own vision of what it means to teach and to learn.

TEACHING QUEER

INTRODUCTION

To out your text creates the illusion that queer texts can be written, that an author's relationship with a text is simply a matter of interplay between two points on a rhetorical triangle. Such a relationship is, however, a multifaceted intersection of shifting bodies, fingers, tongues that speak, not-so-silent emotions, a series of conflicts not to be (re)solved but to be exploded into language.

Jacqueline Rhodes, "Homo Origo: The Queertext Manifesto"

We understand queer *composing* as a queer rhetorical practice aimed at disrupting how we understand ourselves to ourselves. As such, it is a composing that is not a composing, a call in many ways to acts of de- and un- and re-composition.

**Jacqueline Rhodes and Jonathan Alexander,
from *Techne: Queer Meditations on Writing the Self***

Elementary school—when it was time to get in line to walk from the primary classroom to gym class or to music class. There were, without question, the girls' line and the boys' line—the two linear formations in which we were to walk from one room to another. And there was me, always lingering at the end of those lines, floating between them like a small balloon. The narrative begins this way because it continues in this way as I stand now still in this androgynous, passing body, a body that cannot align itself even disciplinarily.

In a 1995 issue of *Educational Theory*, Deborah Britzman asks the question, *Is there a queer pedagogy?* She asked this question at a time when scholars in English and in education were beginning to raise questions about what queer studies brings to teaching, about what conversations would emerge if we imagined queerness in relation to teaching and to the teaching of English. We can mark this time period in the mid-1990s as a moment when scholars began to put the terms "queer" and "pedagogy" side by side, though we might say at this moment that what this pairing of notions means or what it makes possible is still developing. The mid-1990s also marks the appearance of texts such as George Haggerty and Bonnie Zimmerman's *Professions of Desire: Lesbian and Gay Studies in Literature* (1995), Linda Garber's *Tilting the Tower: Lesbians/Teaching/Queer Subjects* (1994), and Harriet Malinowitz's *Textual Orientations: Lesbian and Gay Students and the Making of Discourse Communities* (1995). Malinowitz's book marks a moment when English's queer lens begins to sway toward composition more particularly. Several years later, both *College English* and *JAC* published special issues on queer pedagogies and lesbian and gay studies. In 2008, the publication of Jonathan Alexander's *Literacy, Sexuality, Pedagogy: Theory and Practice for Composition Studies* illuminates the ways the merging of these two fields is still providing active and interesting sites for discussions about the teaching of writing.

Composition, thankfully, has often welcomed the illuminations that have come from outside the confines of its own area of study. In "Feminism and Methodology in Composition Studies" (1992), Patricia Sullivan called for feminism to become a "more fully realized voice within composition studies," urging that if our field did not "understand issues of gender difference and sexual politics, we [could] never hope to achieve the full understanding of composing that has been the goal of composition studies from its inception" (38). Nearly two decades later, in 2009, Jonathan Alexander and David Wallace articulate a call to action about the "critical power of queerness," which, they argue, "remains an under-explored and under-utilized modality in composition studies" (301). They ask questions about "what it means to take the queer turn in composition" (302). I consider it a pedagogical imperative to invest in what this queer turn *could* mean—not only for composition's long-standing commitment to social justice but also for students (and for scholars in the field) *as writers*.

When I examine the ways queer pedagogies are represented in scholarship about teaching, and in particular about the teaching of composition, I notice some interesting patterns. First, oftentimes (as in Malinowitz's book or in Garber's anthology) notions of queer pedagogies seem bound to LGBTQ subjects—queer teachers or queer students. Second, I notice that queer pedagogies are frequently equated with queer texts or the reading of LGBTQ literature. Finally, I notice very few references to student writing *as writing*, meaning that discussions of student writing are bound to discussions of content (how to respond to homophobic papers or how to teach students to respect and honor differences in their writing, for example). I value and make use of all of these kinds of inquiry in my teaching and in my writing about teaching, and I think the work and patterns I refer to here take up very important questions about reading and writing *practices*. However, I understand my exploration of queer pedagogies as more explicitly connected to methodologies or approaches to teaching *and* to writing. In this book and with permission from my students, as collaborators and generators of scholarship, I explore the terrain where queer theory, writing, and pedagogy overlap, intersect, and move into one another. Working through transcripts of class discussions, student writing, teaching notes, and journals, I want to raise questions about the act of writing and the teaching of writing; I want to consider queer possibilities for the teaching of writing with particular attention to college writing courses. I want to continually develop queer methodologies, thinking of queer pedagogies as sets of theorized practices that any student or teacher might engage, sets of theorized practices that as practices were, or could be, queer. I see this work as an extension of what Karen Kopelson describes as a performative or "ambiguous" pedagogy when she writes, "We know, for example, that advocating particular political positions in the classroom becomes much more highly charged and fraught with risks when we are going to be read as occupying somehow 'corresponding' identity positions, and thus as advancing political/pedagogical 'agendas' based on or arising from those identity positions. The question then, the dilemma, is how to advocate those political positions to which we are committed anyway" ("Of Ambiguity" 564). I think a good part of the solution to the dilemma is not about content, not about teaching *about* one particular "issue" over another, but more about the approaches we take to any subject we teach and, more specifically, the approach we take to the teaching of *writing*. Rather than positioning queerness as connected only to queer texts or queer teachers/students, I offer writing and teaching as already queer practices, and I contend that if we honor the overlaps between queer theory and composition, we encounter complex and evolving possibilities for teaching writing. I argue for and employ what I call "queer forms"—non-normative and category-resistant forms of writing that move between the critical and the creative, the theoretical and the practical, the rhetorical and the poetic, the queer and the often invisible normative functions of classrooms. I ask myself, What would happen if the teaching of composition were queerer? What would that look like? What kind of writing would students do? What would happen in that queerer classroom? How would *I* write about that classroom?

In their 2011 article, "Queer: An Impossible Subject for Composition," Alexander and Rhodes arrive at the following conclusion: "[We] have now come to believe that queerness is not simply one of composition's difficult subjects. Queerness is one of composition's *impossible* subjects" (179). They explain that "queerness is essentially about impossibility and excess . . . queerness is the gesture of the unrepresentable, the call for a space of impossibility, the insistence that not everything be composed" (180). Here, Alexander and Rhodes contend with the multiple meanings of "composure"—something perhaps always imbued with normativity. When we "compose" ourselves, we reduce ourselves to available and understandable forms, we get it together, we clean up our messy identities, our emotions, our grammar, and we "produce shapely texts" (194). Here, we can begin to think about whether it is possible to compose queerly, to write queer, to teach writing queer. Alexander and Rhodes suggest that "it seems more important to see how queerness challenges the very subject of composition, of what it means to compose, of what it means to *be composed*" (182). This book, in its composition and its content, seeks to be "de- and un- and re-" composed, to explore the impossible landscape of queer composition, to consider the possibility of teaching queer.

In "The Failure of Queer Pedagogy," a video essay from *The Writing Instructor*'s 2015 special issue entitled *Queer and Now*, Jacqueline Rhodes reveals,

> I struggle with the melding of queer and pedagogy. Can such a thing as queer pedagogy even exist? For pedagogy is about disciplining the subject. Pedagogy is a heterosexed political indoctrination in service of a heterosexed institutional imperative. The queer challenges such disciplining, such assimilation, and resists the demarcation of acceptable and unacceptable, appropriate and inappropriate. There can be and are queer teachers. There can be and is queer teaching, but queer teachers teaching queerly still struggle against the confines of capital "P" pedagogy, which is informed by a logic of mastery, of individual attainment, and of institutional assessment of that attainment.

Rhodes invites us to recall that the teaching of composition in the university is teaching that happens within the norms of institutional, departmental, and programmatic constraints. And, of course, there is no denying the fact of the "institutional imperative." I wonder, though, what locations or positions *can* or *do* exist outside these kinds of constraints? Even when I imagine the most radical places I can bring to mind, not one of them is innocent of the charge of "disciplining the subject." There is, in the end, no outside of institutional constraints even if and when one imagines oneself as outside an actual institution. For Rhodes, then, there is no queer pedagogy; there is only the possibility of "queer teachers teaching queerly" or, as I might put it, teaching queer. The question remains, How might teachers of composition, even from our various institutional locations and fields of constraint, mobilize queer as an act of resistance?

Queer Methodologies

To consider questions about queering composition, I needed to consider myself as a writer first. I needed to consider how I would go about representing the materials I gather, the students I teach, and the questions I want to ask. In considering these questions of representation and methodology, I became invested in writing that enacts its central inquiries formally, and I turned to scholars in queer theory to think about methodology. *Teaching Queer*'s subjects of inquiry *and* its form are informed by my own understandings of what constitutes *queer*. Jack Halberstam, in the introduction to *Female Masculinity*, writes that a "queer methodology is [. . .] a scavenger methodology, that uses different methods to collect and produce information" (13). Halberstam argues that "queer methodology attempts to combine methods that are often cast as being at odds with each other, and it refuses the academic compulsion toward disciplinary coherence" (13). I take to heart Halberstam's call for a "scavenger methodology," and in this book I try to push on notions of disciplinary, bodily, pedagogical, writerly, and scholarly coherence. I do not think scholarship in teaching can pretend to separate itself from the teachers and students who are its subjects; I cannot convince myself (and have no wish to convince readers) that there is some objective distance between the stories of the lives of teachers and the narratives of their teaching. And because I believe, as Halberstam does, that methods "that are often cast as being at odds with each other" can be put in dynamic, productive combination, I try to compose as this scavenger. I collect my work and my students' work alongside one another; I try to move toward the layers of understanding that might emerge. I blur the lines of authorship. I make use of literature, science, personal narrative, and individual experience. I recall my own education; I describe the fragments and fissures of my own life alongside ruminations on the loon, my martial arts practice, the body, dolphins, comets, and my third-grade teacher—all become narrative threads with and against which my students and I can be read and interpreted. In this sense, this project is about writing, *and* this project *is* writing. Teaching writing queer *and* writing queer. Or, at least, as queer as it is possible to teach and write.

In Gary A. Olson and Lynn Worsham's gathering of writers' voices in *Critical Intellectuals on Writing*, Judith Butler responds to a question about her statement that "difficult language can change a tough world." Butler writes, "I believe it is important that intellectuals with a sense of social responsibility be able to shift registers and to work at various levels, to communicate what they're communicating in various ways" (Olson and Worsham 45). In many ways, this book communicates in various ways, in several registers, and in multiplying forms. Because I believe, as Vershawn Ashanti Young puts it, "[r]eally, theoretical discussion cannot be put to better use—I think—than for someone to wrap his life in it and disclose just how closely or loosely the cover fits, just how much warmth the blanket provides or how much cold it still lets in" (13).

Instead of a science project, I wrote what I called "a science book" entitled "The Monarch," and I remember drawing pictures of my family, giving them butterflies as faces. Alongside my father and mother, my siblings and their butterfly heads, I composed narratives that made use of all the science projects I could see in the room. I remember writing down the names of planets, which I used as the names for the characters with the butterfly heads, who were also my family. I remember there were volcanoes, and I remember trying to describe the anatomy of a fly—something Joey Lavarco, who had to repeat third grade twice and whom I loved for his irreverence, was working on in the back row. This is the first time I remember writing queerly and having a teacher who celebrated that sensibility in me.

Johnnie Hart, a student in one of the first-year writing courses I examine in this project, writes in his midterm course evaluation form,

> It's like I keep going to write something down, but I feel lost. I feel like there is not much I can say for sure in this class. So I guess my biggest question is how do I write if I can't say anything for sure about anything? In high school I was supposed to pretend to be sure when I wasn't in my writing and lots of other things come to think of it, but now, now being sure is a sign of weakness when before it was a sign of strength. My thinking feels all watery. It's hard to fight the urge to freeze it back up.

It is easy to note Johnnie Hart's narrative gift of metaphor—how he is able to imagine his way through the literal circumstances of his experience with the readings and with the course. I am interested in his sense of liquid, of his thinking being "watery." I am interested in that water as a kind of alternative epistemology, a way of thinking and writing. I am curious about how I might more explicitly encourage student work that functions as liquid, as fluid. For me, this means I must contend with fluidity in terms of reading, writing, thinking, and interpretation, as all of these kinds of literacy practices overlap and move into another when students engage the practice of writing, or when anyone does.

One of the things I notice, again and again, about the work of queer theorists (and really, the work of many writers I love) is the fierceness with which they are willing to interrogate the self, identity, and language. We need not reach very far into the pockets of queer studies to find this interrogation: Foucault's interrogation of discourse and the repressive hypothesis in volume 1 of *The History of Sexuality*, Butler's interrogation of the category of "woman" in *Gender Trouble*, or Eve Kosofsky

Sedgwick's interrogation of "coming out" in *Epistemology of the Closet*. Sedgwick writes, "But, again, the extent, construction and meaning, and especially the history of any such theoretical continuity—not to mention its consequences for practical politics—must be open to every interrogation" (88). In fact, even to think of Butler's move to imagine drag as a kind of potentially subversive "trying on" of gender is also a way to imagine the courses I teach as a potentially subversive "trying on" of queer teaching—a kind of inductive experiment. Queer pedagogy is not liberatory pedagogy, not critical or feminist pedagogy, but something else. And as Sedgwick additionally asserts, "[a]ntihomophobic inquiry is not co-extensive with feminist inquiry, but we can't know in advance how they will be different" (83). The same holds true for queer pedagogical inquiry and other types of pedagogical inquiry. I teach writing courses with interrogation in mind—interrogation that would inevitably involve interrogations of language, identity, and self. I try to begin my courses with an interrogation into perhaps one of the most sacred culminations of language, identity, and self: gender. After all, male/female "functions as a primary and perhaps model binarism affecting the structure and meaning of many, many other binarisms" (Sedgwick, *Epistemology* 84). I have the idea that if students do work in thinking through this powerful system of meaning, it would not only help them to understand how selves are made and how systems of domination operate, but it would also help them to write more interesting and more complicated work, writing that proceeds without the assumption that meaning can be contained. Just as Sedgwick characterizes her project as a writer, I, too, would characterize my project as a teacher of writing: "[r]epeatedly to ask how certain categorizations work, what enactments they are performing and what relations they are creating, rather than what they essentially *mean*, has been my principal strategy" (Sedgwick, *Epistemology* 83). How categorizations "work" is a question of theoretical function and construction as opposed to what categorizations "mean," which would suggest first that we could even know what they mean and second that they have inherent or fixed meaning. While queer pedagogy would not be the first radical pedagogy to aim to disrupt binarisms, it does seem that a queer pedagogy might ask that students and teachers disrupt binaries in some very specific, embodied, sexed, and gendered ways—ways that cut right to the heart of who we think we are, or who we think others are. These categorizations, of course, have something to do with gender and bodies (*kinds* of people), but they also have everything to do with form (*kinds* of writing).

It seems to have started quite early—the idea that some things that I found so strange and terrifying were, to others, quite obvious and comforting. There was, however, some consensus, like the idea that I should accept the invitation to join the third-grade "Gifted and Talented Reading Group" at Forest Brook Elementary School. I don't remember any of the books we read in that group except one. It was a book titled Call It Courage, *by Armstrong Sperry, and it was about a young boy whose mother was killed by the sea in a hurricane; of course, the young boy, Mafatu, was terrified of the sea and felt cast out by his community, which valued courage above all things. As narrative would have it, Mafatu goes out to sea alone to face his fears. Mrs. Sullivan, the beautiful librarian who painted on her eyebrows and drove a gleaming red car, chose me for the reading group. I had been a "library aide" for two years, and I suspect while my grades weren't always strong, she chose me because of the sheer number of books she had watched me check out. To this day, I am not exactly certain if I read any of them. But* Call It Courage *I did read. I read it on the school bus, on the way to Little League practice, late at night when just enough hall light (which I insisted be left on) shone through the bedroom door. I was obsessed with Mafatu's fear, and with the idea that there seemed to be no one else in his entire community who feared the sea. I had a hard time believing this, and when I told Mrs. Sullivan that there was no way no other kid was afraid of the sea except Mafatu, she said that even though we lived on Long Island we had no concept of how close Mafatu lived to the sea. And living so close, she explained, the sea was just part of everyone's life, so it is believable that no one living that close to the sea and looking out to the sea each day would be afraid of it in the way that Mafatu was.*

The Question of Narrative

I had asked my students to read a chapter from Judith Butler's Undoing Gender. *Danielle says Butler is impossible. Maria jokes, "Doesn't she have anything better to do than be completely impenetrable?" Johnnie says, "This woman does talk in circles, I'll give 'em that." I fear this is the start of the coup—the moment when my students forge an ever-strengthening uprising to overthrow the queer text they have been given. And by extension they seem to threaten to overthrow me, their queer teacher, and also to leave little room for the possibility of value in queer and difficult texts. I feel simultaneously angry and guilty. But I need to hurry, to decide what approach to take. There is, of course, the "eat your vegetables, they are good for you approach," which I have to say usually ends with my students rightfully feeding my metaphorical vegetables to the metaphorical dog. There is the "therapeutic" approach; this is when I say, "Are you frustrated by this text?" and perhaps I make the ever-predictable move of "take us* to a place in the chapter you found so difficult or frustrating to understand." There is also the "I hate 'the man' too" approach, in which I validate their revolution. I say things like, "Yes, Judith Butler is impossible." I say, "Yeah, I don't know why this theory stuff has to be so dense on purpose." I say, "We want theory for the people!"

I can't say that I like the teacher (me) in this narrative very much. I can't say I find the students that compelling either—how could they be compelling when they are so erased by my own inner neuroses? What my students are saying to me is quite interesting, though because I categorize their response to Butler as "resistance" or, even more problematically, as a "coup," it can be difficult to see how their responses are interesting. However, I suppose my anxiety, which is what causes me to see their responses as a kind of "coup," does interest me. The anxiety speaks to some of the complicated questions of power present in all classroom scenarios. And as queer theory's interventions in pedagogy can tell us, power is not fixed; it is ever shifting, even in moments when we are reaching for its fixity. Knowing this, I need to find ways to work *with* the moments I can feel the power shifting between myself and my students, who can also feel power shift. My internal monologue both amuses and disturbs me at once because if a shift in power is happening in this moment, none of the "approaches" I consider above seems to be conscious of that power shift. Each move is an attempt at taking power back, or asserting its fixity, rather than moving *with* the shift of power *in* the direction of my students. So, perhaps I can tell the same story another way.

When my students say Judith Butler is impenetrable, I laugh. I say, "Don't you think it's kinda ironic that we're calling a butch lesbian queer theorist 'impenetrable'?" They look stumped. Finally, Johnnie says enthusiastically from the back, "Oh, I get it. Impenetrable, like won't be penetrated. Like by a man." The students shift uncomfortably in their seats. "Something like that," I say. I'm a little worried I've said something "wrong" but hope I'm hiding it well. I hope I am teaching my students that penetration is a something we can collectively consider as an intellectual term. When my students then say Butler is impossible, I feel sad, defensive even. So I read from Butler page 29: "Possibility is not a luxury; it is as crucial as bread." Interesting, I say, that we are accusing a person who says possibility is as crucial as bread of being impossible. Does anyone else find this interesting? From the back again: "It just proves her point," Johnnie says. I am sweating. I know in my mind that I have my clothes on, but my body feels naked. And Johnnie, the other "visible" queer in the classroom, is wearing his compassion on his sleeve. I can tell he wants to help me. We are of the same impossible body, after all. Him with his purple beret, skinny-girl jeans, and beautiful queer lisp. Me with my unruly chin hair and a voice that I can only describe as my father's. How will Johnnie and I lead the students out of impossibility? "This woman does talk in circles," Johnnie says, "I'll give 'em that."

I don't know about this teacher either. And clearly the representation of students is just as problematic as their erasure. I don't know if I should or how I should write about my students' bodies or if their bodies and fashion choices move the narrative in another theoretical direction. I don't know if I have the right to say what Johnnie's cooperation means. I do know there is always something different about a classroom in which there is a queer body, a queer sensibility. This narrative is about trying to make Butler *possible*—not accessible, or easy, or even pleasurable but possible. There is much at stake in recognizing her possibility because if she is *impossible*, I also am impossible. Johnnie is impossible. Queer pedagogies, impossible. Queer bodies have certainly the potential for pushing up against what is possible, and this potential can cause us to be deemed *impossible*. This is not necessarily a problem; in fact, it is sometimes desirable to be impossible, illegible—to become the difficult text. Can this teacher, who is me, really make an ironic joke about penetration with first-year students? Is that even possible or ethical or "appropriate"? What context would a narrative need that says this? What teacher would we allow to say it? Narrative exposes our vulnerability as teachers (and often the vulnerability of our students) endlessly. Sometimes I wonder if it is the vulnerability itself that gives classroom story a bad rap or turns classroom narrative into the little brother some like to bully. But narrative almost always raises complicated questions about representation. And as queer theory also tells us, representation is already impossible before we even begin—identity itself is moving beneath our feet as we teach, as we write about teaching.

Much of my teaching is waiting. I try to be patient—I try to wait the way I wait for the train. Confident it will arrive. Not exactly sure of the precise moment, but soon. Each class a series of waitings. On this particular day, I am waiting for one of my students to make a comment I am able to see as possibility—the piece of a discussion that we will all remember because without it, the conversation might have fallen to pieces. They have read Judith Butler for the first time. There is the sense of struggling, maybe even of suffering in the room. Comments are made about difficulty, about big words, about density. One student even heckles Butler a bit. I am waiting still. This woman does talk in circles, Johnnie says, I'll give 'em that. By "them," he means the other students. He means he agrees with them about the denseness and difficulty of the text. But what I am interested in most are the circles—what it means for a writer to approach her task "in circles." What shapes do people usually talk in? I ask. At first, they seem to think a little that I am teasing. Then Danielle sees that I am not and says, "I think of essays more like boxes that connect." On the board, I draw a picture of circles spiraling into one another and then boxes that connect. We end up drawing a geometrical diagram for every essay that follows (both the course readings and the students' essays); we try to graph their shapes as a way of understanding the content. Some students grow to like the talking in circles—the way ideas slip back into one another again and again—and each time they are changed. This won't be the last time a queer text moves us to draw essays, to talk about structure and shape in new ways.

It's hard, even for me, to see these three narratives as speaking about or telling the story of the same classroom moment. But each one does describe the same period of time. I move them *in* time. I begin at a different moment. I skip over time. Narrative time becomes as fluid and movable as power and identity. I offer these narratives not because I see them (or any narrative) as instructions for writing pedagogies but because the questions narrative produces for me are distinct and essential to teaching practice and to queer pedagogy as a theoretical field of inquiry. I thought to begin this introduction by finding a teaching narrative in which someone attempted to record or describe queer pedagogies in composition. And each time, I noticed the way I treated the narrative more like an object, like an opportunity for critique. I noticed myself pointing to the limits of narrative *first*, before thinking about its possibilities. So I decided that I might raise some questions about my own teaching story—it might be important or illuminating for me to risk my own narratives to start—to offer a moment when both narrative possibilities and pedagogical possibilities intersect. Every one of these narratives is problematic—narratives are never *not* problematic. But I am also interested in asking questions about what narratives make visible. And as someone who is interested in the intersections between queer theory and composition studies, I am curious about the ways teaching stories shape understandings of what queer teaching might mean or make possible. I do, after all, agree with Butler that "[p]ossibility is not a luxury; it is as crucial as bread" (*Undoing* 28).

This exploration of where queer pedagogies might be or begin, like my own body, refuses linear formations, refuses the category of discipline. The investigations are narrative, theoretical, fluid, a series of constant movements between gender studies, queer theory, pedagogy, and composition theory. I both argue *for* an approach to teaching *and* try to invite my reader to embody that approach—self-conscious, weblike, and fragmentary. I do not believe the story of my scholarship is separate from the story of my life or the body I live. And while narrative has certainly played a role in composition studies thus far, I want to offer a particularly queer understanding of what narrative might mean to theory and, dialectically, what theory might mean to narrative. I most closely link my own understanding of the scholarly use of narrative to Nancy K. Miller's understanding in *Getting Personal: Feminist Occasions and Other Autobiographical Acts*. She writes, "By the risks of its writing, personal criticism embodies a pact . . . binding writer to reader in the fabulation of self-truth, that what is at stake matters also to others: somewhere in the self-fiction of the personal voice is the belief that the writing is worth the risk. In this sense, by turning its authorial voice into spectacle, personal writing theorizes the stakes of its own performance. . . . Personal writing opens an inquiry on the cost of writing—critical writing or Theory—and its effects" (24). While I have no intention of glorifying or romanticizing the "personal," I do intend for the narrative to become spectacle inasmuch as it "theorizes the stakes of its own performance." The word *spectacle* can, of course, imply a certain kind of regretfully public moment, a disaster of sorts. But I want to read this term as carrying, at once, all its meanings and connotations—spectacle as public, open, in plain sight, and even the possible disaster of putting into view that which should be kept out of view, behind the scenes. As this project is simultaneously about writing, about teaching and about my own selfhood, it aims not only to articulate queer pedagogy's possibilities for teaching composition but also to *enact*, in its very writing, a kind of queer pedagogy—one that tries to both expose and complicate the life that leads to the study of writing and queer pedagogy in the first place.

My mother went to great lengths to convince me, as a child, to wear shirts, to wear the tops to my bathing suits in the swimming pool. I tore the First Communion dress and rubbed my hair violently against the velvet couch to dismantle the "body wave" the hairdresser constructed for the special day. The body of Christ. And I learned how to hold my hands to receive it, how to stand in line with the others. Mostly, in the late afternoons, when I'd ride my bike into the woods, I'd pull off my shirt and ride the dirt pathways with the sun lighting up my small back. No one was there to see me.

I am working, in some sense, in a tradition in composition of using the personal narrative or the materials of experience in or for scholarship. And I hope to stretch and push on that tradition, opening up new possibilities for what counts as scholarship—blurring the creative and the critical, the linear and the nonlinear, the personal and the public, the theoretical and the "practical." I hope the ways in which this project is, ultimately, about me offer productive sites of inquiry—expanding the project and exposing its vulnerabilities (even as a kind of spectacle) as I try learn about and to put into view my own teaching practices. I might contend, even, that every book you have ever read is about its author. I have kept, in my mind, William E. Coles's book *The Plural I: The Teaching of Writing*, which he referred to as a kind of "novel of the classroom." I have read with great interest not only scholars writing about queer pedagogies but also scholars who have disrupted notions of the academic and the personal, scholars like Richard Miller in his book *Writing at the End of the World*, or Frankie Condon in her book *I Hope I Join the Band: Narrative, Affiliation, and Antiracist Rhetoric*. I have also kept close Paul Kameen's important and groundbreaking book *Writing/Teaching: Essays toward a Rhetoric of Pedagogy*, in which he takes his students and his experiences to be some of the central research materials of his project. He writes,

> One could argue, for example, that what I offer here is either too practical or too local to be legitimately scholarly, that these are, after all, *only* teaching materials or *merely* autobiography or *simply* personal reflections. And they are, of course, all of those things. I present them, though, not specifically for what they say about the context out of which they emerged—my personal experience—but for the things that they attempt to *do* with the kinds of change, especially for the teacher, that are part of the stakes, tacitly if not expressly, in any pedagogical enterprise, most especially one that has an overt political component, as this course clearly did. (6)

Like Kameen's characterization of his course, it is easy to see the writing courses I draw from in this project as "overtly political." However, I also want to raise questions "that are part of the stakes . . . in any pedagogical enterprise." And I want to raise these questions through means that are quite "legitimately scholarly," but perhaps not quite obviously, at times. I present the theory, autobiography, teaching materials, and personal reflections *as* scholarship, as a kind of research—a looking again—into the teaching of writing. And while the particular courses I examine are primarily first-year writing courses, I expect the possibilities for queer pedagogies would be relevant to most courses and teachers of classes within the humanities. I am aware, as I begin, of the way in which my body, my identity, the events of the story of my life and education inform the way I construct this writing, my thinking, and the stories of my classrooms. I cannot read without my body. I cannot read without the presence of a fleeting masculinity, androgyny, contradiction, and movement. And because I have come to see this position as a kind of blessing, I try to find ways to offer contradiction and movement to my students—especially those students who have come to understand themselves as solid, as fixed and named forms who can make fixed and named assumptions about reading and writing. I seek to (as tenderly as I can and with acute awareness of the responsibilities) disrupt this kind of learning, as I believe it limits our capabilities and places us (without our consent) into a state of unconsciousness. It leads us, unfairly and without self-implication, to walk the boys' line or the girls' line, endlessly, through each door of our lives.

Before I knew the names of identities, before I had traveled the long years of "mistaken for a boy," before I knew the word "butch," before I stumbled upon the XY chromosome in my "female" body, I am no older than six or seven. And each month the Highlights Magazine *arrives at the house. And I am giddy with excitement to complete my favorite task. It's a game called "What does not belong?" in which the child (in this case me) is meant to identify in a picture the object or subject that does not belong and then use scissors to rid the picture of its not belonging piece. I can remember cutting out what appeared to be a bird from inside what appeared to be a body of water of some kind. The bird appeared to be swimming, so my mother happily hands me the red-handled kid scissors. She watches me and is proud of how smart I have always been. "Careful," she says, "don't accidentally cut out a fish." And here I am remembering back. Here I am a writer who knows, of course, there is such a bird called a loon—in the air a bird, flying, but in the water a winged fish, swimming.*

Body of Knowledge

The phrase "body of knowledge" is most familiar to us as institutional, a set of sanctioned practices—this body of knowledge is understood to be located outside the self. It is something we can grasp toward, something we can know, something we can teach, but it is not, however, something that we are. In this model, I *have* the body of knowledge; my students do not. However, even as I have this body, this does not mean I *am* this body or can ever be it. Our bodies are forbidden to *be* this body of knowledge; our bodies are meant to be outside, separate from the body of knowledge. What we know, then, is not supposed to be at all about embodiment. The body of knowledge replaces the body, substitutes institutional sanctions in its place, intending to forever codify and compartmentalize what we know from what we do, from what we are, from the lived experience of our bodies. The political stakes of this "body of knowledge" are then quite high. It evens paves the way for us to dismiss or disregard what the body knows in favor of what the institution knows.

It is no accident, then, that the idiom *body of knowledge* takes the metaphor of body—steals it *from* the body in order to *disembody* education. But in the echoes of the idiom's erasure of the body, we can still hear that somehow what we know, or what we come to know, is part of bodily expression and bodily composition. What happens when we ourselves become bodies of knowledge? Most of us do not want to talk about our bodies, at least not here in the brainy mindspace of academic discourse, and especially when it comes to teaching and students. Part shame, part fear, part binary of body and mind, this hesitancy can be particularly amplified for queer bodies, or bodies like mine. The queer body always calls attention to what the body knows. Institutions must put students with appropriate (read: composed) straight folks who won't have sex with them (read: make them gay), nice straight folks who will erase themselves as bodies (read: straight people have invisible bodies unless they are queered in some other way), or who have the luxury of seeming to do so. At sixteen, when my close friend says to me, *if you want to be a teacher you better take off those freedom rings and stay in the closet. You can't be queer around kids; people don't like that.* And later in college, the education professor who taught my educational psychology course saying, *especially for you, Stacey, it's important you keep your classroom door open, and that you do not touch your students for any reason.*

I used to teach tai chi to a group of women from a church in the suburbs of Pittsburgh. Some of them referred to me as "he," some as "she." They don't seem to notice the disparity between their pronouns. Once, I was showing Evelyn, a seventy-six-year-old two-time cancer survivor, how to stand. I pressed my hands gently atop her shoulders and pressed down. Her back and shoulders relaxed. I placed my hand at the small of her back and pushed softly forward. Her knees bend as she falls into a stance known as "wu ji," the most balanced and relaxed a person can be—perhaps another way to think about a body of knowledge.

In teaching tai chi, the physical relation is obvious, necessary. Even when I am not touching my students, they watch my physical movements intently, looking for when to step, when to circle their hands, how to use their waists to lead the rest of their bodies. In the college classroom, the body's force is less obvious, or perhaps less admitted. In his essay "A 'Sisterly Camaraderie' and Other Queer Friendships," from the anthology *The Teacher's Body*, Jonathan Alexander writes about the ways his particular "embodied queerness had intense effects on his teaching and relationship with his students" (163). Most students, and most people who meet me for the first time, watch for clues for what might be underneath my clothes, what body of knowledge my body conveys. What does it mean for my queer and uncertain body to teach students to write? What does it mean for my queer ambiguous hand to write words *about* my students' work? And do I also, in writing about their work, write about their bodies?

Bodies do matter. A body of knowledge has everything to do with bodies. As a person whose scholarship draws most often on students and student writing, I have to contend with their bodies—or at the very least, acknowledge the body. I have to raise questions over and over again about how, if, and when to represent students' bodies as part of their writing or their classroom presence. I have to make decisions about what representations are ethical or necessary. I have to consider my own fears about being a queer scholar who pays attention to bodies. I am supposed to be one of those good queers, if I am to be a teacher, one who says "appropriate" things, unerotic, eunuch. I am supposed to ignore my students' bodies. Of course, the question arises, *Can I really do this when so many of my courses ask students to think about gender, sexuality, and embodiment, when I ask my students at times to write about themselves, their bodily experiences?* Take, for example, the following passage, written by a student in one of my first-year writing classes. I had asked students to spend the five days between two class meetings keeping a gender journal, one in which they were to take notice of anything they saw that they thought might be connected to gendered bodily expression. Kelsey Fagan writes,

> When I am walking down the street alone, I rarely make eye contact with other people who are passing me. I never thought of this attribute as a female one. But I think maybe it might be. When I walked down the street, I tried to make eye contact with people I passed. I noticed it was much harder to make eye contact with other women than it was for me to make eye contact with men. I think if it's because women evaluate each other in secret. Like we look at each other's clothes and stomachs and stuff to see how we compare. With guys, who cares.

Does it help in trying to read her writing to know that Kelsey's body is a white body, a conventionally attractive normatively gendered young woman, that she looks me in the eyes all the time? Do I say I am uncomfortable saying that? Do I say she wears rings on every finger, that she closes her eyes when something is hard to think about in class, that she rolls her eyes whenever a particular classmate speaks, that she crosses her legs always when she sits and has a habit of biting her nails? I learn, in Kelsey's passage, that I am easier for her to look at, that our bodies are not in competition, that Kelsey and I are not "women" to each other. This is Kelsey's body of knowledge as I read it, as I am not supposed to be reading it. We know our students' bodies; we sometimes know the emotional terrain that is expressed through them. We are, by the very notion of an institutional "body of knowledge," encouraged to erase this embodied knowledge, to find it irrelevant to our classroom practices. To acknowledge Kelsey's body would be, in part, to explode the myth of my own objectivity as her teacher, to admit there is more to my comments, more to my scholarship that cites Kelsey, more to the grades I give Kelsey inside the institution, the grades that mark her position with respect to writing's ambiguous, shifting body of knowledge.

The truth is, this is what I am reading when I read Kelsey's papers, when she raises her hand to speak in class—her body always part of my interpretation. I can hear Kelsey's voice in her response because I know the sound, because I recognize the sound, because I have watched and listened to the sound of her voice, because I even know the sound she makes the instant before she speaks—the quick taking of breath, the tight shift of the eyebrows. Reading student writing in the context of physical classroom means always to read a body alongside or behind a text. Reading student papers is quite distinct from reading a novel, from reading a book of scholarship by someone whose body you have never seen, whose body you do not know, whose body might intentionally erase itself—something I am trying to work against. Reading student writing and representing that writing in our scholarship is always a representation of body.

It's 1986. I'm nine. All I can think about is Don Mattingly. Mattingly was a no frills hitter. There was something endlessly compelling about how relaxed he was—his hands loose around the grip of the bat, his eyes clear and meditative. It would be easy to hit like Dave Winfield, who had a distinctive high stance, who waved the bat above his shoulder like a flag. But it was Don Mattingly I wanted to be. I recognized a certain evenness in him. Mattingly never stood still after hitting a home run to admire it; he never strutted. But people still called him "Donnie Baseball" or sometimes "The Hit Man." So I'd watch the Yankees games holding my peewee Louisville Slugger. I'd stand in the living room and mirror him. My mother yelling from the kitchen, "If you swing that bat in the house, I swear to Holy Lord." I was careful. I'd wait until my mother was a safe distance from the room. I'd make sure there was no chance of hitting anything in the room. Sometimes, if I needed to, I would use the new camcorder held up to the television to tape Mattingly's at bats, so later I could play them in slow motion. Being Don Mattingly, I felt more like myself, though, of course, I was not Don Mattingly. At least not until one glorious day in Little League when Brian Poulos's dad says to my dad—loud enough for me to hear, after I had hit a single to right center, rounded first base, and put my hands together for one single clap, just like Mattingly—he says, your kid hits like Donnie. My dad chuckled, I remember. But my body lit up inside.

Here is an excerpt from Kelsey Fagan's essay "A Journey to Womanhood." The first passage is from the beginning, and the second from the closing to her essay. She writes,

> I was six or seven, and I was playing in the yard with all of my neighbors, all of whom happened to be boys. We were playing Star Wars and since I was the only girl I of course was Princess Leia. We set up the rules for the game and started to play. Only I wasn't running around with light sabers

saving the galaxy. I was sitting in the tree house waiting to be rescued. Since I was the princess, I needed to be rescued.

. . .

If I could go back and have a conversation with little Kelsey, while she was waiting to be rescued by the boys, I would give her a few pointers. I would tell her that she should do what she wants. If she wanted to be Luke Skywalker, she should go be Luke Skywalker and if she wanted to be Princess Leia waiting for the boys to come rescue her then she should be Princess Leia. Either way, she rescues herself in the end by making a conscious choice.

Composition, of course, as a field, has known for a long time that the idea of some official "body of knowledge" in our discipline is contradictory, even impossible. Consider how much time we spend reaching into other disciplines, blurring and contesting the boundaries of what counts as composition. Consider the ways we tell and retell histories of composition, knowing all along that the "body of knowledge" that counts as composition is not a stable, predetermined body. Consider the work compositionists do in thinking about identity, knowing that this body of knowledge is connected to, rather than outside of, some notion of self. But what recent turns in queer theory—turns in which the field of transgender studies makes a tremendous impact—can tell us is that the idea of a "body of knowledge" is not only linked to identity as a concept but also linked to actual material bodies, that, in fact, identity is inextricably linked to actual material bodies. This is the pressure transgender theorists are putting on some areas of queer theory—a pressure I want to put on our practices of pedagogy and on our writing about our students and their work. In the *Transgender Studies Quarterly* inaugural keywords issue, Francisco J. Galarte provides an extensive flushing out of "transpedagogies," a term coined by Vic Muñoz and Ednie Kaeh Garrison in *Women's Studies Quarterly*. Galarte writes,

> In a transpedagogical approach, processes of learning become political mechanisms through which identities can be shaped and desires mobilized and through which the experience of bodily materiality and everyday life can take form and acquire meaning. Transpedagogies supply a discursive mode of critique for challenging the production of social

hierarchies, identities, and ideologies across local and national boundaries. They represent both a mode of cultural production and a type of cultural criticism for questioning the conditions under which knowledge of gendered embodiment is produced. They provide a space for affective engagement, for the affirmation or rejection of values, and for the inhabitation, negotiation, or refusal of culturally prescribed gendered subject positions. Understanding pedagogy as a mode of cultural production in this way underscores its performative nature. It is how theory becomes practice. (146)

I want to bring the body back to knowledge, to acknowledge all the material realities of our classrooms—the student who shakes my hand firmly and introduces himself on the first day of class, the student whose hungover and vodka-seeping body slumps in the back row, me (their teacher), whose voice rings of her father's voice, whose broad shoulders curb her fears of earning no authority. There is no bodiless pedagogy, no disembodied scholarship to represent disembodied students and teaching. I wonder what would happen if we stopped pretending there were, if we considered the meaning our bodies make, if we showed up (mortal, subjective, messy, and vulnerable as bodies are) to, as Kelsey says, "rescue ourselves in the end by making a conscious choice."

Teaching Queer

What follows is both my attempt (which also involves my inevitable and deeply necessary failure) to teach queer, to develop and cultivate queer methodologies in my classroom and in my writing, to experiment with what happens when I invite my students to take queerer approaches as well. The first chapter here takes up questions of the teaching body—this body that shows up vulnerable in a first day of class. A teaching body will always be waited for, looked at, put on its front-of-the-room stage as the first kind of student knowledge, the first body of knowledge. In chapter one, "Becoming the Loon: Queer Masculinities, Queer Pedagogies," I offer a hybrid-genre, theoretical meditation with the hope of inviting teachers to see their bodies, to confront the fear, defensiveness, and erasure that constitute what it means to *be* a teaching body. In this chapter, teaching queer means quite literally teaching *as a queer body*. And while I link this theoretical meditation on the body to my own experience and lived material existence, I also think this chapter calls on the figure of the teacher to consider their queerness, whether that queerness is linked to gender-specific instantiations or not. The body is queered by all sorts of non-normative markers, and those markers become perhaps more visible as the body stands as a spectacle on stage for the eyes of other bodies: the body queered by disability, the body queered by race, the body queered by beauty, the body queered by pregnancy, and so on. Some might argue that a pregnant body, for example, is not queer, perhaps because of a presumed connection to reproduction. But the way I want to understand *queer* in this particular context is as a kind of deviant mark, an excess, a bodily expression that exists outside a normative construction *of* the body. In this sense, we can imagine the pregnant body marked with *queerness*, how the body moves around the stomach, how the presence of another body is imagined within it, how the practices that may (or may not have) produced this pregnant body become part of the body's interpretative possibility. Chapter one takes the loon as its central metaphor. The loon's body, like my own, is a blurring body—attributes of fish and bird.

In chapter two, "Courting Failure," I draw heavily from Jack Halberstam's *The Queer Art of Failure* to consider how teaching queer means always, in some sense, to court failure, to bring failure into view as a necessary, illuminating, and imperative part of any attempt to teach (or to write) queer. I ask students to think about structural failures—terms like "structure" and "organization"—that circulate frequently in their discussions of one another's writing. In this chapter, I wonder if, or how, notions of order can survive in a queer context. What does queer structure look like? Is that an oxymoron? The notion of "writing queer" is one I both relish and problematize in the chapter, trying to understand if there might even be such a thing and why I would ask my students to try it. I consider how teachers of writing conceptualize failure with students through an examination of my own failing class participation policies and my own complicated understandings of silence.

In chapter three, "Alternative Orientations," I consider the documents informing and circulating around one in the composition courses I draw from in this book. These documents include: the University of Pittsburgh first-year composition mission statement, my own course description and instructor's statement, and the sequence of assignments themselves. I consider this chapter an inquiry into the course documents that reflect and contribute to course logics and ideas. I offer some glimpses of the writing students composed in response. This chapter introduces the dolphin as another site of interpretative possibility. As a child, I was not exactly a reader. I always wanted to be, but I just could not seem to stay interested for long. That is, until a class trip to an aquarium, where I saw a dolphin for the first time. Because of its curled body and what seemed at the time like joyous dives, I read. I read anything about dolphins I could. Sign posts, encyclopedia entries, children's stories. It became a kind of marker of my expertise: relatives brought dolphin T-shirts to my birthday instead of "girl" presents I would refuse to engage with. I posted dolphin photos in my room. I had a dolphin key chain—its mouth lit up if you pushed on its fin. It is likely no accident that, as a child, I was drawn to creatures that could do amazing things from, in, and because of water. Like many scholars of queer theory over the past twenty years, I am drawn to notions of fluidity, though I am also interested in the notion as it is connected to water itself. Consequently, in chapter four, "Becoming Liquid: Queer Interpretations," I consider what it might mean to *queer* literacy and to consider interpretation as an integral aspect of that queering. Drawing from the work of my students, I want to ask questions about their interpretations, about moments their writing seems more like water. As I think about this water, I am brought back to Johnnie Hart's words: "My thinking feels all watery. It's hard to fight the urge to freeze it back up." I read Johnnie's notion of freezing as a kind of permanence, a turning from water to stone. Chapter four considers ways of moving students, or helping them to move themselves, away from dualistic constructions of body, of argument, and of categorical placement. The chapter takes my own martial arts practice of tai chi as part of its own movement. It is through my own body—both through its shifting gendered position and its daily martial practice—that I try to understand what it means to *become water*, moving water, which, in the end, resists its own freezing up. In the final chapter, "Queer (Re)Visions of Composition," I develop three threads of composition that I believe are crucial not only to the work of this book but also to the work of queer compositionists as we continue to develop the relationship between queerness and composition. I consider narration, naming, and "scavenging" (a term I pull from Halberstam's

Female Masculinity but also stretch for my own teaching goals) as imperative and paradoxical aspects of what it might mean to teach queer.

What I loved most about Mrs. Sullivan was after school hours, when I'd stay to laminate book covers in the back room—a job given to only the most careful and efficient library aide. Mrs. Sullivan had taken to using a nickname she called me only in private. She'd come to the back room and say, "How many books covered, Sir?" She'd say it in this military way as though we were performing some wartime version of book covering. Or sometimes she'd walk me out to the late bus and say, "See you tomorrow, Sir." And we'd both smile. Something seemed fitting about it. I liked it. It didn't feel judgmental in the way it did when rude old ladies asked my mother if I was a boy or a girl or the way it felt when the other kids teased me. It felt right. I didn't feel as though I needed to defend myself, or my "womanhood," against this claim. Sometimes I had dreams I married Mrs. Sullivan next to the ocean. And I was a man, and I was dressed in that perfect black-suit way I had seen my father dressed a few times. And I was wearing a tie, the blackest, shiniest tie, though I wasn't flashy. I was Donnie. I was the Hit Man, the kind of man for whom being a man was nothing special, nothing imitated, nothing forbidden.

CHAPTER ONE

BECOMING THE LOON

Queer Masculinities, Queer Pedagogies

To learn and to teach, one must have the awareness of leaving something behind while reaching toward something new, and this kind of awareness must be linked to imagination.

Maxine Green, *Releasing the Imagination*

The body implies mortality, vulnerability, agency: the skin and the flesh expose us to the gaze of others but also to touch and to violence. The body can be the agency and instrument of all these as well, or the site where "doing" and "being done to" become equivocal.

Judith Butler, *Undoing Gender*

The wild foxes, uncertain, walk across the frozen river, listening beneath for the sound of water. If they hear nothing, they may cross to the other side.

David Rothenberg, *Blue Cliff Record*

Legitimate Bodies

Imagine what the neighborhood folks might have called a tomboy. Tomboys are, usually up until the age of ten or twelve, seen as benign—a to-be-expected imitation of masculinity. After all, who wouldn't want to be a boy? Their toys are more engaging, their clothes more comfortable, their privilege already visible to the young girls, who, for a time, want to be them. Still, families will make sure to find excuses—the tomboy has too many brothers, the tomboy has only a male parent, the tomboy does not have a male parent, the tomboy has only neighborhood boys to play with. Why else would she turn to stickball or manhunt? Tomboys are formed through imitation. This comforts those who believe something imitated is not original, not real, not authentic. I was a gifted imitator. And yes, we can, if we need to, blame my brothers, who I watched intently to find out how to do boy—how to take up space, how to call "do over" in the street when a car disrupts play, how to lace up my shoes loose, so they barely appear tied. My mother wished I had more girls to imitate. That would have been more authentic, more real. And we all tell ourselves we want the ones we love to "be themselves." Who can be themselves if they're always walking around trying on the identities that aren't supposed to belong to them?

As children, we get some of our first lessons in difference and domination. Find what is different in the picture. Dominate that difference. Stabilize the difference. Remove it. Categorize it elsewhere. Toss it into your plastic Peter Pan garbage pail. It does not belong. I have dedicated many of my adult years to teaching and to building a pedagogy that blurs difference and tries to call systems of domination into question—heterosexism, racism, classism, sexism—and to call the ideologies that form these systems into question as well. I have selected for my courses numerous texts that aim to disrupt hierarchies and expose systems of privilege of all kinds, particularly with regard to gender and sexuality. I have resisted, for a long time, many male teachers whom I saw as constructing and using masculine domination to lead a classroom. Pedagogy's interesting intersections with gender and masculinity are striking. And while it is not within the scope of this project to examine the history of pedagogy through the lens of gender, I do want to offer an example of the *kinds* of historical moments that interest me in terms of the stakes of the classroom practices I intend to engage.

The loon is the only bird with solid bones as opposed to the hollow bones of other birds. This is what makes the loon a brilliant diver.

Mariolina Rizzi Salvatori's edited collection *Pedagogy: Disturbing History, 1819–1929*, provides a lens through which we can begin to think about masculinity and pedagogy and, importantly, about the complex relationship between pedagogy and identity. What strikes me about so many of the documents in Salvatori's collection are the many ways definitions of pedagogy struggle with essential philosophical and political questions of what it means to be in a body, what it means to *be* in the lived world, what it means to learn. Gabriel Compayré, in one of the documents (written in 1910) aiming to define pedagogy, writes the following: "The science which claims to establish the laws of education, which would instruct and raise the child and form the man, cannot with certainty construct its inductions and deductions unless other sciences have taught it what man is, what child is—in body, in soul, in his individual nature and also in what he must be in terms of his destiny, his social role" (Salvatori 32). There are several things that seem notable about this passage, of course. But rather than put pressure on the term "science" as an understanding of pedagogy or put pressure on the masculine understanding of who is worthy of being taught, I want to focus first on the ways this passage links pedagogy ("the science which claims to establish the laws of education") with ontology, with concerns of *being* ("what man is"). Compayré is quite aware that in order to begin to understand what it means to teach, we must also begin to understand bodies, souls, nature—in essence, being—meaning that pedagogy is not alone a question of education but also a question of ontology, a question of identity, physicality, theology, and ecology. This, of course, is one of the reasons pedagogy is endlessly contested and summarily reduced to one thing or the other. What can we know about what we are? About what "the child" (who is to become the "man") or the student (or even the teacher) is? And if our vision is always blocked or otherwise blurred by these limits, how can we see what we are becoming, or being, in order to educate ourselves not only *about* what we might become but also about what it means to teach another being, another being who is also becoming? I ask these questions to remind myself that when I am talking about teaching, I am, without question, talking about and making assumptions about *being*, about who I imagine myself to be and who I imagine my students to be—though I understand both states of being as temporary and mutable, even if, for a moment, we might find ourselves stable, fixed, or seemingly still.

Loons often swim all day—paddling and pushing through the water. Their leg muscle fibers are mostly red. Loons rest their wings most of the time, though their wings are made of red and white fibers because when loons do use their wings, they use them furiously and steadily.

Nearing the end of this document, Compayré writes, "We must hope that the day will soon come when a scientific schematization will finally be accomplished" (Salvatori 34). He indicates that we will someday be able to *know* what pedagogy is after science has finally determined what man is. For Compayré, once we know what "man" is, we can know what it means to teach him. Perhaps these questions of "what man is" are part of the reason pedagogy has taken its modern home at times in composition—because writing has something to do with *being*, because composing thoughts, composing writing, and composing a self permeate every aspect of being. But how do we bring questions of being to questions of pedagogy more explicitly? What will be said of our doing so? What is man? Who is the man who teaches him? What kind of man am I?

I am told by doctors that I have both an X and a Y chromosome (read: male). I look, talk, and walk like a man (read: male). I am carrying what we call here at this historical moment and in most cultures, a "woman's" body (read: female). But this body alone cannot make a theory of teaching writing. I must, as any writer must, put myself at risk. Writing, much like reading, risks revising the self, having the self in question, even at times in annihilation. I am then a woman who is a man, or, to put it another way, a man who is a woman.

The university classroom, in its long history, is a masculine place. As Pierre Bourdieu points out in *Masculine Domination*, "The particular strength of the masculine sociodicy [a term he uses to mean the justification of a masculine society as it is constructed] comes from the fact that it combines and condenses two operations: *it legitimates a relationship of domination by embedding it in a biological nature that is itself a naturalized social construction*" (23, original emphasis). Bourdieu points out how domination is linked to the masculine but that the masculine is linked to "biological nature." And anything linked (despite its social construction) to "biological nature" is going to be seen as natural. As R. W. Connell suggests, "True masculinity is almost always thought to proceed from men's bodies—to be inherent in a male body or to express something about the male body" (45). In this sense, domination is natural, the masculine is natural, masculine domination is natural. Of course, many gender theorists know this not to be "true." Many gender theorists have shown us that our sense of the natural is actually made, constructed—that what is natural is always in question. However, I am interested in what happens when masculinity's "truth," its fragility or fluidity, is exposed via the body, in my case via the "female masculine" body.

I am interested in the way my masculinity (read often as illegitimate because it is *perceived* to be *not* linked to "biological nature") might provide a site for a complicated performative pedagogy in which the now destabilized masculinity becomes a site of contention, disruption, or even horror and melancholy, for students; in other words, the both-at-once-ness of my body itself might launch any course I teach as already disruptive. I could, and at times have wanted to, ignore this disruption; I could proceed to teach as if the disruption is not there. To an extent, most teachers have. We often teach as though the baggage of ourselves has been left at some metaphorical door. We are in the classroom. We are teachers now. We are not women or men. We are teachers. Through this project I have begun to ask questions about the man who teaches my course, the man who is me, who is also a woman.

The word loon *is said to derive from the Scandinavian word* lom—*which means clumsy and awkward person. The loon gets this name because of how graceless it seems on land, its hind legs too far back for walking. It moves in strange jerks and diagonal patterns on the ground. One can always recognize a loon's sporadic walking.*

What I am calling the "illegitimate masculine" (the masculine not lived in a "male" body) is most visible when it comes into contact with or is put under the gaze of "legitimate masculinity." I am sometimes working alongside male masculine students who seem to fold their arms in refusal when I walk in the room in my suit and tie, who challenge my authority in various complicated and sometimes comical ways, or who might sense my gender performance, perhaps rightly so, as an embodiment of a pedagogy that is asking them to change the way they think about identity. I am fully aware that there are a variety of reasons students might act in these ways; however, over the past seventeen years of teaching courses in the university, I have become acutely aware of resistance that is gendered, that is an embodied response. I can feel this (for different reasons and in different ways) both when I run into a female student in the public bathroom and we both shift our eyes toward the walls, shift our weight from foot to foot with the sense that I do not belong there (despite her "knowing" I am a "woman") and when a male student looks over my clothing the way my cousin, who is a serious skateboarder, might look at a boy in "skateboarder" wardrobe who cannot "actually" (whatever that means) skate or cannot skate well—or look "natural" doing so. I am a "poser," illegitimate and nonauthentic. My performance can never be the "real deal," the real masculine deal. I have not learned my masculinity or been given the "masculine habitus" (a name Bourdieu gives to the set of sometimes invisible codes for masculinity and domination that are taught, reinforced, and handed down in any given society) in an authentic (meaning natural) and institutionally approved way. I am the self-made masculine or, in Bourdieu's terms, an autodidact:

> Because he has not acquired his culture in the legitimate order established by the educational system, the autodidact constantly betrays, by his very anxiety about the right classification, the arbitrariness of his classifications and therefore of his knowledge—a collection of unstrung pearls, accumulated in the course of an uncharted exploration, unchecked by the institutionalized, standardized stages and obstacles, the curricula and progressions which make scholastic culture a ranked and ranking set of interdependent levels and forms of knowledge. (*Distinction* 328)

Bourdieu's notion of the autodidact is certainly useful in talking about masculinity and about how masculinity is read by the larger culture and often by students in a classroom. The autodidact, then, "has not acquired his culture in the legitimate order established." *He* betrays; *he* is "a collection of unstrung pearls." The butch performance clearly echoes the description Bourdieu offers of the autodidact. In this case, it is I who have not had my masculinity sanctioned and approved by the legitimate order. It is my own body (and performance) that "betrays" me, that reveals "the arbitrariness" of classifications—my body standing at the chalkboard, fleshy proof that masculinity might be worn, might be acted out by one who does not have "birthright." Consequently, my body *betrays* and in doing so becomes a kind of *betrayal*. I betray my students, so that in addition to reading seemingly radical texts (like Kate Bornstein's *Gender Outlaw: On Men, Women, and the Rest of Us*, or Vershawn Ashanti Young's *Your Average Nigga: Performing Race, Literacy, and Masculinity*, or Michael Warner's *The Trouble with Normal: Sex, Politics, and the Ethics of Queer Life*, or Judith Butler's *Gender Trouble: Feminism and the Subversion of Identity*, or Gloria Anzaldúa's *Borderlands/La Frontera: The New Mestiza*), my students are also faced with a teaching body and performance that betrays them. They have difficulty reading or interpreting the texts I give them or the text I am to them to the point that these texts (my body) may seem impossible and illegible. College students might already feel a sense of betrayal in those contexts in which their high school skill sets or former interpretative strategies appear not to work in a new university context. This sense of betrayal could be further intensified when the teacher requires a different set of interpretative strategies in order to be read or understood.

Loons find their prey not by heat or scent, but by sight. They need, in order to survive, to see clearly. For this reason, they look for clear lakes.

Perhaps my interpretative act here, me giving my students' hypothetical feelings a temporary name—betrayal—is a kind of projection of my own fear, the fear of being, ultimately and forever, illegible. Erased. A poser, indeed. Here, Bourdieu would seem to agree with Halberstam's assertion, in *Female Masculinity*, that masculinity "becomes legible as masculinity where and when it leaves the white male middle-class body" (2) and that "female masculinity is generally received by hetero- and homonormative cultures as a pathological sign of misidentification and maladjustment, as longing to be and to have a power that is always just out of reach" (3).

Kimberly Wallace-Sanders, in her essay "A Vessel of Possibilities," writes, "The academy largely insists on the body's erasure because the body is the undeniable reminder of our private selves. Our bodies betray truths about our private selves that confound professional interaction" (188). While on some level this erasure can serve to protect or function as a kind of safety having to do with sexual harassment or with the unequal power distributions that circulate also dialectically between teachers and students, the erasure still functions as a denial of materiality. The academy is so often a disembodied place—a place where we might be asked to distance ourselves from our bodies, to leave them behind in favor of some intellectual practices that we imagine happen outside of or independent of the body. But our bodies are with us always. We cannot, as it were, teach without them.

There were several long days of snow that year. The students seem tired, having stayed up late figuring the snow would cancel their buses and leave them asleep and warm. I have been teaching at this small high school in central Pennsylvania only a few months. And after the eleventh graders have turned in their papers on "the whiteness of the whale" in Moby Dick, *one student stays behind. She leans awkwardly against my desk. She looks down at the patches she has sewn to her backpack. One reads, "If you can read this, you're too fuckin' close." I almost giggle—knowing the school's policies about the display of such language. "What's up?" I ask her. "I'm pregnant," she answers. And we both stand quiet under the horrible fluorescent light. She begins to cry. I cannot come close to her. I cannot comfort her. I have listened hard during my teacher training meetings: Do not touch your students under any circumstances. Do not touch them. They cannot be touched. You cannot trust what they will say. You cannot touch them for any reason.*

Embodied Practices

It can certainly trouble both teachers and students when they come face to face with the materiality of the body. It helps me to understand both myself and my students if I think of my masculinity as a kind of embodied betrayal—not because I believe that, as their teacher, I commit a kind of falseness but because understanding the dynamic as a perceived betrayal helps to explain what, for many students, is a challenging and unusual interaction—the androgynous body, the men's ties I wear to class, the deep voice, the "female" pronoun. The body that betrays "professional boundaries" by *not* being able to be rendered invisible (a body that appears legible in its normativity *might* be able to be rendered invisible) is a body that must be reckoned with as one of the classroom's primary texts. One cannot avoid or ignore it any more than one could avoid or ignore the work of a course that must be done in order to complete it. To be intelligible then might mean to be invisible even if that intelligibility is only a perceived intelligibility. As Judith Butler reminds us, "There are advantages to remaining less than intelligible, if intelligibility is understood as that which is produced as a consequence of recognition according to prevailing social norms" (*Undoing* 3). In other words, it is not necessarily a sad story to be an unintelligible body, to be something other than "produced as a consequence of recognition according to prevailing social norms." To be intelligible is to be seen through the lens of what already is, or what already appears to be. To be unintelligible is to be, quite literally, a becoming. Butler goes on to say that "if I have no desire to be recognized within a certain set of norms, then it follows that my sense of survival depends upon escaping the clutch of those norms by which recognition is conferred" (3). In this sense, my students do not recognize me, and that they do not recognize me is integral to my survival—that is, if I want to be the person I continue to become and still teach classes in settings where the social norms "by which recognition is conferred" cannot be said to apply to me. I do not have the desire to be "recognized within a certain set of norms," and so Butler is spot on that this lack of *desire* means that my survival "depends upon escaping the clutch of those norms." I am always aware, when I am teaching or thinking about my teaching, that my pedagogy is, at its heart, about my own survival, or about the survival of *my kind*—those of us living outside "those norms by which recognition is conferred." There is a selfishness, I fear, to this pedagogy, though most of the time I suspect all teachers are trying to survive, asking students to try on new ways of thinking so that we might live in a more layered world—one ringing more loudly with possibilities for writing, for knowing, and for becoming.

A newly born loon can dive and swim on its own the second it is born, though most newborn loons will rest on their parents' backs for the first few weeks of life. They do this primarily to maintain heat and to avoid predators.

The cyclical process of disruption and recognition brings to light some of the differences between the body and embodiment—"embodiment [which is distinct from but also inextricably linked to notions of the body] moves in conjunction with inscription, technology, and ideology" (Hayles 196). N. Katherine Hayles suggests that embodiment "moves," that it is moving in accordance with inscription (which might be understood as what is "written on" or inscribed upon the body, a kind of labeling that implies meaning); with technology, as it changes what can be known and done about bodies; and lastly with ideology, which tells us what bodies mean. Embodiment, Hayles writes, is "the specific instantiation generated from the noise of difference" (196). Hayles understands embodiment as being created *by* difference; without difference, or the perception of difference, there would be only bodies. The "noise of difference" rings loudly in classrooms—between students, between our performances to and for one another, between their gendered embodiment and my own. Such a curious, cacophonous, seductive, beautiful, and tragic noise—a noise that calls out in my writing of assignments and in my students' trying to write and work within the parameters that I, in some ways, have little choice but to set. To teach queerly, to teach as a queer, to enact or design a queer pedagogy is, by definition and by practice, paradoxical. If part of the transformative power of queer theory is the concept of queer—its elasticity, its fluidity, its resistance to definition—then queer pedagogy becomes a particularly challenging contradiction. I, after all, make a syllabus, design assignments, ask students to perform within the parameters I define—something I take up in chapters two and three. And though I confess to not always being comfortable setting these parameters, or giving grades as a response to how well students might follow these parameters, I do these quite un-queer tasks in the confines of the institution that disciplines both me and my students.

Loons have considerable and remarkable stamina. They travel and migrate long distances during the winter, and they can live up to thirty years.

Like any social or cultural experience, the classroom has its field of constraints, its norms. Butler calls this the "doubled truth that although we need norms in order to live, and to live well, and to know in what direction to transform our social world, we are also constrained by norms in ways that sometimes do violence to us" (*Undoing* 205–6). And the violence Butler describes has many meanings and layers. There is, of course, the obvious and overt violence, which is easier to see and identify *as violence*. But the part of my challenge (as a teacher interested in the idea of queering teaching itself) is to identify those less apparent moments of violence—moments, without my knowing, in which my norms (my syllabus, my assignments, my set of assumptions about my students) might do their own version of violence. This is not always easy to see and understand. Norms themselves are not violence, but, as Butler cautions, norms can constrain in ways that *do violence*. I think of this violence as a kind of control or limitation that is completely un-queer—without flexibility, elasticity, or the possibility of change. I write my assignments, not always successfully, in an attempt to leave room for students to change and resist the very parameters the assignments set up. But this room sometimes leads to a tricky and difficult negotiation between the violence my parameters might do to students and the violence their resistance might to do me.

In a first-year writing class, I asked my students to do a short writing response to Kate Bornstein's concept of the gender terrorist. The assignment was as follows:

> Re-read the following passage from *Gender Outlaw*:
>
>> For a while, I thought that it would be fun to call what I do in life gender terrorism. Seemed right at first—I and so many folks like me were terrorizing the structure of gender itself. But I've come to see it a bit differently now—gender terrorists are not the drag queens, the butch dykes, the men on roller skates dressed as nuns. Gender terrorists are not the female to male transsexual who's learning to look people in the eye as he walks down the street. Gender terrorists are not the leather daddies or back seat Betties. Gender terrorists are not the married men, shivering in the dark as they slip on their wives' panties. Gender terrorists are those who bang their heads against a gender system which is real and natural, and who then use gender to terrorize the rest of us. These are the real terrorists: the Gender Defenders. (72)
>
> Compose a response to Bornstein's definition of a gender terrorist. Can you think of examples of Gender Terrorism as she defines it? Are we all implicated in her definition? Are you implicated in any way? Why or why not?

Many of my students responded quite thoughtfully and compassionately to the passage, citing examples of having seen people asked to leave bathrooms, talking about their gay or trans cousins, friends, and so on. Many students spoke eloquently about the expectations set by society and about how those expectations caused people to respond or behave. Many students were able to write in a complicated way about their responses, even despite the fact that my final question (a failure of a question, indeed) "why or why not?" sets them up to do one or the other of these things. In reading through the student responses, there is one particular response that seems relevant to my concerns about this idea of *violence*. This response was from a male-identified student who often let out sighs in class (sighs I read as disbelief or a kind of resistance) or sat with his arms folded but rarely said anything. I read these classroom actions as a form of resistance, though I cannot, of course, be certain of what they are. Of course, the student's writing inevitably shapes the ways I understand his classroom actions. I want very much to leave room for his resistance; I want the assignments and the classroom to have room, to leave open the possibility of his discomfort, or his frustration—if that's indeed what it is. In response to the assignment, the student writes, "Bornstein should change this book now that it's 2005. You can't run around calling people who think women look ridiculous and funny in ties gender terrorists. Terrorists are people who fly planes into important buildings. It's horrifying to think her problems are serious at all enough to equate them with terrorists. Even all her examples are funny. When people 'slip on their wives' panties,' they make themselves open to ridicule. I'm not going to feel bad for them" (Anonymous Student C, Untitled writing).

I first notice that Bornstein says nothing about "women in ties," but the student does say something about this. And, of course, I have been standing in the front of the classroom in a shirt and tie for two months by this point, so it is hard to imagine that the student is not talking to me (even though he, technically, is not). Technically, he is talking about a more general and less dangerous "them," a "them" who is not in the room, a "them" who is not me, a "them" who "slip on their wives' panties," a "them" he cannot imagine in any room he might be in. But my reading of his writing is that this student will not take seriously a performance of "illegitimate" masculinity such as mine. I begin to think he imagines me as a "poser," as the autodidact masculine who makes themselves "open to ridicule." Perhaps a serious identity, a valid and authentic identity, is one that matches a body, a "normal" portrayal of gender and sexuality. As I read this student writing, Bornstein's concerns are "horrifying" in that the student is horrified that she would consider her "problems" to be problems of a kind of terrorism. This horror might not be only about the word *terrorism*'s connection to 9/11. Terrorism, the student worries, is not funny. I think we (all of us—students, teachers, writers) would agree it is not at all funny. Bornstein certainly does not say that gender terrorism is funny. As I read it, this student's horror *is* about terrorism; it is about the idea that someone you couldn't see, someone undetectable, someone you might have even trusted, would betray you—your traditions, your culture, your life, your country. This horror is, more specifically, the horror of "passing." It is also the horror of movable boundaries, of blurring, and of coming to see that what we think we know will not stay still, will not, in the end, *become* knowledge.

If threatened, a loon might do what is called a "penguin dance" whereby the loon looks as though it is standing on top of the water, holding its wings at its sides like a penguin would. The loon is a kind of chameleon. The "penguin dance" is a sign of extreme agitation. Birdwatchers advise humans to keep away from loon doing a "penguin dance."

What we think we know will not emerge as a stable truth; it will not, as it were, turn into truth; it will not *become* permanent and knowable knowledge, but it will become a becoming, an emerging, elastic, and changing knowledge—knowledge queered. And the truth is, as I read this student's writing, I understood the various ways he might be terrorized by me (by my course, by this book I had chosen for him to read); I also understood the ways I, too, felt terrorized by him—he's *not going to feel bad for them*. It's the "them" that's terrifying. It's seeing myself as this student's "them." It's becoming the *other* to a single one of my students. It is the fear that every one of my students, however politely, thinks of me this way. They might or might not, of course. On some level, and if I subscribe to my own definition of knowledge, I cannot know what my students *really* think, or how they imagine me. But I am, after all, afraid of my students—as, I think, most teachers are if we are honest with ourselves about what is at stake in offering one's vision—one's assignments, philosophies, and inevitably one's identities—as a site for intellectual inquiry and written exploration.

I got to play Hansel in the school production of Hansel and Gretel. *I had practiced being shoved into the oven. I had watched my brothers intently, practicing my protective boyish faces. And I was a good Hansel. And I felt at home in Hansel's clothing. I felt, at last, like someone's brother. And when the play is over, the audience claps and cheers, my family in the third row—my brothers punching one another and laughing, my mother looking down. But the rest of the room is in love with us. They love the play. They love Hansel. And I am soaking up my boyhood, until Mrs. Toriani says into the microphone, "These children are wonderful little actors, so wonderful that Hansel was played by Stacey Waite, quite a talented little girl." There's a pause. There's the sense of surprise. I'm mortified. I am, in the end, no Hansel.*

Here, Julia Kristeva offers me one interesting way of thinking about the experience of students who are "normatively gendered" when they come into contact with the female masculine body, with my body. Kristeva writes, "It is thus not lack of cleanliness or health that causes abjection but what disturbs identity, system, order. What does not respect borders, positions, rules. The in-between, the ambiguous, the composite" (4). Abjection seems a viable way to describe what happens when students encounter an unreadable body in a pedagogical context. Here, the pedagogy *and* the teacher's body are sites of abjection—both do not "respect borders, positions, rules," both are the "in-between, the ambiguous, the composite." After all, as Karen Kopelson suggests, "A queer performative pedagogy, in fact, often *strives* to confuse, as it strives to push thought beyond circumscribed divisions—strives to push thought beyond what can be *thought*" ("Dis/Integrating" 20). A queer pedagogy aims to put pressure on or stretch those norms of recognition Butler describes. What *can be thought* is already within those normative parameters. And to push beyond *what can be thought*, we must be able to think beyond those norms, to write beyond them, to think of new possibilities. And while this seems compelling, I am aware, as I write this, that I want my students to be able to imagine me, to *think* of me, to make me, in the end, possible.

It is illegal to hunt or kill loons. Many have been found dead with high amounts of mercury in their blood. Many of their natural habitats are being polluted by the pastime of driving one's motorboat or by the spilling of chemicals.

Kopelson argues for a pedagogy and a teaching body that disrupt and destabilize identity. She argues, for example, that "coming out" as any stable identity might be a mistake in a classroom. According to Kopelson, one might only seek to "come out" *as* destabilizing. If we are interested in what queer theory offers us—a productive way of thinking about identity and the body—we might consider the ways we might all "come out" as destabilizing, impossible, unthinkable. I am not interested in arguing here whether certain identities may feel themselves to be fixed or stable; I work with the understanding that there are momentary and even necessary fixities, or particular strategic (and even activist) reasons why one might, at some given moment, name identity as fixed or unilateral. For the purposes of my work, however, I am interested in the idea that fixed and stable identities are not always useful for writing pedagogies. I think that what it means to introduce students to writing in the humanities is to ask students to consider that composition is not a moment when we decide one thing over another or take one side of a two-sided debate—rather, it is an act of wavering and careful consideration in which writers move fluidly through the complicated terrain of their own thinking and the thinking of others. In terms of this fluidity, I would say that while my masculine body is at times troubling or resisted, it can also be an opportunity for confusion of the productive kind, the kind that produces complicated ways of knowing that push the borders of what can be written or thought.

I am in college and taking a course subtitled "Fictional History." I have a professor who practices, in each opportunity for confusion of the productive kind, a "destabilizing" pedagogy. We are talking about why a particular student in the class does not find pleasure in reading a series of Toni Morrison's books. The student says to the professor, "I just think women enjoy books like these more than men, that's all." He says it with no ill will, sort of sweetly. The professor, Professor Hill, says to him, "And do you think I am a woman?" The student grins, sort of. He sees her clearly in her long dress, her full lips, and perfectly feminine cheekbones. We (all of us in the class) "know" she is a woman. She goes on: "What makes you think I am a woman, Charles?" The student doesn't answer again. We spend the better part of that hour, as a class, making a list of reasons we think Professor Hill is a woman. It starts with silence before someone says, "Your first name is Mary." Another student says, "You said you were a mother." She writes them on the board as we list them. We must reckon with our perception of her body. No one ever says she has breasts, but we are all thinking it. We are all thinking of the material conditions we could not (because of boundaries) name that would settle the question once and for all. Professor Hill shows us the holes, the room for possibility in each of our womanhood proofs. We never did get to Toni Morrison that day, or perhaps we did some other way I couldn't name.

Abject Pedagogy

At times my masculinity is read in a way that is advantageous to me. As Deborah Meem writes of her own positioning as a teacher, "Students and faculty see my butchness as powerful, especially as contrasted with femme experience, which is mostly invisible" (in Gibson et al. 82). Like Meem, I also rarely, if ever, experience the space of invisibility she describes here, the space reserved for "women," a space that is sexually visible while intellectually or politically *invisible*. I have no idea what it is like, for example, to be treated as a female sexual object by male students. My masculinity might be said to protect me from this particular gaze, however illegitimate my masculinity may be. And the issues I may have with authority in my classroom are rarely public—most male students do not, for example, challenge me publicly (as they might do silently or in their papers). This may be in part because of my enactment of teacherly authority, but because of the ways my teacherly authority is inextricable from my masculinity I often wonder if this lack of public or classroom challenge comes from a fear that my illegitimate masculinity may somehow supernaturally trump their "real" masculinity. Feminine "women" might not be feared in this precise way, though they are, of course, feared in others. Masculinity worn on the "female" body can change an environment in specific ways, can change the bodies in that environment, can call the entire notion of the body and the environment into question, because it troubles their meanings. After all, as Kristeva also points out, what is abject has much to illuminate with regard to meaning: "If the object, however, through its opposition, settles me within the fragile texture of a desire for meaning, which, as a matter of fact, makes me ceaselessly and infinitely homologous to it[,] what is abject, on the contrary, the jettisoned object, is radically excluded and draws me toward the place where meaning collapses" (1–2). The "desire for meaning" is not merely a desire for any meaning at all or for multiple meanings. The meaning of legitimate masculinity is a singular, fixed meaning according to those who establish and perpetuate its singularity and static-ness. So when, as Kristeva asserts, "the abject" brings us to the place "where meaning collapses"—*the place the bird hits water*—we are, in turn, horrified (and perhaps intrigued as well). We are faced with a moment of crisis about ourselves and about our notions of how the world is named and ordered. Written texts can have this effect as well, but I want to emphasize that the body is most rooted in desire, and in shame, and that its appearance creates the intense and visceral site of abjection that Kristeva describes. While I have taken only part of Kristeva's theory of abjection as a lens through which to look at female masculinity in the context of my classrooms and their discourses, I read her notion of abjection as a lens that allows us to theorize the in-between, the ambiguous, and the unnamed in the classroom.

The abject can often be seen as criminal. And there is a sense in which I have "stolen" masculinity, a sense in which I have taken an inheritance that does not belong to me or to my line of people—namely, "women." Masculinity, is, in a sense, a type of inherited capital (the male body) that prepares a man for his acquisition of cultural or social capital (what Bourdieu would deem the masculine habitus). In this way, we can understand Bourdieu's thoughts about education alongside the model of female masculinity I have described above. Bourdieu explains, "Likewise, in every relationship between educational capital and a given practice, one sees the effect of the dispositions associated with gender which help to determine the logic of the reconversion of inherited capital into educational capital, that is, the 'choice' of the type of educational capital which will be obtained from the same initial capital" (*Distinction* 105). Bourdieu writes about educational capital as a series of titles or stages achieved through masculinity, the inherited capital masquerading as achieved educational capital. To become a gender, we must learn it; we must receive an education in it; we must learn masculinity. Some of us, though, are perceived as having inherited it as part of our *natural* right. This system of reconversion applies to the inheritance of masculinity and finally to how masculinity is passed down—educationally, culturally, socially. As for the female masculine, we must resort to stealing pieces of the masculine educational capital regardless of our living in a society that tells us we have little or no right to that capital. We have no inherited capital, as women. The inheritance of masculinity belongs to men. While of course Bourdieu's claims are linked to other kinds of identity, I am interested, for the purposes of this inquiry, in the connections he makes to gender and masculinity. I am interested in thinking about how women (and genderqueer-identified people) become thieves of masculine capital. I think of myself as this kind of thief, someone who has attained masculinity without any right to it, someone who is a writer—another kind of thief altogether.

There is always the sense that students find their teachers strange outside the environment of the classroom. For me, however, there is the sense, in certain moments, that this strangeness is amplified. When my composition course breaks halfway through, I stand nervously with the women in my class as we wait for stalls in the women's room. They are nervous too. We do not speak. We look at the white floor. Or I do. There is the sense there is a man in this room. There is the sense of invasion, of the criminal.

The title of this section is, in a sense, dramatic. Abjection conjures up the perverse and repulsive. Kristeva gives as material examples: corpses and shit. Do I really believe my body is abject—and moreover that students might experience my body as abjection? Or, is queering itself abjection? Is the queer subject always abject? In his book *What Do Gay Men Want? An Essay on Sex, Risk, and Subjectivity* (2007), David Halperin traces abjection's path prior to Kristeva's *Powers of Horror*. Halperin writes, "Abjection therefore has a particularly precise and powerful relevance to gay men as well as to other despised social groups, who have a heightened, and intimate, experience of its social operations" (69). I, my students' teacher, am a member of one of these "other despised social groups." Often, some of my students are members of these groups as well. Whether one might call my body transgender or intersex is not clear. The truth is I often do not want to contend with this reality, which only furthers the notion of abjection—a casting out of perversity, my queer and impossible nature. If abjection, as Halperin asserts, is about social power and social experience (perhaps more so than it is about psychoanalysis), we need only look to popular talk shows that often display those of my kind preying on traditionally gendered and heterosexual innocents. We need only look at media representations of Thomas Beatie, the pregnant man, or the discussions surrounding the gender of the South African Olympic runner Caster Semenya. The headlines: "Tests show that controversial runner Caster Semenya is a woman . . . and a man!!!!!" There is outrage, horror, exertion of social force: abjection.

Driving through the back roads of rural Pennsylvania several years back, I stop at a rest stop along Route 28, a winding mountain road that takes me from graduate school back to the small town where I went to college. I have to go to the bathroom. I consider pulling over to use the woods but am running of out gas. When I step out of the gas station bathroom, I find myself against the brick wall of the building, a forearm pressing into my throat. And when I look into his face, he is young and handsome and wants to kill me. I think of a vigil there might be at the college. I think of my mother who will wish I had done more to fit in. I think of the woman inside this man who will kill me. I think she is terribly beautiful.

Halperin goes on to discuss the work of Jean Genet and focuses his attention on the abject as embraced by the queer, as a way of reversing its power to dominate or humiliate. My classroom is a room inside the social world; it is an extension of that world. So to think of my classroom, and my body, as a site of abjection is not dramatic, is not an overstatement of the social dynamics at work in the world and in the teaching situation. To many of my students, I am abject. As I am to myself. As I must be to survive. But why? Why would I find value in pedagogies of abjection, in the abject? Why would I give my students the book *Gender Outlaw*, knowing how likely it is so many of them will cringe at Bornstein's mention of golden showers or butt plugs? Halperin, through his work with Genet, offers another understanding:

> Far from glorifying domination, abjection achieves a spiritual release from it by derealizing its humiliating effects—by depriving domination of its ability to demean the subject and, thus, robbing it of a portion of its reality. As a result, social persecution loses some of its crushing power and changes its meaning (hatred is transformed into love). Only once domination has been defied through being resignified can it be transformed into a vehicle for attaining beatitude. (*What* 78)

In the abject itself, in the experience of abjection, is the possibility of changed meaning, of transformation, of resignification, of, finally, a kind of spiritual blessing. And Halperin echoes here the Christian term "beatitude" as a way of enacting the very resignifying he describes. There are layers of meaning here as to how this notion of abjection speaks to teaching, to my teaching. First, I value the abject experience and believe that experience is one that can happen in many ways—in literal social experience, in reading, in the discussion of ideas, in behavior, and in writing. This value is, admittedly, quite personal. If I am to value my own life (and I do), I am to value abjection. Second, I believe that writing has the transformative potential of abjection. And finally, as the existence of Halperin's book suggests, gender and sexuality (especially when we think of abjection in social terms) exist at the contradiction of shame and pride. Abjection exists always in contradiction; Kristeva and Halperin are in agreement about that. And, in returning to my first layer of meaning, whereby I claim to value abjection, I then value, in my teaching and in writing (my own writing and my students' writing), the capacity to live, write, and learn in contradiction. This is asking a lot of myself and of my students. In an earlier book, *Saint Foucault*, Halperin writes, "Queer is by definition *whatever* is at odds with the normal, the legitimate, the dominant. *There is nothing in particular to which it necessarily refers.* It is an identity without an essence" (62, original emphasis). What could be more contradictory? What could be more disorienting? How can I understand or explore queer pedagogies if, according to Halperin's definition of queer, it is a pedagogy without an essence?

There is a federal law called the Migratory Bird Treaty Act, which protects loons from the harassment of humans. This includes violating low-wake or no-wake zones. The aggressive movement of boat wakes can wash away loon nests at the shoreline.

Pedagogy of Melancholy

In her essay "Melancholy Gender/Refused Identification," Butler describes how gender creates a kind of grieving, which accompanies this sense of abjection I am interested in; she calls it "a mourning of unlived possibilities" (32) in which gender is always already about loss. In this case Butler is talking about a compulsory heterosexual model in which one becomes a girl, for example, by not desiring another girl, but then mourns the girl she is and therefore the girl she cannot have. This model means that succeeding at one's gender means to succeed at not lusting after one's own gender; one becomes a woman by refusing to want another woman. Desires not being met can certainly qualify as a kind of abjection in that when our desires cannot be met, there is a clashing between the world as it is and the world as we wished or thought it to be. Then, following, we must grieve that loss—the loss of the world as we wished or thought it to be in order to try to move the world as it is—whatever that means—into its place. This is not to suggest that there is a "world as it is" but rather that there are moments of seeing, flickers of clarity in which we are either affirmed or challenged in our seeing—or some combination of both. If we are challenged and find that what we see destroys some other version or vision we had, we experience the melancholy Butler describes—the melancholy, the mourning of the person we are and the person we cannot be/have. There is, or can also be, a kind of exhilaration in this loss. There is, or can also be, a kind of gaining—a layering whereby our prior understandings become part of new understandings creating a more complicated, more both-at-once vision. A simultaneous, perhaps even paradoxical, vision.

Bird watchers have said is it virtually impossible to tell the difference between a female loon and a male loon. There is sometimes a difference in size, but nothing distinct to mention. Nothing that allows us to see the loon and know it.

Students, like everyone, have visions of the world, have visions of themselves inside it. And when they come into contact with texts/bodies/ideas that do not fit that vision, there can be great risk for them; they can lose vision, can lose some version of themselves they hold dear, can experience great loss. For example, in teaching Peggy McIntosh's "White Privilege: Unpacking the Invisible Knapsack" (in which she lists more than fifty privileges belonging to white people only and only by virtue of their skin color), I received the following response from one of my students: "I was brought up to believe all people are equal. I find it hard to believe that in this day and age that these privileges hold to be true. If they were true, I would have to feel pretty bummed out that my success was so fake" (Anonymous Student C, Untitled writing). There is so much in my pedagogy, in my body, in the content of my courses that may have students "pretty bummed out" or that may get them feeling that their realities are at risk as "fake." The student's discussion of the possibility of being "bummed out" if what McIntosh says is true is a real sense of loss for this student. If he reads the essay in a way that allows his version of equality to be challenged, he loses something: his own sense of "success," which is important to him, as it is to all of us. By assigning this essay, by bringing to class a contradictory identity, a movable body, I put my students at risk. I ask them to purposely put their realities in danger and, in a sense, to embrace that danger. This is no small task, despite the fact that our identities and realities are always in danger.

There is no immovable place, no permanent understanding, though we may proceed as though there were. We don't often want to look there, to find this danger and walk in its direction. And what is to say the risk will be worth it? What might we all (students and teachers alike) gain in spite of these abjections, risks, and losses? This melancholy pedagogy in which we lose, again and again, what we believed to be permanent and stable visions. My gender performance, in this sense, undoes a version of reality even as it undoes me. Or, my gender performance might reaffirm what is already thought, reify those norms of recognition—making my gender performance, again, abject.

Understanding how female masculinity might function inside a classroom can offer an approach to teaching. Kopelson writes, "Performative pedagogy is thus a 'doing' that disclaims 'being'—or at least a doing that disclaims the idea of 'being' as singular, unified, and static" ("Dis/Integrating" 25). This performative pedagogy might help students to develop critical and political positions from which to read and write if they are reading and writing in a classroom in which the instructor's body will not lie still on the specimen table of identity. The instructor will not "be" their identities. They will only perform identities. It is important that teachers move, (even in the sense that Professor Hill moves) that we create moments of abjection from which our students can emerge, from which we can emerge.

Fishermen are dangerous to loons. A loon can mistake lures and jigs for live prey. Loons die each year from entanglement in fishing line or from swallowing lures, which can cause them to die of lead poisoning.

I mean not at all to compose a heroic narrative of how my "butchness" makes for good teaching. In fact, this inquiry began from my own frustrations and failures, from the difficulty and challenges of teaching in my body rather than from any promising pedagogical moments I might have. My butchness, in fact, like most categories of identity, makes for complicated teaching, for teaching that confuses. Teachers' bodies, our raced, sexed, classed, spiritualized, clothed bodies, when they become visible, or are made visible to students, complicate our pedagogies whether or not we choose to acknowledge how. As Kopelson reminds us, "*Queer* is a term that offers to us and our students an epistemological position—a way of knowing rather than something to be known" ("Dis/Integrating" 25). This epistemological position is a movable position, one that wavers; it may, in fact, not be "a" position at all, but multiple positions, *ways* of knowing rather than *somethings* to be known. Our ways of knowing are inextricably linked to our ways of being, our becoming. In this sense, this project is both an epistemological and ontological meditation on pedagogy, as it is also tied to a shifting self.

The loon song is one that has inspired cultures for centuries. On northern lakes where they nest in the summer, loons utter long, drawn-out, wailing cries and screams at night. Early Inuit cultures buried loon skulls in graves. Because of its mournful song, the loon was thought to act as a guide into the netherworld.

On my first day of every course, I walk in terrified, the shake of voice, the sweating, the stomach turning over and over at the thought of interpretation. My students need a pronoun with which to refer to me; their language demands it. Years ago, I would avoid the pronouns altogether until once, a kind, hard-working, and well-meaning student (as most of my students are) does something on the first day he never quite forgives himself for. He's late for starters and then says loudly to a classmate, "Did *he* give out the syllabus yet?" The classroom rings with discomfort. I can hear several giggles, several students shifting in their seats. The other students have "figured out" by now that I am not a man—at least not in a way they are used to. The student sinks down in his chair. He does not look at me for weeks. He believes he has done something hurtful, I think. I suspect he thinks he has offended me, which (of course) he has not. These days, I begin with pronouns; I talk about my gender in those first few moments of introducing myself to my students. I try it comically and gently: *If you think you're not quite sure about my gender now, wait 'til you read these books on the syllabus.* They laugh, sometimes nervously. *My parents refer to me as "she"; you may do the same. But it doesn't mean you know anything about how I throw a ball.* Again, they laugh, less nervously this time. We try to work it out together, the stories of one another's bodies. We spend the semester "undoing" the texts we read, undoing the texts of our bodies. And there is risk, and sadness, and horror, and seduction, and the sense that nothing is as it first appears. I assume things, too, about them; they teach me again and again that I cannot do so.

The Work of Assumptions

The loon's red eyes, caused by pigment in the retina, allow them clear underwater vision. They can dive up to two hundred feet deep for as long as ten minutes.

In talking with students about gender, I sometimes begin by asking them to notice their assumptions about what feminism is and what a feminist does or looks like. I ask them, "What are some stereotypes about feminists?" And this is a question they readily answer with (and these are just some of their responses): doesn't shave, is a lesbian, overassertive, loud, manly, finds fault with everything, militant, overcritical, and doesn't know when to shut up. As we construct this vision of a feminist in our minds, as we look at this list on the board together, I can't help but straighten my tie and wonder if I might just follow up the list on the board by saying, "Well, now that you've met me. . . ." There is the sense that when my students arrive in my composition courses focused on sexuality and gender, they are reading my position from the moment they step in the door. It figures, after all, that a short-haired, manly, overcritical "woman" would teach a course that starts in with the whole feminism thing right away. My position is being read one of two ways by my students: (1) I am trying to "convince" them to be feminist radicals because I want them to think I am okay; in other words, my intellectual interests are reduced to personal investment only (and perhaps there is always some truth in this assumption for all teachers), or (2) because my body inhabits the space that it does, I must certainly be the holder of the body of knowledge of all that is feminist and butch lesbian (perhaps there is some truth in this assumption as well). All semester, my students and I dance around one another's identity. They suspect me and I, in turn, suspect them. In her essay "Identity Politics in the College Classroom, or Whose Issue Is This Anyway?" Katherine Mayberry suggests that "the politicization of identity, knowledge, and authority have changed" much about the way students and their instructors interact, "introducing an identity-based definition of *credibility* as an entirely new precondition of professional authority" (3). In fact, I find myself wondering how I might begin to discuss my authority or my credibility with my students, to engage in a dialogue about the way we are reading one another as bodies in terms of gender and the assumptions we make about what we are trying to get one another to do. For example, at times, I suspect my students of being polite and refusing to assert their "real" beliefs in fear of literally "hurting my feelings." But often, identity begins there, with feelings. As Laura Micciche reminds us, "Emotion matters to *writing* teachers, who remain indebted to Dewey's belief in the democratizing function of education, because writing is mediated by language, bodies, and culture; writing involves sticky attachments that evolve and materialize through the writing process, including emotioned attachments that find their way onto the page sometimes against our will or without our conscious intent" (106). We guess at one another's feelings; we project our fear and desire onto one another. And through writing, our bodies are both obscured and made vulnerable to one another. There are also times I suspect my students of being overly resistant to texts because they feel threatened not so much by the text itself but by me, by my body and its lack of a satisfying explanation. At the close of a composition course, I gave my students the following prompt:

> Return back to your papers this semester and read through my comments. Write a letter addressed to me in which you consider the following: What kind of writer am I asking you to be and why might I ask you to be this particular writer? What kinds of questions do I seem to be wanting you to ask? How do you feel about my challenges to your ideas, and where in the course did you see my reading of the text and yours as drastically different? Why might they be different? What about you or about me might cause us to read a text so differently? Use specific examples from my comments to make your points.

I was terrified to get these papers. But there is so much I have to learn about the relationship between my students and myself in terms of identity in order to teach them about reading and writing. One of my students, whose permission I have to use her writing but not her name, discusses what she calls our "totally opposite ways" of reading the following claim by Kate Bornstein. Bornstein writes, "In living along the borders of the gender frontier, I've come to see the gender system created by this culture as a particularly malevolent and divisive construct, made all the more dangerous by the seeming inability of the culture to *question* gender, its own creation" (*Gender* 12). The student writes,

> I think the whole reason that Bornstein doesn't really affect me as much with this line is because I want to keep my gender. Although you don't seem to go as overboard as Bornstein, it seems like you want things that go against what is expected for women, so it would make sense that you'd see gender as malevolent. What I want is to stay a woman, to play that role and maybe I said what I said about Bornstein because she wants gender to be "performance?" and I think there is something more internal, spiritual even, about it. I want to be a woman. I know that you probably know more about gender than me but I cannot believe that gender is "a creation of culture." I just can't. (Anonymous Student D, Untitled writing)

This student, quite astutely I think, articulates something about reading that she may not have articulated before: that our reading of a text is somehow located in "want." She *wants* to be a woman and suspects I have been more "affected" by Kate Bornstein's book because I want something different from the world than she does. Of course, I did not have to tell my students explicitly that this particular text illustrates many of my own ideas about gender, but they have positioned me with the text—*partially* because I am the instructor and I have chosen the text but also, and more so, because my performance of gender, as the student says, "goes against what is expected." The student positions Bornstein as "going overboard" and positions me as perhaps a less militant version of Bornstein. She ends her response with the words "I just can't," which I think reveals another way that desire and the body become visible in the teaching of composition. In this short paragraph, the student comes to the conclusion that there is something about "want" and about willingness that positions a reader who is considering these ideas about gender. Another student in this particular composition class writes,

> Next to where I wrote "Feminism itself might be a reason for inequality," you wrote to me "In what sense?" And I don't know why but I felt like you were annoyed with me in a way, not that "in what sense" is a mean comment, but there is a possibility that you didn't know what I meant. OK, let me get this out right. If Kate Bornstein (and you I think) believes that gender is a myth and that it being a two-choice system is what creates all the problems, then wouldn't feminism also be setting up a two-choice system. OK, because if feminism is about women being equal to men then it's about women and men, which means gender has to exist. I think you

want me to agree with Bornstein and agree with feminism, but you haven't proved to me why I guess because the two things are saying reverse ideas. I know you're gonna say it's wrong, but I think it's true. (Anonymous Student E, Untitled writing)

This student articulates a contradiction in what he sees as two of the ideologies represented in my course and represented by me—perhaps by the very existence of my body itself. He had no idea how happy I would be to read his response. He assumes that I am trying to "prove" to him that feminism and this text, *Gender Outlaw*, are supporting arguments I want him to "agree" with. The student positions my emotional reading of his text, that I was annoyed with him when I wrote "in what sense?" He then ends by saying, "I know you're gonna say it's wrong." Of course, I think my question "in what sense?" is a generous one, but I have to be honest in saying I did assume that he was suggesting that feminism creates inequality because women then want to surpass or be better than men. Perhaps I assumed he meant this because I read him as a man, as a white male college freshman who is "probably threatened by feminism," never mind the queer content in Bornstein's book. In actuality, this student and I are concerned about the limits of feminism in some of the same ways. In fact, we are perhaps both "postfeminist" in that sense, both concerned with a kind of gender multiplicity.

The loon is a water bird. Loons build their nests at the edge of the shoreline. They bring up vegetation and reeds from the bottom of the lake. They rise up on the water to dry their wings and collect pieces of tree branches to bring to the nest.

This assignment changed my relationship with many of my students. As we discussed some of their responses in class, it became clear that with each excerpt we looked at, we became more human to one another; we became physical, intellectual, and emotional beings—all of us having sets of assumptions shaping our interpretations, shaping our interactions. I don't discuss this assignment as a "magic trick" to composition but rather one of the ways I was able to make the assumptions about desire, body, and intention more visible, a way to address the question of my gender, and of theirs, and how these genders and bodies shape the texts we read and the texts the students write.

Loons need up to one-half mile of build-up running in order to lift themselves up into the air. Once they do, they can fly up to sixty miles per hour.

Notes on Teaching (the Teacher)

Our histories are quite similar in terms of how we come into being, how we arrive or are said to arrive in the world. The body is the first text. There might, as it were, be a sonogram to locate the presence or lack in the child's body as it is submerged in the fluid that holds in warmth and nourishment. The doctor will announce the presence or lack. What the child is, how the child is to be interpreted gets named into being. The first interpretative act is one enacted upon us, one we cannot control or enter into a conversation about. We will then be born into a body, and we ourselves will begin to interpret our world in this gendered body, this first trap of unconsciousness, unwavering, perceived as certain. A careful set of cultural rules will instruct us that our genders are natural, that they go always without question. We learn first what not to question. We learn first the antithesis of knowing, to accept without wondering, without asking or probing. We learn that these expressions of our named gender are natural. Butler, in *Gender Trouble*, describes the process, writing, "There is no gender identity behind the expressions of gender . . . identity is performatively constituted by the very 'expressions' that are said to be its results" (25). Expressions of gender are naturalized through the process I describe above, but they are not natural. They are named and contained into being.

Usually only two loons inhabit one lake. They are territorial birds. They often return to the same lakes but don't always continue last year's courtship.

This is often where names come from; they come from a desire to contain wonderment. It is here that my students and I must commit to teaching one another to wonder how we know what we know, what ways of knowing have led us to know what we know, and (finally) how we will enact ways of knowing that have the potential to make new knowledge about our names, about our bodies, about reading and writing, about the lives we imagine. The construction of masculinity, of the body, of a reader, of students, of the body of their teacher. For many of us, many of the ways of knowing we have learned are ways that cover the tracks of acquired knowledge, invisible ways of knowing that then appear naturalized; they appear as found knowledge rather than made. To teach, inevitably, means to engage with and be responsible for constructions of identity. And one of our first tasks is to expose that constructedness; however, that will not, in the end, be enough. As one of my students reminded me in an anonymous midterm course evaluation in which I asked what questions they were hoping the rest of the course would address, "I guess, what do we do if everything we know is just a bunch of spoon fed ideas about who we're supposed to be or who everyone is? It seems like we don't know anything then." This student reminds me of something very important: it is not enough to expose identity as unstable or fragile, or to expose its constructedness. Something more needs to happen. The student feels stuck. I start to feel stuck. Yes, what do we make now of identity knowing full well what it has tried to make of us?

Just as this project seeks to sound off in a number of registers, so does identity. Each register is its own way of knowing. To know lyrically might be thought something quite aside from knowing theoretically. To know narratively, something quite distinct from knowing politically. And so on. And when the lines begin to blur, I think we can begin to *make* new ways of knowing, ways of knowing (actual knowledge and teaching practices) that are in themselves unstable and fluid.

It is summer. I have been swimming most of the day in a small lake in northern Maine. I am watching two dogs chase a loon out into the water. A man calls after his dog, Here Shelby. Shelby, come. And as the dogs move toward the loon, it sinks down into the lake. And the dogs turn back as if it had never been. Identity does sink down into the water, does disappear as we come closer to it. Still, we think we know what we've seen. We think if we return to the place where identity was, we'd hear it echo; we'd follow that sound to its origin, which, of course, is (as echoes are) only a memory of a sound having been made.

CHAPTER TWO

COURTING FAILURE

In Composition Studies, we've long talked about conversation rather than mastery, about collaboration, decentered classrooms, shared power, about leaving teacherly authority behind, but each of these noble goals relies, ironically, on the ongoing authority of the institutionalized pedagogue, of the teacher, to make it succeed. Teaching queer means risking failure; it means opening conversation that cannot be closed.

Jacqueline Rhodes, "The Failure of Queer Pedagogy"

The development of a professional identity is inextricable from personal identity and when personal and professional development are brought into dialogue, when teachers are given the opportunity to compose and reflect on their own stories of learning and of selfhood within a supportive and challenging community then teachers can begin to resist and revise the scripting narratives of the culture and begin to compose new narratives of identity and practice. They can begin to author their own development.

Joy S. Ritchie and David E. Wilson, *Teacher Narrative as Critical Inquiry*

A story is told as much by silence as by speech.

Susan Griffin, *A Chorus of Stones*

Learning to Fail

It would be impossible to engage in acts of teaching or acts of writing without coming up against notions of failure. If we understand coming to terms with ambiguity (gender or otherwise) as an experience of abjection, it is not a far leap to say that, in our current moment, failure is also abject. Failure is the moment we mourn what could have been: success. In *The Queer Art of Failure*, Jack Halberstam writes, "Failing is something queers do and have always done well" (3). As the first chapter of this book, in some ways, positions my own masculinity as a kind of perceived (and perhaps actual) failure, this chapter takes up failure as its central lens through which to consider writing and teaching. In her video essay in *The Writing Instructor*, "The Failure of Queer Pedagogy," Jacqueline Rhodes tells us that the "energy in queer teaching comes from the failure of queer pedagogy and the discomfiting, uncentered, unstable joys within and without the classroom." There are some ways in which the field of composition has always been drawn to failure. We know failure in our discussions of assessment (how we fail to assess writing over and over); we know it in our desires to understand "the logic of student error" (Shaughnessy 13); we know failure in our contradictions—writing as both a product *and* process, literacy as both constraining and liberating. As a field, composition is no stranger to the study of failure. And we are no strangers to the notion that maybe failure isn't the thing we thought it was. But Halberstam offers another way of understanding what failure means and how failure itself might be a queer pathway through which we can "dismantle the logics of success" (*Queer Art* 2). This is something Rhodes and Jonathan Alexander point to when they call for "acts of de- and un- and re-composition" (*Techne*). Inevitably, queer composition would indicate a failure to compose. Likewise, queer pedagogy would signal a failure to teach.

In the opening to *The Queer Art of Failure*, Halberstam offers one of the final scenes from the film *Little Miss Sunshine* to articulate a vision of queer failure:

> With her porn-obsessed junky [sic] grandfather providing her with the choreography for her pageant routine and a cheerleading squad made up of a gay suicidal uncle, a Nietzsche-reading mute brother, an aspiring but flailing motivational speaker father, and an exasperated stay-at-home mom, Olive is destined to fail, and to fail spectacularly. But while her failure could be the source of misery and humiliation, and while it does indeed deliver precisely this, it also leads to a kind of ecstatic exposure

of the contradictions of a society obsessed with meaningless competition. By implication it also reveals the precarious models of success by which American families live and die. (4–5)

The film suggests in this scene that viewers will see Olive's failure as illuminating the insidious, normative, and absurd models of beauty, gender, childhood, sexuality, and success that create a beauty pageant in the first place. Through this scene, Halberstam suggests that where there is "failure," we might look to the system that set the scene for the failure in the first place. And that perhaps the failure is a radical critique (whether it knows it or not) of the very system that produced it as a failure. I want to extend Halberstam's queer theory of failure to examine how we understand writing and language, how we understand student writers, and how we understand our own classroom norms.

I'm in college by the time they add the "Q" to the LGBTQ Resource Center's acronym. The student cafeteria is ablaze with jokes. I overhear a guy who lived in my dorm call it the "LGBT-ABCDEFGHIJKLMNOP" center. He thinks he is pointing out how ridiculous we are—all our names, all our letters, all our endless expanding out, language failing us.

The Body Paragraphs

One failure that I think about often as a teacher of writing is the failure of the available language we have to talk about writing in the first place. In teaching both composition and creative writing, I have had many conversations with other writing teachers about our frustration with the limiting effects of "workshop talk" or of the typical language students use (and are given to use) to talk about writing. In my earliest years, I would often forbid students from using certain kinds of feedback during workshop—feedback like *this doesn't flow*, or *give more examples*, or *needs a stronger thesis*.

In any one body, there are two types of muscle: voluntary skeletal muscles and involuntary smooth muscles. In this sense, only some movement is about choice.

My students and I are having a writing workshop. The subject under discussion is writing introductions. We have been looking at several students' introductions to their essays on a first-draft assignment.

The assignment asked students to focus closely on an idea or writerly approach taken by one of the writers we read in the course and to consider that approach as both connected to writing *and* connected to lived experience. Some students wrote about humor, some about sentence fragments, some about the act of reflection itself. One student, Jennifer Bracken, took up the subject of questioning as a writerly approach and as what she believed to be an important aspect of writing and of being in the world. The following is her first-draft introduction to her essay entitled "There Are No Stupid Questions":

> When I think all the way back to elementary school, I remember teachers telling my fellow classmates and me, "there are no stupid questions." Then of course once you get to high school you hear the jokes that go, "Yeah, there are no stupid questions, just stupid people who ask questions." Regardless, questioning is something we have all done; even Benjamin Franklin, the man who discovered electricity, certainly asked questions on his way to accomplishing something great. Of course I wasn't present when he did this, but had he asked no questions, there would have been no motive for him to put that key on that kite to see what happened. This is the essential reason questions are important, they lead us to form new ideas, learn about ourselves, and to turn these new ideas into reality. They also help us to complicate our thoughts when we question the thoughts of those around us—not to judge or find one idea better than another, just to try to better understand one idea in order to complicate another.

During this particular workshop, I asked students what they were most interested in about this paragraph, which sentences they felt most connected to and why. Students, almost unanimously, pointed to the first two sentences of the essay as the most compelling, offering reasons like, *it's actually what she's thinking about* and *you feel like someone is actually talking to you in those sentences*. To be honest, I thought what might follow was a discussion of voice in an essay, but this isn't what happened at all, not that it is at all unusual for me to be surprised by the directions my students take me. While in some workshops the student writer is asked to remain anonymous or silent, I ask that my student writers participate in the workshop as the writers. So, part way through the conversation, Jennifer Bracken sits up in her chair and says, "It's weird, the first two sentences are the only sentences it feels like I even wrote. The rest are like format sentences." I'm intrigued by what Jennifer has said. *What are format sentences?* I ask. Jennifer and the class erupt with answers like *the Ben Franklin thing is the linking sentence* and *yeah, the sentence that gives three reasons why questions are important is the thesis,* and finally, *that last sentence is the transition sentence where you transition to the body paragraphs.* "Yeah," Jennifer says, "it's like the essay's all great if I take out the thesis and stuff." The class laughs a bit. I shift some in my chair. I try, as a teacher of writing, to value my students' prior experiences with writing and to honor the teachers who may have offered them these kinds of experiences in writing introductions, experiences that have brought them this far, to a university. Besides, the trouble here is not with the names for these sentences or even what the names were intended to do but rather with what the names have come to mean. Class comes to a close in the middle of this conversation—one, I tell the students, that we will continue in our next class meeting. That afternoon, Jennifer visits during my office hours. *Should I not have a thesis?* she wants to know. *Is that what you want me to do, take the thesis out and the Ben Franklin thing out?* I ask Jennifer to hold her questions one more day until the class meets again. Truthfully, I needed time. What did I want? If I am trying to queer the essay, should there not be a thesis?

*When my parents move, after I have grown and moved out, they tell me to come to collect a few boxes of things that belong to me. I drag the boxes of yearbooks, old trophies, and schoolwork to my small apartment in Lewisburg. One night I discover I have written "*DYKE*" over Emily Mott's face in the sixth-grade yearbook. I hadn't remembered doing so, though the handwriting is recognizable. I do cry some. "How could I have done that?" I say to my college girlfriend, whose shirt is wet with sink water from leaning into the dishes. And it's impossible to know now why, but the ink is dark blue; the lines of the letters have been repeatedly traced over. I don't even remember her, Emily Mott. But now, I cannot forget her blue-lined face, the violence of the pen having revisited the word so many times. "You couldn't have known," my girlfriend says. And I start to feel angry. "Yes, I could have."*

I spent that evening thinking about names, about the names given to sentences, and inevitably about the names given to identities, to places, to human beings. I thought about the failure of names, the failure of language to *be* who we are, the failure of language to contain the living act of writing. I wondered how I could invite students to resist and question the ways the conventional ways of talking about writing had failed them, and the ways that failure might illuminate what is wrong with a system that tells us we can, once and for all, talk about writing in the "right" way, the way that will enable writing to be containable, teachable, repeatable. In a sense, I began, in my mind, to do the very assignment I had given my students to do—thinking carefully about a writerly approach, about its connection to lived experience. I began thinking about Kate Bornstein, who writes in *Hello, Cruel World: 101 Alternatives to Suicide for Teens, Freaks, and Other Outlaws*, "I have this idea that every time we discover that the names we're being called are somehow keeping us less than free, we need to come up with new names for ourselves, and that the names we give ourselves must no longer reflect a fear of being labeled outsiders, must no longer bind us to a system that would rather see us dead" (36–37). I remember that for queer bodies, new names are a matter of survival. If there are not new and shifting names, I myself as the genderqueer teacher of this class cease to exist as myself. When I first began teaching composition courses just over fifteen years ago, I was (and it seemed at times my students were as well) frustrated with the language already in place to talk about being and about writing, and this was the problem of the current teaching moment at hand. While I do not think, for example, that "thesis statement" as a name for a piece of an essay is inherently problematic, I do think that the name has come to limit rather than expand or stretch our ideas about what essays are and, perhaps more importantly, what essays can or might do. And so, in the spirit of "queering the brew," as Harriet Malinowitz (252) puts it, I thought I might ask students to invent new names, new ways of calling into being what their essays can do. Perhaps, as a class, we might practice naming together, inventing a common language among us, a new language, one that we create, one that captures what we think we are doing. This is the first of what will become many times I ask my students to rename, to give their own voice and invention to a set of writing terms or notions. I will ask them to consider new names. I will ask them to let go of the terms a bit: thesis sentence, linking sentence, transition sentence, introduction. I will, I think to myself, ask them to let go of the "body paragraphs."

All the children are laughing. The two first graders: Lucy Cavaro and Craig Larson. They each have rocks. Lucy is taunting, "Are you a boy or a girl? Boy or girl?" I don't say anything. I keep doing what I do whenever I feel cornered like this. I look off through the green fence and picture myself as capable of movement. I picture myself faster than I am, as fast as a boy, I suppose. I see myself leap the tire swing and head for home. But Lucy won't quit. She hurls one of her rocks at my feet. "Can't you even talk?" she wants to know. I can't rid myself of the fire rising in my small round belly. There's a pasty coating on my tongue, and the lump in my throat is growing, expanding like a party balloon. I can't breathe. When Miss Sherri finds us, she's angry. When I tell her Lucy does this to me, she wants to know why I don't answer. "Tell her you're a girl," she says. But I can't think of what to tell—the way I can't think of any sins to tell the priest at confession. I saw a face of contradiction; I was frozen, unnamed on a playground.

At the beginning of the next class, I put all these terms on the board: thesis, body paragraph, introduction, and so on. I begin class with the sort of nervousness that emerges whenever I am depending on my students. I don't have control over what they will say; I cannot dictate the new names they will give to these forms. I have to trust their creativity, their perception, and their language. I have to forget my own notions about what these sentences are meant to do and what they are called.

I want us to rename the thesis, I say. *Let's call it something else. Think for a moment about what the "thesis" is for, what you hope it will do. What could we call the thesis, instead of calling it the thesis?* They don't think for long. Danielle looks up from her notebook: *the thesis is the heart, you know, like the heart of the matter, the core, the inside*. It's hard to know which of her terms to lock into. I find the heart metaphor a little cliché. But before I have time to write the "c" in "core," Tearsa says, *the heart, I like that. It is. It's like the heart of the essay, the thing that keeps it alive*. I become more interested in the heart in this new elaboration by Tearsa. I write it on the board. Iggy leans forward. "It's a little cheesy," he says, "but not if you think of it like a real heart." *What do you mean?* I ask. Iggy explains: *like if the essay has a heart, a real beating heart, and that's the thesis, then the rest of the essay is like the places the blood is pumping to, like hands and feet and stuff*. There is some laughter, though I am fascinated by what my students are doing. *Well*, Johnnie says, *if that's the case, then if we're gonna change all the names of this stuff that's fine, but we gotta keep calling them body paragraphs*. I am interested in this renaming as well, that now we can keep the name, though it will mean something different—now that we imagine an essay with a body, with a heart, with hands, and muscle, and veins. *Okay*, I say, *we've got a heart and a body. What about this linking sentence? If it's a part of this essay that is also a body, what body part is it?* Students offer several options. They think, of course, of connectors: joints, muscle, bone. I have them vote. The class settles on "muscle." Before I have time to shift to the transition sentence or the introduction as something we might rename, Laura says, *the heart's made of muscle, you know, so that means the tissue that holds the thesis together also holds other parts of the essay together.* Maria raises her hand: *it's weird if you think of the whole essay as a body . . . like it's sexual, like it wants something.* The class laughs some. I am laughing too. *But it does want something, doesn't it?* I ask. We sit a moment in the language of desire. I am thinking about what an essay wants, who it wants, what it wants to do to those it wants. *Yeah,* Iggy says, *that means when you quote someone else, you're kinda into them.* More laughs. Kelsey offers a rebuttal: *maybe, or maybe quoting someone is more like punching them or wrestling them.* The possibilities become endless. At this moment, my students are talking in more nuanced ways than ever before about what it means to engage with another text, about the ways one might perform that engagement. *Or pinching their cheeks like a grandma,* Kristin says. I am trying to keep up, writing their phrases on the board. Erasing the thesis, I am trying to draw a picture of a body: a heart inside, a fat hand like a boxing glove, other stick figure bodies surrounding this body.

The class continues to make connections between things a body can do and things an essay can do. They turn from the kinds of questions I was asking about renaming the parts of an essay to asking questions about how the metaphor works. *What would be the lungs?* a student asks. *Yeah, does an essay breathe?* I am still intrigued and compelled by what they are doing, but I begin to wonder how the conversation will translate, how the students will absorb, or enact, this conversation in their writing, or if they will be able to. Or, even if they tried to, what would it look like? So as we close class, I begin to ask them about this kind of transference. *As you think about revising the essays you've just written, how could you account for this conversation? What could this metaphor we've been creating offer to your writing process?* They're quiet. It has been much easier to collaboratively create this body metaphor than think about applying it. *What will we do? What would I do as a writer?* I have asked a hard question. I give the silence some time, which is hard for me, as a teacher, to do, though I practice it. I practice being quiet. After a few minutes, Iggy offers a possibility: *Well, I guess if I think of my essay as a body, it's like a person instead of an object.* I'm interested but still not sure what he means, what this means he would do to his essay. *Can you say more?* I ask. Iggy gives his answer: *Uh, okay, if my essay is a person with a body, then it needs* to have like a personality, and be attractive. *I gotta dress it up.* There are, again, some giggles. With all the discussion of gender and drag in this class, it's hard not to laugh. Tearsa interjects: *I think, if we're gonna revise using this, I'd use more physical words, like things a body would say.* I'm running out of time. It's hard to know exactly how to help them, though they are doing an honorable job helping themselves. *Try it,* I say. *Bring in just your first paragraph revised in light of this conversation today.* Students turned in revisions of their introductions, and some pretty interesting things happened, particularly with Jennifer's writing. Here is her revised introduction:

> When I think back to elementary school, I remember teachers proclaiming, "there are no stupid questions." Then of course once I got to high school, boys in baggy jeans heckled from the back of the classroom with jokes that went, "Yeah, there are no stupid questions, just stupid people who ask questions." And who wants to be that stupid person who asks. The boys in the baggy jeans don't want questions. They are too cool to ask. But without questions, we make no discoveries. Benjamin Franklin discovered electricity through questioning. Of course I wasn't standing with him in a thunderstorm when he did this, but had he asked no questions, his hands would never have put the key on that kite to feel static electricity. Questions, like Franklin's lightning, can feel wild and dangerous. They can also start sparks. This is the essential reason questions are important, they lead us to form new ideas. The boys in baggy jeans are no Ben Franklins for sure. A writer is like an inventor. We need to ask questions. I seem to be able to do this questioning in my life more often, now that the baggy jeans boys have disappeared into my old town memories, but questioning while writing is another thing altogether. It's harder. My hands start typing what I know instead of asking questions.

I'm actually not particularly interested, at this moment, in talking about this piece of writing as better than the first piece, though I can imagine some ways it might be. What interests me is the set of choices Bracken makes in revision. First, I notice the actual bodies that appear in the essay—the boys in baggy jeans, Ben Franklin now "in a thunderstorm" and having actual hands that put the key on the kite, Bracken's own hands in the place of that "transition sentence" to the body paragraph, this paragraph itself becoming more of a body paragraph, more *embodied* by both the cast of characters it makes use of and more embodied by

Bracken herself. I notice the ways Bracken embodies herself as a writer of the piece, talking explicitly about being a writer, about the body (her hands) moving in knowing fashion without questioning. Bracken's embodied writing enacts a kind of contradiction—a hand with a mind of its own, a hand bound to an act of expression that is not a question.

Bracken also gives questions a shape, a kind of embodiment of questions whereby they are turned into sparks, through the image of Ben Franklin's lightning, lightning that leads her to the sense that questions are "dangerous and wild." Something about our discussion seems to press Bracken toward the figurative: the writer is like an inventor. The baggy jeans boys disappearing, their bodies leaving the scene of Bracken's writing as she tries to leave them behind. I notice the newly shaped "we" in this revision—her first draft invoking an abstract *we*, an "all of us," while this version seems to imagine the "we" as writers, as thinkers who "need" to ask questions. I find the verb *need* striking, too, its connection to desire, to the talk of relationality. And where, I ask myself, as I read Bracken's revision, where is the thesis? It's hard to answer. But when I ask myself where the essay's heart is, I imagine a complex web of investigation whereby Bracken writes to explore the notion of questioning, to even go so far as to implicate herself in not always being able to ask important questions. The truth is, and I suspect this is likely true for many writing teachers (especially writing teachers who are writers themselves), very few of the books and essays I admire have a thesis sentence, but every one of them has a pulsing heart, has an embodied presence, has a writer who appears (even if perhaps in different ways), has a kind of muscle tissue, reaches out to other places (whether they be texts, experience, or language) to touch, in some way, something outside itself.

My father's best friend, Mike Bird, who I loved for his name and his willingness to sit on the floor and help me find the edges of puzzle pieces, had a habit of calling me "bruiser." I had no idea what the word meant—only that it lit me up inside. I knew it had something to do with fighting. I wasn't much of a fighter unless a fellow underdog was under siege, but I liked to think of myself as a fighter, to think of myself as capable of answering back.

Kenneth Burke writes, "Indeed always beneath the dance of words there will be the dance of bodies" (288). Of course, Burke is not talking specifically about the writing of an essay, but he does remind me that voice, that subject I thought my students and I were going to discuss at the start of the first class meeting I describe, comes from the sense that someone is speaking, that there is a mouth speaking words, a body who makes them.

One of the things queer pedagogies and queer theory itself have been called to more fully contend with is the material body and embodiment. The transgender studies field, through the work of theorists such as Susan Stryker and Jay Prosser, has been bringing the question of the material body more prominently back to theoretical discussions of gender, sexuality, and identity. What this renaming reminds me of, and what is queer about the namings my students enact, is the inevitable and infinite ways there are *to* embody. In an essay in the journal *Pedagogy* from 2006, Amy Winans writes, "Ultimately, queer pedagogy entails decentering dominant cultural assumptions, exploring the facets of the geography of normalization, and interrogating the self and the implications of affiliation" (106). I believe Winans's comment connects not only to understandings of sexual and gendered identities but also to our understandings of writing. I want to suggest that not only are there dominant cultural assumptions about gender and sexuality that can be disrupted by queer failures but that there are also dominant cultural assumptions about writing that can be disrupted by queer failures, including the assumptions that writing is something that happens in the mind and not in the body, that it is a production of the body's capabilities but not an actual embodiment, that writing is something that can be contained by formulaic sentences, that it is something we can "know about" in some definite way. In this sense, the renamings I ask my students to do are, as Winans puts it, "decentering." If I am to ask my students to question the processes by which identity and writing are made, if I am to ask my students to decenter themselves in relation to the materials of my courses, my teaching must also embody this very decentering—not merely apply the concept of decentering to teaching. I must be willing to decenter myself, even my notions of teaching and research. I must ask of myself the same complicated renamings. My students, the writing they produce, the comments they make, and the questions they ask are a kind of archive I draw from to try to further articulate queer notions of theorized practice.

The connections, for me, are quite evident in terms of the relationship between queer theory (which I understand as a particular way of looking, a particular methodology) and the teaching of writing. Jonathan Alexander and Michelle Gibson, in their essay "Queer Composition(s): Queer Theory in the Writing Classroom," remind us "how deeply and intimately rhetorical queer theory is, for queer theory asks us to question, at the most fundamental levels and in the most essential ways, the nature of authorship, representation, and the process of coming into being through language" (8). I think our teaching of composition asks us to do the same. It asks us to help our students "come into being through language," and to come into being means, in part, to become embodied, to appear as a body, to let Ben Franklin appear, to let your authorial hands appear. And perhaps we might, as I first thought, call this some notion of voice. Our teaching of composition asks us to engage with paradox, with difficulty, with failure, with the ambiguous blurs of articulation; it asks us to give new names to the interpretative and writerly moves we make, to revise those names when they fail us, or, as Bornstein puts it, "every time we discover that the names . . . are somehow keeping us less than free"; it asks us, as teachers, to "decenter" our practices, and this might mean collaborating with our students, this might mean temporarily moving out from the center of our classrooms, it might mean generating new languages with each class rather than *providing* the language our students should use to talk about form. To be clear, I do not mean to suggest here, or elsewhere in this book's inquiry, that the student work in writing and discussion, or my own work as a teacher, should be reproduced as some sort of "best practice"—such that another teacher might say to her students, *let's turn the essay into a body*. What is here is not meant to prevent or enable the use of this body metaphor in another class setting; the point, however, is the process of generating new names, new language, a strategy I return to again and again, a strategy that drives work in queer theory and queer activism, a strategy that values new *ways of knowing*, rather than merely offering new knowledge.

My first-grade teacher was Mrs. Killian. She lets me take home the class gerbil on weekends. I do not like the gerbil, but I understand the gesture. My teacher is old and fragile and thinks of me as the caretaking kind—responsible and sound in judgment. She catches me and Jillian Becker trading kisses in the jacket room. She tells my mother I am "confused about my role—

perhaps it's the four older brothers," she says. And she's kind and gentle enough for my mother not to be threatened or alarmed. But my mother does begin to dress me more gender appropriately, crying one morning when I refuse the dress and barrettes. Second grade, Mrs. Walsh. I remember her very little. She did not like my handwriting and gave me my first B grade—penmanship. I spent second grade failing at the alphabet sheets, not touching my capitals to the top line, missing the cursive letter z over and over. I cry at the bus stop. My mother says no one's perfect and signs the report card without hesitation. My father leaves my mother for his nurse. He leaves a note on her pillow that says he "went with plan B."

Knowing Failure

The primary function of muscles in a body is to cause motion or produce force. To do the work of contracting and expanding, muscles need oxygen and energy, provided from the body's blood. Some muscle fibers are relentlessly diligent and will allow a body to work for a long time, repeatedly stretching and pulling, stretching and pulling. This intense motion calls for a constant supply of blood. Muscle fibers that need a rich supply of blood and can work intensely without rest are red muscle fibers.

In her book *Repurposing Composition: Feminist Interventions for a Neoliberal Age*, Shari Stenberg writes, "Our students will be better prepared for cultural participation—in the workforce, in their communities, in their families—if they are offered an education that invites them to engage multiple, even conflicting, perspectives; if they are encouraged to inquire, explore, fail, and try again; if they are valued as intellectual, emotional, embodied subjects" (149). In my courses, I want to put the model of "inquire, explore, fail" into practice, but I also want my students to, at times, begin with failure, focusing on the already failing extent of our various knowledges. In their essay "Flattening Effects: Composition's Multicultural Imperative and the Problem of Narrative Coherence," Alexander and Rhodes write, "A simple way to begin might be by having students not write about what they believe they 'know' about one another, but what they suspect they do not know" (445). Here Alexander and Rhodes are specifically talking about what students know "about one another," but we might also interpret their statement as a call to turn our attention more fully to what we do not know and, even more importantly, what we cannot know not only about one another but also about ideas, identity, writing, teaching, and the world itself. I have always encouraged students to explore contradictions in their writing, to write about what they do not know as opposed to adhering to the old adage to "write what you know." But what does this writing about what you do not know mean or look like? In first-year composition courses, at the moments in my courses that invite students to invent their own projects and essays, students very often want to choose "topics" they feel passionate about: abortion, gay marriage, the death penalty, the drinking age in their state. In the earliest years of my teaching, I would turn down any proposals from students who seemed to want to participate in the "abortion debate" or other popular "debate" topics. I did this because I wanted my students to explore, to discover new ideas rather than head off to the library or the Internet to find sources to advocate for their already formed positions. It would, in fact, have been my contention that this kind of writing is not useful if we are interested in writing as a transformative, self-reflexive, and exploratory act, which I am. So I wondered what would happen if, instead of turning down proposals that wanted to take up these contemporary "debates," I invited students to write about these subjects in ways that might illuminate the limits of their own experience and knowledge, in ways that might reveal their own failure to know. I came up with an assignment in which I would require, if they wanted to take up one of these contemporary hot topics, a pre-project essay. I was surprised how many of the students wanted to engage in this extra work so that they could focus on the subjects they wanted to focus on. This prompt would later become one I would give before the majority of self-directed papers in my writing courses. Here is the prompt:

> Your writing project aims to take up the subject of _____. Before you begin this project, you should compose two lists that form a kind of lyrical essay. There should be 20–25 sentences on each list. The first list will be 20–25 sentences that start with the words, "I do not know." And the second list will be sentences that start with the words, "I cannot know." This assignment calls you to begin with what you do not and cannot know about this subject. It asks you to begin by recording the limits of your own knowledge and experience. It asks you to take seriously the idea that you don't already know, in a full way, your position on this subject, even if you feel that you do. It asks you to acknowledge that all knowledge is partial knowledge, and to begin your project with a full examination

of what you have failed to know, uncover, or see about this subject. If you want to write about this subject, you must consider how to make your essay or project reflect both what you think you know and what you do not, or cannot, know.

I want to feature one student's response to this assignment because I think it speaks to challenging moments for many of us who teach writing. This student focuses on the drinking age. When students take up subjects like the drinking age, I am reminded of Lad Tobin's essay "Car Wrecks, Baseball Caps, and Man-to-Man Defense: The Personal Narratives of Adolescent Males," an essay that points out how difficult it is to read and comment on the "car accident" paper or the "sports" paper. But it is also an essay that chronicles, self-reflexively and honestly, Tobin's own failure to respond to these essays. The "lower the drinking age" essay is reminiscent of the essays Tobin describes—often written by a male-identified student who wants to advocate his right to drunkenness. It was indeed a male-identified student who took up this subject in my course as well. Here are some selected sentences from his required lists:

> I do not know the legal history of how the drinking age was decided on.
> I do not know anyone who actually doesn't drink before the legal age other than a few really religious people.
> I do not know if I have kids if I will want them to drink younger than 21.
> I do not know if alcohol addiction happens more to people who drink younger.
> I do not know statistics about how many teens die from drinking, if any.
> I cannot know if the results of lowering the legal age will be good or bad.
> I cannot know the physical capacities of other people's bodies for alcohol.
> I cannot know if other people, besides just me and my close friends and family, do ok drinking at younger ages.

This particular student noted in his email with his assignment attached that he had a hard time writing the lists, but he also said, "I found it hard to write the lists about things I didn't know, so then I tried writing a list of things I did know and that was even harder." From his lists, and from his email, it seemed to me that the student had already learned something about focusing on what he did not, or could not, know—that the assignment had illuminated that the argument he wanted to make (that the state should lower the drinking age) wasn't informed by his actual knowledge or a broad range of experiences. I am particularly interested in the ways his lists form a commentary on the impossibility of knowing the experiences of others—something I tried to work on in so many other ways during class discussion when I put pressure on my students' use of "we" to mean everyone, for example. I was curious to see how the lists would affect this student's paper about underage drinking. Below is an excerpt from his paper, which he titles, "Let Them Drink Beer":

> If other 18 year olds are like me, then they are totally capable of drinking beer on a Friday night. Also they are totally capable of finding out the consequences of drinking *too much* beer on a Friday night. I have seen just as many 21 year olds drunk in a pile of their own puke as I have seen 18 year olds. Nothing magical happens in three years. In our society, we assign each age, and weirdly it is different state by state, with something you can do. At 16 you can have sex that could lead to you having a baby, at 15 you can get a job, at 18 you can get married, go to war, vote, smoke, and at 21 you can drink. So are they just making sure you are not drunk when you go to work, have sex, get married, go to war, vote, and smoke? Are they making sure these prior decisions are made while you're sober because it seems to me that drinking beer seems a less life-altering experience than going to war?
>
> However it could seem that way to me because as far as I can tell I am not addicted to alcohol. While I have found myself hung over or a little nauseated from drinking endeavors I have never ended up in bed with a stranger or in a car wreck or accidently married in a chapel in Las Vegas. (Anonymous Student F)

There are two moments in this student's essay that stand out for me in terms of their relationship to failure. First, the student seems to be paying close attention to his perspective *as a perspective* with language such as "if other 18 year olds are like me" and "it could seem that way to me because. . . ." These moments reveal the student as being palpably aware that he sees the world from his own subject position and that others might not share that particular vision. This turn toward what he might not see, what he might fail to see from his particular angle on the world seems significant and certainly affects the way he writes about this subject. Second, I notice the student's use of "we" seems different than in his prior essays. In earlier writing, this student had often used "we" to mean he and others like him. But in this excerpt, he writes the phrase "in our society, we assign." Here he aligns himself with those who assign meaning to specific age groups instead of only aligning himself with those who are capable of drinking at a young age. This may seem like a small moment, but I believe it is a significant writing moment, an example of when writers are seeing themselves as both implicated in and trying to critique a problem they are writing about. I do think that turning students' attention toward failure, toward impossibility, toward the limits of their own understanding, makes this more complex and more self-reflexive writing possible.

Queer Participation

"She's talking like her brothers on purpose," my father says when he is trying to convince my stepmother that the depth of my voice is not inherent in my voice itself. "There's too many men around," he says. And this is without knowing about the hockey boys, the hockey coach, the weekend trips to the batting cages, the neighbor boy's barn where I had jumped time and time again from the hayloft door. They "sit me down," as parents call it. My stepmother teaches me to lift my voice, to let more air into the words. I try not to answer the phone, to get mistaken for one of my brothers or, worse, my father. At night I have dreams that my voice box is made of ink, that when it runs out I won't be able to say another word.

I've heard, many times, myself and other teachers say that they learn more from their students than their students learn from them. We say it so much it seems rather unremarkable, cliché. But we don't talk about it too specifically; we don't frequently write about our failures as teachers, about those moments our students show us to ourselves, and we do not sparkle under the light they shed on us. I want to stand for some time in the light of my own failure. I want to illuminate how pedagogical change might happen, how one student can shift everything until you see your own assumptions about learning, and about the world, sink to the bottom of a murky lake, suddenly blurred and eventually unimaginable.

First, I should say that before Andy Dejka was my student there were things I took for granted—that class participation means *talking* in class, that class participation is good, that the best students will participate in class, that the best model for teaching writing is a model in which students talk out loud to the group. I would have aligned myself with scholars such as Stephen Brookfield and Stephen Preskill, who argue in their book *Discussion as a Way of Teaching* that discussion "encapsulates a form of living and association that we regard as a model for civil society" (xv). I should also say that before I read Andy's essay, I saw myself as a radical. After all, I am a scholar of queer pedagogies; one might even say I have expertise in non-normative thinking, in alternative ways to imagine identity, behavior, and meaning. And since Andy, there's a shift in the way I think about teaching, about silence, about participation, and about the shards of my own life that leave me clinging to what I can only now call a kind of conservatism. I won't delete that word. I let it hang there. I listen to what it tells me. I dwell a moment in the possibility that queer, intersex poet/scholar/activists might need to think about their own conservatism.

As Cheryl Glenn points out, "Little wonder, then, that speaking or speaking out continues to signal power, liberation, culture, or civilization itself. That seeming obverse, silence, signals nothingness" (3). And while Andy arrived in my classroom in 2011, I, like many scholars of composition, had read Glenn's book about the rhetorical art of silence quite a few years *before* this course. In 2009, I read Mary M. Reda's *Between Speaking and Silence: A Study of Quiet Students*. I have truly valued the work of many scholars who have followed Krista Ratcliffe's lead in making engaged listening (which can often involve silence) part of our pedagogical understandings. I knew another version of silence; it had actually been explained to me many times. And I nodded and thought to myself, *yes, of course*. But I do not *practice* a politics of silence—especially not in the classroom. I think we, teachers, think we "know" a lot of things; we don't always enact what we know. I knew that what I called "class participation" was not *only* about talking in class. For example, here is the excerpt from my syllabus (an excerpt I have been using in one form or another for quite a few years) in which I describe what "participation" means in my courses. This is the version from the composition course in which Andy Dejka was a student: "The success of our course together depends very much on your active participation and contribution to class discussions. Your class participation and attendance grade will take into account your attendance, your attentiveness and engagement in class, the quality of your contributions to class discussion, and your energy toward the course itself."

I imagine a blurb from a syllabus, one very much like this one, is familiar to most teachers. I can see myself, in this writing, theoretically understanding that participation is not only talking in class. But I also convey to students here that "active participation and contribution to class discussion" are essential to the "success" of the course. I wonder now about what other meanings this active participation might have; I wonder about why I thought, and often continue to think, that a course's "success" depends upon this participation. What does it mean for a course to be "successful" and why do I want that? Or, what kind of success is that? Is a course with less talking a failure? Is a student who talks not at all an obstacle on this path to course success? Andy spoke twice over the course of the semester, both times because I spoke directly to him, and because the students were doing a kind of "go-around-the-room" participation. Andy was, for the most part, silent—though any look over to his corner of the room on any given day, and Andy was locked in. His eyes are a pale green-blue, reflective in a quite striking way, which is not surprising, given that this student is probably one of the most intensely reflective students I have had the gift of teaching in many years. *Your class participation and attendance grade will take into account your attendance, your attentiveness and engagement in class, the quality of your contributions to class discussion, and your energy toward the course itself.* I can hear myself trying very deliberately to value aspects of participation that are not just talking in class. I use words like "attentiveness" and "engagement" and "energy," though I can see the many ways I often do not define, measure, or reflect the meanings of these words in how I measure and *grade* class participation.

At the age of seven I notice how my mother's silence shapes her. And from my seven-year-old viewpoint, her silence seemed very much like weakness. My father slept with his secretary, she was silent. He took the house and the money despite his adultery, she was silent. Through years of my father's need for control, again silence. I remember thinking that silence meant compliance, that her silence was passive, or that her silence had no power.

Andy is an A student. And at his midterm conference, he is not surprised when I tell him things like, *You convey such sharp ideas in your writing, I just really wish you'd share these ideas in class* or *To get an A in class participation, you're going to need to at least try to contribute to class discussion.* Contribute. I'm always telling my students to think about their word choices. And sometimes I need to think about mine. If contributing means helping to bring about, or adding to, how can I describe the ways Andy contributed? What did he contribute? How, and of course why, might I have failed to recognize his contributions?

It's worth noting that "class participation"—speaking in a group during class—is not only a composition program or English department value. It's a normative university value often posed as a problem for teachers and programs to solve—often asking questions like, How can we get *participation* from students? or, How can we signal to students that participation is good for them, like eating their peas? And while, at universities and colleges, we may often be skilled at the art of inquiry, at allowing questions to remain questions, some questions do not remain questions. For example, the title of Raymond C. Jones's article, "The 'Why' of Class Participation: A Question Worth Asking" (2008), suggests he might consider the question of "why," but Jones does not really commit to allowing class participation to remain a question. Jones concludes, "Students should share rather than withhold their insights. Both the professor and the other class members should be able to profit and move forward thanks to the contributions of individual students. The obligation is to give as well as to take" (62). I can only imagine the number of years I would have taken for granted this kind of statement. Of course students should "share rather than withhold their insights." First, it makes it easier for me—someone not comfortable with silence, and someone who enacts power through speaking—to teach my class. Second, if students withheld their insights, how could I facilitate a course? How could I teach at all? Jones's assertions are not unlike the ones in my syllabus. And somehow, both of us seem to align student vocal participation in class with conventional understandings of success.

There were other versions of silence that emerged as I grew up. My mother became an alcoholic after my father left, and I learned another silence—the kind that ignores, the kind that is denial, the kind that is so powerful, and so terrible, that it infects a family with a complete inability to acknowledge any truths about themselves or others. So while I might have understood the silence I observed as powerful, that power was not something I wanted, not something I thought others should want or enact. Silence moved from signifying weakness to signifying sickness, or dysfunction.

Andy Dejka illuminates this very idea in the essay he composed for a course in composition. That essay was written in response to the following prompt:

> In *Just Girls*, Margaret Finders writes, "I became aware of two literate systems in operation: sanctioned literacies (those literacies that are recognized, circulated, and sanctioned by adults in authority) and what I have come to refer to as 'literate underlife' (those practices that refuse in some way to accept the official view, practices designed and enacted to challenge and disrupt the official expectations" (24). Here Finders makes a distinction between literate practices that happen under the authority and gaze of institutions *and* literacies that happen outside those bounds. The "literate underlife," according to Finders, can "disrupt official expectations" and assumptions.
>
> Writing Project #2 invites you to consider a literacy practice or a literacy event that you think is disruptive in some way to traditional understandings of literacy. The disruption can be major or very subtle. In your project, you will want to consider the following questions: What kind of literacy is the one you are describing? How does it operate? What are the discourse communities that take part in or form the audience for this kind of literacy? How does one learn to be literate in this particular kind of literacy? Is there a literacy event associated with this specific kind of literacy? Is it public or hidden—and in what ways? How does the literacy practice you are writing about shed light upon, challenge, or complicate Finders' assertions about literacy? And finally, how does looking at this literacy in your project enrich or expand our notions of what literacy is, what counts as literacy, and how literacy works?

Dejka's essay, "Stupid Is as Stupid Does," takes on the university's common view of silence in classrooms and articulates what he calls a "myth of extroversion" in the humanities. Dejka writes, "Silence in a classroom is quite frequently, even at levels of higher education, taken as a sign of dysfunction" (3). What I find remarkable about Dejka's assertion in his essay is not only the echo of dysfunction but also the heavy weight of the words: *even at levels of higher education*. This phrase is one worth spending time on. It indicates to me that Dejka expects more of us and that he is surprised that *even* at the university level, where some teachers earn doctorates and get sabbaticals to think our deep thoughts, silence is still interpreted and, most importantly, evaluated, in a noncomplex and frankly pretty normative way. At least this is how I have engaged with silence in my own practice of teaching. And I hope this essay illuminates how my own histories shape that engagement.

I should also say that one of the reasons I was able to hear Andy, to listen to the argument of his essay with the kind of consideration and rumination often reserved for "expert" texts is because of Jack Halberstam's *The Queer Art of Failure*. Halberstam positions failures as "ways of being and knowing that stand outside conventional understandings of success" (2) and argues that these failures have the potential to expose the contradictions or hypocrisies embedded in normative systems of value. In his essay, Dejka tells a compelling and powerful story about his brother, who was diagnosed with selective mutism and often seen by teachers as not intelligent, or even illiterate, because of his silence. And while Dejka does not identify himself with the diagnosis, his writing captures his identification with his brother, his sense that quiet is positioned as failure. What Halberstam helps me to see is that this failure is a way of "being and knowing" that is, indeed, "standing outside conventional understandings of success" (2). The interpretative frame Halberstam offers allows me to see *not* Andy's failure but the normative extroversion so cherished in education—and, not surprisingly, in my own life. Andy's "failure" to speak highlights the illusive and unexamined normativity of one of my most valued classroom practices. Suddenly, as Halberstam suggests it might, the refusal or failure to speak exposes the systemic failure of education—quite the same way a good drag show might illuminate the systemic failure of gender—that is, if we recognize what we've just seen as disrupting our sense of normative order.

I was a teenager in the nineties. I attended a small liberal arts college in central Pennsylvania at a time when queer youth were gathering together to encourage one another to "come out" or "be out." We considered it both a political responsibility and a personal triumph to speak out, to say who we were. *We're here, we're queer. Get used to it.* We read feminist and queer authors as biblical. When Audre Lorde told us, in essays and on bumper stickers, *your silence will not protect you,* we took that to heart.

Silence meant oppression. It meant your voice would not be heard. It meant you were implicated in all the systems you might want to challenge. In "The Transformation of Silence into Language and Action," Lorde writes, "I have come to believe over and over again that what is most important to me must be spoken, made verbal and shared, even at the risk of having it bruised or misunderstood. That the speaking profits me, beyond any other effect" (40). From this essay came also the idea that "Silence = Death," as Lorde characterizes death as the final silence. I hear that word "profits" again. And I am thinking about how my speaking out as a young queer person "profited me," which sometimes it did. Of course, sometimes it didn't. And not just because other people might be dangerous and react violently to this speaking out (which happened often) but also because speaking out is not universally better or necessarily more powerful than silence. It never occurred to me that silence could be productive. *Silence = Death. Your silence will not protect you.* Lorde isn't wrong, I suppose, about the kinds of silence she describes, but I think it sank in for many of us as reaching out even beyond the politics of oppression and into the politics of education, the politics of group participation, the politics of personal interaction.

The human ear is responsible for detecting sound, for listening. It is also responsible for balance, for the ability to maintain position.

What's remarkable about Andy Dejka's essay is the way he does seem to find a way to speak out about his silence. His essay itself is a nonsilence, a speaking out for the silent. In this sense, I very much recognize his moves, his efforts to make the lives of the silent visible. Andy, after all, doesn't seem to want to be *invisible*. His silence is not at all about disappearance or death. In fact, through his silence, Andy shows up. I started to recognize this *after* I read his paper. I started noticing the energy around his body in the classroom. I started to truly understand participation as a kind of embodied practice. Andy leans into a conversation. He's not afraid of it, he's not refusing it. He listens to it without interjecting. And not because Andy is passive. In fact, he is as much a generator of ideas as he is a sponge for them. Others' words (in speech and in reading) wash over him. Dejka writes,

> Some students learn by thinking out loud, bouncing ideas off the professor and their fellow classmates, and find discussions vital to their understanding. Conversely, those students like myself, who often require more time to effectively articulate their ideas, and who enjoy selecting those words which most accurately convey their thoughts, will appreciate writing projects and discussion board posts. We tend to "soak in" the class discussion and spend time out of class processing or ruminating. (6)

I take Dejka's reflection on his learning processes quite seriously. And his essay leads me to think more about how I can create more contexts for my students to write about *how* they learn and what they value in that process. It's strange that I find myself enacting, in my pedagogy, which I would have thought quite conducive to consciousness and rumination, practices that might get in the way of rumination, practices that fill up the silent possibilities of a classroom with voices. I am not suggesting that suddenly I find talking to be of no, or little, value. I am suggesting that this is a time for me to come face to face with my fears about silence and what it means. I am suggesting that when I pose a question to my students and they don't respond right away, I pose it another way. I ask them why they're so quiet. I shift gears, even though I know that often the questions I am asking them are difficult ones, perhaps even unanswerable. The questions I am asking them may require silence—or that silence may even *be* the answer to the question. In her essay "Cultivating Listening: Teaching from a Restored Logos," Shari Stenberg suggests that "a logos that places listening and speaking in opposition prevents us from the kind of receptivity necessary to overcome other dualisms that limit genuine dialogue" (251), and Andy Dejka was a student whose capacity for listening was beyond what a "speaker" like me can even imagine. Stenberg describes the kind of listening that leads to "genuine dialogue" as connected to Peter Elbow's description of what it means to "dwell" in the ideas or texts of others (252–53). It seems strange to me that I recognize this idea of "dwelling" as something I ask students to do with *texts* but not something it occurred to me to ask them to do with each other. Of course, like many teachers, I encourage my students to be respectful when others are talking. But the kind of engaged silence Stenberg describes is not just a matter of quiet. It's a matter of rumination, of dwelling in the voices of the classroom. I wonder how I might cultivate (to use a term from Stenberg's title) this dwelling in practice.

Upon entering graduate school, I would learn, at least theoretically, to rethink silence through a more extensive exposure to and study of queer theory. I read Foucault, so I knew that the production of discourse is not necessarily liberating or empowering. I learned that an "incitement to discourse" (much like the imperative for queers to "come out" and offer language that captures who they are) doesn't necessarily signify that you are finally free. I knew that saying, out loud, the words of who you are, enclosed you and encapsulated you even as you felt liberated in the saying. I knew the complex directions in which power could move and shift. I had thought a lot about whether "coming out" was really the answer to the problem of normativity. I, as a graduate student instructor, did classroom experiments in which sometimes and in some classes I "came out" to students as gay, or queer, or intersex. And I also experimented with not "coming out" as anything in the performative ways scholars and teacher-scholars like Karen Kopelson have described. I played with silence. I watched the powerful effect of coming to meaning through others' perceptions without giving them language to place on top of who you are. It is true that language can, indeed, be powerful. I find, in queer theory, a very complex relation to language, and I don't think it's an accident that some of the most prominent queer theorists—Foucault, Sedgwick, Butler—have intellectual ties to discourse study and speech act theory. What we say is important, yes. But only as important as what we don't say, or won't. This is the paradox: discourse is regulation, and silence is regulation. Or the reverse is also the paradox: discourse is empowerment, and silence is empowerment. And if there is not a universal interpretation for what silence means, why have I been teaching as though there is a universal interpretation that silence is a sign of *disengagement*?

The truth is, sometimes language covers up rather than reveals the self. While I learned as a kid that silence can cover up or make invisible, I also learned, as I moved through high school, that talking is perhaps even more effective at covering or making invisible. As an intersex person, I have always been kind of queer looking. Chubby maybe, "butch," masculinized, deep-voiced, hairy. I was a freak of a teenage girl, bench pressing more than my male classmates, ruling the arm-wrestling table in the lunchroom, singing as the only female tenor my music teacher had ever cast in the chorus. And I knew I was weird. I had heard my biological father say to my stepmother, *there's something not right about that kid*. And I knew what he meant, and I knew I had to find ways to cover up this weirdness, to make up for it in the eyes of family members and particularly other kids. But how?

So I started learning how to erase, or obfuscate, my difference through humor and extroversion. I had seen it done many times: Chris Farley, John Candy, the character "Chunk" in *Goonies*. I saw outcasts and fat guys become legends—all because they knew what joke to make or they knew how to use language to create a version of themselves that seemed more normative, less threatening. My older brother, Michael, had one of these friends growing up. My brother was friends with fit and handsome Italian kids, like Nicky Mangano and Blair Roccio. But watching them come up the street from the bus stop made one thing clear: an outsider had infiltrated—a very large, very nerdy outsider they called "Stubby." But Stubby was so funny and so good at football, his difference was forgiven, even celebrated. So I followed in Stubby's footsteps. I constructed an extroverted funny-man version of a girl. I was permitted to walk in groups with those far out of my social range. I watched other students who were different, but quiet, have very different luck. To be an introvert exacerbated rather than hid one's difference. It was talking, speaking up, saying jokes out loud, that made my difference forgivable, relatable, something the community was willing to overlook. I don't think this version of difference is uncommon. It speaks to just how self-evident patterns of extroversion and speech production seem to be in our current models of success and normative function.

I think if I really listen to Andy and dwell in the possibility of his ideas, I have to consider that the stakes for his *being himself* (if being himself means silent) are not entirely different from the stakes of me being *myself*, whatever that means. Dejka does consider his silence a kind of identity. In fact, he writes, "I suspect my social aversion is genetically rooted" (4). And in his statement I can hear the genetic or biological arguments made (for better or for worse) around issues of identity. Our identities can (whatever their roots) certainly feel connected to some core of who we are. Dejka opens his essay with a scene of reading, one in which his brother is being asked to participate in reading aloud, in giving voice to a text. He writes,

> [The teacher] pressed him further, but he could not speak. Pointing to a sentence in Frog and Toad are Friends, an easy-reader children's book she held in front of his nose, the woman insisted in an exasperated tone, "Adam, won't you please tell me what this line says? What does Frog ask Toad?" He wanted desperately to follow her command, but his mouth refused to obey. His eyes shifted furtively from the book to the woman and then back to the book, searching for any escape. Of course he could read the sentence; he wasn't stupid. The woman asked again, but he endured it, suffering, and shuddered imperceptibly. At last, the lunch bell rang. He was free. (1)

Silence is read, in this instance (and I think in many others), as either an inability (a dysfunction, as Dejka calls it) or a refusal to participate or follow convention. Adam, as his brother artfully suggests, knows how to read and even "wanted desperately" to participate in the teacher-ask-student-answer model. But he does not. And, in the end, Dejka says it's Adam's mouth that "refused to obey." There is, indeed, something queer about silence, but only when it is employed in environments that require speech as a model of success. As an audience member, for example, silence is required. But in a classroom, normative functioning means speech, especially in many English classrooms. Adam's refusal (and also Andy Dejka's own refusal in my course) to speak is a failure not of the mouth or of student identity. It is a systemic failure.

The Queer Art of Failure is not about classrooms; mostly, it is about animated films and characters who embody fantastic, silly, and even absurd failures. But Halberstam's ultimate conclusion seems to give those of us interested in shaping classrooms that value non-normative ways of being in the world—those of us committed to pedagogies aware of and informed by the potential of difference—an essential challenge. Halberstam asserts, "Queerness offers the promise of failure as a way of life . . . but it is up to us whether we choose to make good on that promise in a way that makes a detour around the usual markers of accomplishment and satisfaction" (186). As part of my work on queer pedagogies, I often ask myself how to make my classroom queerer, how to queer my own and students' understandings of identity, desire, and narration. But Halberstam's remarks remind me that it isn't just the writing process or the rhetorical choices made by my students in their writing that seems to demand a bit of queering. It's also ideas about education itself, ideas about what it means to be a student, to succeed at the game of school in and outside the university. I start to think of the other kinds of norms that shape a classroom—class discussion (requiring normative understandings of participation), group work (requiring normative ideas about collaboration and sociality), sustained engagement with texts (requiring normative notions of attention). The list could, of course, go on. And I am not claiming here to have all the answers, or the perfect list of activities in alternative educational universes where we might, as Halberstam suggests, "revel in and cleave to all of our own inevitable fantastic failures" (187). But I think if those of us in composition are serious about the "social turn" or the "queer turn" or the "turn toward difference" in our field, we have to *continually* ask ourselves how we are implicated in reaffirming the very ideas about difference we seek to disrupt. Or, put another way, how is my classroom just one more normative set of hoops through which students must jump?

I began this chapter with a quote from Ritchie and Wilson's *Teacher Narrative as Critical Inquiry: Rewriting the Script*, and I take quite seriously their claim that "when teachers are given the opportunity to compose and reflect on their own stories of learning and of selfhood . . . [they] can begin to resist and revise the scripting narratives of the culture" (1). Continuing to compose my own story of selfhood alongside Andy's, alongside all my students as I understand and gather their work, I make my own subjectivity more visible to myself—something I ask of my students all the time. I am able to see the parts of myself that are, as I said at the opening of this chapter, conservative. If I am committed, as I imagine myself to be, to being a teacher who can "revise the scripting narratives of the culture," I have to admit to myself and to my colleagues (and ultimately, to my students) the ways I have written the very scripts I seek to subvert or transform.

I know some friends and scholars in queer theory or queer studies might not like the parallel I'm drawing here. They might say, Is being silent really *like* being gay, or being genderqueer? And I think that while this question comes from an important place, a place where those of us who are queer resist having the term "queer" co-opted and used anywhere someone finds it a useful analogy, it's not actually the right question. To be clear, it's not really analogy (or *like*-ness) I am trying to understand; it's methodology, a way of looking. And I think queering as a methodology (or a set of expanding methodologies) is something that every one of us should advocate. Sometimes I get tired of this question about who queerness belongs to and how it can't belong to everyone. But that worry, that worry that somehow everyone in this world will someday look at things in queer ways all the time, and that worry that then queerness will just be the norm and therefore not queer anymore, that worry is one I'd welcome. I would love to actually *have* this problem, to one day think to myself, "Aw shucks, now everyone is thinking about things in queer ways! Just what will we do now?" So while I know that Andy Dejka's identity as a silent person is not the same as my identity as a queer person, I do know that queer ways of knowing help me to see myself, and Andy, with a mind of possibility—a habit of mind I try to cultivate alongside my students all the time.

Thinking queerly about participation might mean thinking about my students' bodies, about Andy's expression of body in the room. Thinking queerly about participation might mean valuing a student comment that is "inappropriate" or socially awkward. It might mean becoming more embodied, more "inappropriate," or more silent myself, somehow trying to rebuild my classroom as a space where dominant narratives about class participation aren't useful, don't function as success. It might mean actually articulating how failures to "participate" might also be productive, fantastic, and generative failures. I would never have argued that the writing process was not an inevitable failure, so it strikes me that it never occurred to me that the process of participation might also be one in which failure could be desirable. It might also mean that I ask myself to truly enact, in the actual classroom when I am interacting with students, the decentering I often claim to value. I might need to stop *participating*, stop talking. Take the cue from Andy, and listen. I am grateful to Andy Dejka for his elegant and honest writing and for the ways his presence in my classroom and his willingness to compose an essay that troubled a normative understanding have shifted my view. I am sure it wasn't easy for him. After all, he wrote an essay that critiques extroversion as it is valued in the academy—something he knew very well that my classroom (and I) was doing.

There is, in the end, something inevitably quiet about where I live now—its endless stretch of sky, the silent vulnerability of standing underneath it. It's hard not to think I'm meant also to quiet down, to shed the skin made of noise, to pull the sound out from my throat, let it fall silent at my feet. "Quiet down" was what my father used to say when we had crossed the threshold of his short fuse, quiet down as in **make your father a moment of peace,** *as in* **leave him some room to think for once.** *But what my father found when my brothers and I fell silent in the backseat was nothing but the open road, nothing but the car engine—the world gone so quiet, he could hear his eyelids touch when he blinked.*

CHAPTER THREE

ALTERNATIVE ORIENTATIONS

> Subversiveness, rather than being an easily identifiable counter-knowledge, lies in the very moment of unintelligibility, or in the absence of knowledge. If subversiveness is not a new form of knowledge but lies in the capacity to raise questions about the detours of coming to know and make sense, then what does this mean for a pedagogy that imagines itself as queer? Can a queer pedagogy resist the desire for authority and stable knowledge; can it resist disseminating new knowledge and new forms of subjection? What if a queer pedagogy puts into crisis what is known and how we come to know?
>
> Susanne Luhmann, "Queering/Querying Pedagogy?"

> I try to teach my readers to become conscious of their mental moves, to see what such moves produce, and to learn to revise or complicate those moves as they return to them in light of their newly constructed awareness of what those moves did or did not make possible.
>
> Mariolina Salvatori, *The Elements (and Pleasures) of Difficulty*

Queer Habits, Queer Values

I often return to Jacqueline Rhodes's assertion in "The Failure of Queer Pedagogy" that a queer pedagogy might not be able to exist, that pedagogy itself has always been about "disciplining the subject" and has always been "informed by a logic of mastery, of individual attainment, and of institutional assessment of that attainment." I find myself thinking of all the ways that schooling cannot be queer. I think back to high school, the bells ringing, marking at what moments we were to rise from our chairs, move from one class to another. I see myself, hand on heart, saying the Pledge of Allegiance, taking standardized tests, changing in the girls' locker room, where I would not have liked to change. And perhaps colleges and universities have their differences—no Pledge of Allegiance, no bells ringing. But we cannot escape our other institutional norms—our syllabi, our course objectives, our program reviews, our grading systems, assignments, due dates. It all, indeed, sounds very unqueer—a house made of norms. Often I design courses and writing sequences with attention to queer pedagogy both by assigning texts that engage with queer studies (giving specific attention to what Jonathan Alexander calls "sexual literacy") and by trying to develop, during the course itself, queer teaching practices or methods of instruction. But, as Rhodes suggests, there are times that college teaching, in and of itself, seems antithetical to queer approaches. But, in thinking of all structures or guidelines as normative, we might miss the queer possibilities of structure itself. Judith Butler allows for this when she writes that although "we need norms in order to live, and to live well, and to know in what direction to transform our social world, we are also constrained by norms in ways that sometimes do violence to us and which, for reasons of social justice, we must oppose" (*Undoing* 205–6).

One of the first sets of norms made visible to students in our courses is the syllabus we have made, the writing *we* have produced for them. I design my syllabi and assignment sequences in my first-year writing courses as the very body who writes this book. In fact, as I discuss in this chapter, I often ask my students to do the same—to begin where they are, to begin in their own bodies and identities—how do I write assignments that begin there, assignments that ask students to develop critical sexual literacy while at the same time keeping in mind that a writing course *is* a course about writing?

In this chapter, I focus on one particular first-year writing course that is representative of many of the courses I teach. This course, called Seminar in Composition, is one that fulfills the requirement for first-year writing at the University of Pittsburgh. Writing is the "material" I am institutionally expected to teach in the course. So the question is, Why do I think queer theory would help me do this? Might gender, sexuality, the subject of sex itself actually distract my students from the important work of learning to write? Perhaps it might be useful here for me to provide the institutional expectations and context in which I have taught the composition courses I draw from most frequently in this book. The University of Pittsburgh currently describes, as the aims and goals of any Seminar in Composition course, the following sets of values:

SEMINAR IN COMPOSITION AT THE UNIVERSITY OF PITTSBURGH

Seminar in Composition is the introductory writing course most undergraduates at the University of Pittsburgh take during their freshman year to fulfill the first of three writing-intensive ("W") requirements in the School of Arts and Sciences. Although sections of the course vary, all students in Seminar in Composition address a semester-long sequence of assignments demanding sustained attention to a complex subject. Each sequence is carefully designed to require students to do the following:

Engage in writing as a creative, disciplined form of critical inquiry

Students in this course use writing to generate ideas as well as explain them. Through writing, students form questions and explore problems as they work toward nuanced understanding of a multifaceted subject. Sequenced assignments serve to deepen students' engagement with writing and reading, assist them in examining their own experiences and observations, and encourage them to make productive use of their uncertainty rather than come to hasty conclusions.

Address challenging questions about the consequences of their own writing

This course approaches the essay as a flexible genre that takes on different forms in different contexts. Much class time is devoted to scrutiny of the purpose, logic, and design of students' writing, which they are given opportunities to revise in response to comments from their teacher and peers. This focus on their own texts increases awareness of what is at stake in representing an issue or problem in one way instead of another, thus helping students make more attentive decisions as they write.

Compose thoughtfully crafted essays that position the writer's ideas among other views

Rather than merely stating their own opinions, students learn to write essays in which they develop informed positions that reflect understanding of the positions of others. Analyzing as well as summarizing the ideas and writing strategies in assigned texts, students compose interpretations reflecting close attention to their own and others' specific language choices.

Write with precision, nuance, and awareness of textual conventions

Students work on crafting clear, precise prose that effectively uses a variety of sentence and paragraph structures. They are required to learn the conventions for quoting and paraphrasing accurately, responsibly, and adeptly. They are also assisted in developing editing and proofreading strategies that reflect attention to the relation between style and meaning.

I notice, of course, the word "disciplined" appearing almost immediately in the document. But I also notice the values of uncertainty, flexibility, and nuance. As I look carefully at this document, I do understand it as an accurate reflection of what it means to teach composition at the University of Pittsburgh, and I took very seriously its values. I am also aware, as I look at the language and theory of composition above, how very deeply I have been shaped by the institutional contexts in which I work. I am aware of the different meanings it might have to teach writing elsewhere, though in the three institutional locations where I have taught, these principles would still seem to hold true. I also read this document as reflecting a fascinating tension between the language of skills and the language of disposition, or what is sometimes called, in education circles, "habits of mind."

The word *dolphin* comes from ancient Greek. The translation of the word turns out to be something like: *the fish with a womb.*

A *habit* might be understood to be something automatic, something so automatic the term is often paired with *bad.* Smoking, a bad habit. Biting your nails, a bad habit. But we can also become aware of our habits; we can continue those habits with that new awareness or even form new habits. Unlike practices or skills, habits suggest inclinations, tendencies, even a kind of spirit. Habits might be understood to be difficult to change, and they might actually be; however, I want to consider the idea that habits (like orientations) are more mutable than we imagine—and that habits of mind are more conceptual than skills. It is true that there are skills and practices associated with writing and with the teaching of writing. Some of them, in fact, are mentioned by the document I provide above. But I want to consider the idea that these skills and practices might not be very useful if, for example, they were used and approached through a one-dimensional framework. That I can execute the "conventions for quoting" in an essay I have written does not mean I can engage with another author in a meaningful and layered way. The parts of the University of Pittsburgh's Seminar in Composition document that interest me most are those parts that suggest specific habits of mind—*productive use of uncertainty, sustained attention, an awareness of what is it at stake*. These are a few of the habits of mind I see above and ones that are reflected, even if at times called something else, in my own teaching practices.

Dolphins use echolocation to explore their environment in a blurred ocean world where using their sight is of little help. Their brains make rapid analyses of a complicated environment. Using their nasal clicks, dolphins fire off signals that bounce back to them as sound waves, and dolphins measure the distance between their bodies and others by the time it takes for the sound of themselves to return to them.

There are thousands of books and essays out there that intend to teach students to write or to instruct students about what it means to write in the university. There are explicitly rhetorically arranged readers, such as *The Bedford Reader* and *Patterns for College Writing*, which give students a rhetorical taxonomic approach to thinking about and doing writing. These types of textbooks, grounded in the rhetorical tradition, are still best-sellers in the United States. Each of these readers does ultimately propose certain habits of mind, though they rarely call them that or rarely call attention to the habits of mind they support or endorse. *The Bedford Reader*, for example, describes its own taxonomy as follows: "each of the ten chapters explains a familiar method of developing ideas such as narration, description, example, cause and effect, and definition" (Kennedy, Kennedy, and Aaron 3). Often composition and writing textbooks focus on "familiar methods" or traditional taxonomies that aim to categorize and label kinds of writing, asking students to practice one kind of writing at a time. I do not want to argue that there is no value at all in teaching in this way, and of course there are a number of successful textbooks that resist these taxonomies. But I do want to consider alternative habits of mind we might cultivate as we think about our teaching and as we ask our students to think about their writing. David Rosenwasser and Jill Stephen have edited and composed an interesting writing textbook entitled *Writing Analytically* in which they do explicitly call attention to particular habits of mind. In a chapter called "Counterproductive Habits of Mind," Rosenwasser and Stephen write to students:

> Most of us learn early in life to pretend that we understand things even when we don't. Rather than ask questions and risk looking foolish, we nod our heads. Soon, we even come to believe that we understand things when really we don't, or not nearly as well as we think we do. This understandable but problematic human trait means that to become better thinkers, most of us have to cultivate a more positive attitude toward not knowing. Prepare to be surprised by how difficult this can be. Start by trying to accept that uncertainty—even its more extreme version, confusion—is a productive state of mind, a precondition of having ideas. (18)

While it would not be my approach to cite a "human trait" as a reason for our resistance to uncertainty, I do think Rosenwasser and Stephen are raising an important point—that resisting or ignoring confusion or uncertainty does not make for interesting intellectual work. I want to read Rosenwasser and Stephen as quite purposeful in their word choice in this passage, and I want to pay particular attention to the terms "cultivate" and "state of mind, a precondition of having ideas." I usually begin thinking about my writing courses by considering the habits of mind I want the course to explore and try on, habits of mind that seem to be essential to powerful writing and even more particularly to queer writing. Habits of mind can be cultivated, and cultivation is in itself a process, one that must be repeated. Without repetition, there is no cultivation. In the assignment sequence I discuss in this chapter, I want to consider how my own assignments ask (or sometimes fail to ask) students to cultivate particular habits of mind and how that cultivation might lead to particular kinds of writing. But before I talk more explicitly about these assignments, I want to spend some time considering one other way of thinking about these habits of mind.

I failed one test, to my memory, in grade school. It was a geography test whereby we, as students, were meant to label the continents and some important countries inside of them. I remember doodling on the test, tracing over the lines that were the boundaries between one place and another. I could remember so few of their names. The words for each country empty of meaning, missing their contents. Other words I could put things inside. Having learned the word sarcastic *from my brother Michael, I could then, whenever I heard the word, put my brother inside of it, his telling me from the top of the hallway stairs, "It's when you say one thing but mean something else."*

Alternative Orientations

Sara Ahmed, in her book *Queer Phenomenology: Orientations, Objects, Others*, offers me another way of understanding habits of mind. She begins her book with a discussion of *orientation*. She asks, in her very first sentence, "What does it mean to be oriented?" (1). She considers that orientation has something to do with "how we reside in space" or "to be turned toward certain objects" (1). We might think of habits of mind as orientations. And if orientations have something to do with space—and, as Ahmed reminds us, "queer theorists have shown us how spaces are sexualized"—then in this sense orientations are always sexual, always the body in position, in relation. Asking someone to change or consider alternative habits of mind may actually be as intimate and confounding as asking one to consider alternative orientations. For example, Rosenwasser and Stephen are asking students to be oriented *toward* rather than *away from* uncertainty. I use this example because I am asking, in my own way, for the same shift in orientation from my students. This understanding of orientation shapes much of the syllabus and assignments that follow. Take this shift in thinking alongside the sexualized and "queer" content of much of the course, and there is no way around the fact that what I am asking students to do is quite difficult, perhaps even controversial. After all, can one just change one's orientation? Isn't orientation often taken to mean *either you are or you aren't*? You're either down with confusion, or you're not. You can't *make yourself* see confusion differently. What if you're *just not attracted* to confusion? What if you were *born that way*?

I dress up in airports. The airport is already such an unstable and uncertain space. We are without homes, however temporarily, and because of this sense of movement and uncertainty in the travelers, we hold tight to what we know: our bags, our cell phones connecting us to certainties, our social graces, our tickets leading us out of transitional space. So in Detroit I decided on the men's room, knowing how the men do not look up in their restrooms; they look only at the sinks and urinals they are using. Usually, I pass. I have the sense that my body feels male to them. But when there's not much space between the sink and wall and I (being socialized as some sort of woman) put my hand on a man's back just for moment to indicate that I am passing behind him, the smoothness of my performance breaks down (as it often has in the women's room). He turns quickly around and pushes me backward. "What the fuck?" he says. "What the fuck?" he says again. We stare at one another. We both cannot tell what we see.

While habits of mind, or orientations, are not writing itself, I want to argue that without certain orientations, writing in a critical and engaging way is not possible, or at least far less possible. So what are they? How do they create or cultivate the conditions under which writing can grow? What do they have to do with grammar, punctuation, and argument-making? Why are queer approaches a compelling orientation for teaching and writing? I want be clear that, like all of us who strive for and fail at queer pedagogies, I do not know what exactly queer pedagogy is, nor do I want to make the claim that queer pedagogies are the *best* ways to teach writing. What I want to highlight is what queering pedagogy might make possible for the teaching of composition, even if it is also impossible to do. This does not mean I am suggesting that queer orientations are the best or only ways of thinking about composition, and it's certainly not meant to suggest that uncertainty is the sole property of queer kinds of thinking. Composition scholars have been grappling with uncertainty for some time, implicitly or explicitly. But perhaps when uncertainty is valued and expressed through queerer understandings of identity and relation we might begin to imagine new possibilities for writing and for the teaching of writing. And I approach this writing, as I approached the teaching of the course on which it is based, with the same orientation toward uncertainty I ask of my students.

Dolphins make several sounds, though they have no vocal cords.

As I try to return to the documents of this course—its syllabus, class transcripts taken by individual students in the class, and student writing—I am, in a sense, reading them for the first time, reading them for both what I thought I was telling students and what words now seem to stand out as touchstones for the course. Surely in the course description and a piece of writing I call the "instructor's statement" I might find the particular language for the habits of mind and orientations I value. I want to read for my own key terms, paying close attention to the possibilities and impossibilities of my own queer pedagogical positions and concerns. The course description reads,

> This course is perhaps unlike most courses you have taken. It will ask of you a kind of composition that may feel at times uncomfortable, strange or even impossible. The course content is structured around constructs of gender, race, sexuality, the body, writing, class, politics and art. The assignments in this course will ask you to access parts of your consciousness you may not even know are there. They will require you to think critically about gender and its relationship to various cultural and personal identity categories and constructions. The assignments will also ask you to revise, challenge and expand what you know of as "papers." As you know, "papers" are assignments given by instructors for students to "complete." I encourage you to think of the writing in this course as prompting you, daring you, even at times provoking you but never to "complete"—only to compose (like a musician, you might say, or a painter, but not at all like a "student"). If you think you might find it interesting to reconsider all you have learned about writing thus far, all you have learned about bodies, about gender, about sexuality and about the world in which you live, you are sitting in the right course.

I am struck immediately by my own perhaps naïve ambition; the course seems to promise (or hope for) a rather life-changing experience for students, my desire shining through despite years of teaching and learning experience that tells me courses are rarely life-changing. I find in the third sentence a list of subjects I call the "course content"—a list consisting of "gender, race, sexuality, the body, writing, class, politics and art." At first, I wonder if a one-semester course could do justice to all of these "subjects" at once, or if they are subjects at all. I notice the complicated relationship between what I want my students to know about and what I want them to be able to *do*. In one sense, I care less about the *knowing about* and more about the *knowing how* because I see knowing and being as a kind of doing.

The land ancestor of the dolphin is said to have looked like a wolf, hunting in shallow waters and eventually evolving: forelegs turned into flippers, hind legs became fluke, the fur fell away, and nostrils became the blowhole from which dolphins do their conscious breathing.

But I remind myself again: what writing course is not about the ideas on this list? We do not often acknowledge the possibility that every writing class is, explicitly or implicitly, tied to this list. Every writing class is about identity: the identities of the students, the teacher, the dynamics between the various expressions of those identities in writing and in the classroom. To say otherwise would be to fool ourselves into thinking that our pedagogies, our teaching choices, were about something other than ourselves.

My parents signed the permission form for me to take a seventh-grade health class called Human Sexuality. Mrs. Berger was our teacher, and she asked me to stand in the hallway as punishment. I was not able to say "penis" and "vagina" in unison, along with the other kids, without laughing. "Sexuality is no laughing matter," she said.

It's not a surprise to me that my course description seems to value writing as a kind of artistry, asking students to "compose" rather than complete assignments. This language has to do not only with the fact that I am a writer, a poet, but also with the fact that I see myself as a maker, as composing identities *and* composing the writing that represents and reflects those identities. And I am both interested in and suspicious of the ways I am asking my students to try *me* on, to become the kind of maker I see myself becoming. And I describe this process as one that will be uncomfortable, strange, and even at times seemingly impossible, acknowledging, I hope, the difficulty of reading and writing and the difficulty of becoming something other than what we might already understand ourselves to be.

I am particularly interested now in the verbs I chose to use: revise, challenge, expand, provoke, dare, prompt, reconsider, encourage, think critically. While several of these may seem benign—seem the goal of any writing teacher—it is the provoking and daring that seem to speak to the "danger" of my courses, the possibility for provocation and the opportunity to, playfully I hope, accept the dare. Frankly, I am asking the students in this course to be brave, to look into the face of that which brings them discomfort, fear, bewilderment, and even anger. It is a kind of affective, as well as political and intellectual, project. This is, I think, a lot to ask, though I have to say, for me, it is an imperative asking.

I kept a journal in tenth grade. I wrote, "The other kids who are supposed to be in honors English said Ms. Zuccaro's class is hard and that she's strict. I think they only think that because they don't like poems and stories. Just this week Ms. Zuccaro read a passage from Street Car Named Desire, *the one where Blanche says that deliberate cruelty is not forgivable. She says it is the one unforgivable thing. And you could tell Ms. Zuccaro felt the same way; her eyes teared up when she was reading, and so I like her. I like teachers who have feelings, not the ones who pretend they don't. What's a kid supposed to think that growing up means stopping feeling? Grown ups pretend a lot I think. Anyway, Ms. Zuccaro wears her heart on her sleeve. Ain't her fault if some honors kids who don't like poetry think she's strict. Wanting more from people isn't the same as being strict. And Ms. Zuccaro likes me I think 'cause I want more too. And anyhow, that's really why Holden Caulfield is so sad too, 'cause he wants more. And why shouldn't he?"*

Looking back now at my course description, I admit I am somewhat troubled by my own writing—puzzled by what I mean and how I mean it. I write, *The assignments in this course will ask you to access parts of your consciousness you may not even know are there.* I am troubled by my own presumptions, as I often am, that students do not know themselves or that there are parts of themselves they do not know are there. On one level, this seems innocuous enough—all of us are in some way in the dark about ourselves, groping in that dark to touch a self we might come to know. However, my implication that this part of consciousness is already there waiting to be discovered seems, ironically, to go against my own theories and claims about how knowledge is made and produced. My regret here is not so much that I am asking students to go searching for themselves but more about where I am asking them to search. This is a tension I want to read for in the course materials and one I struggle with. Like gender itself, our notions of ourselves are both already there *and* always in the process of being made, a contradictory and paradoxical relation between what we experience as internal and what we experience as external—a question again returning us to orientation, our relation to ourselves and to the world existing simultaneously and inextricably.

The "instructor's statement" that follows the course description in the syllabus is my attempt at telling students more explicitly about my own interests in queer pedagogies and about what they can expect as far as what I value and what I do not value. What I want is for my students and for myself to attempt to begin in agreement about these values, or at the very least, to accept that these values are what counts in this course, what they can count on, in a sense. I also try, in this statement, to negotiate a kind of queer authority. I subscribe neither to a critical pedagogy model (in which I am the guide who leads my students into the light) nor to a model whereby I pretend to have no authority—or pretend that my students and I are "equals." Institutionally and, quite honestly, socially, that is not possible, which is not to say that I am the one who always has the "last-word" authority in grading—the location of power shifts, but I am not afraid to hold it, temporarily, to express, in sometimes more solid terms than I prefer, a kind of certainty about what is valued. Of course, even in that momentary certainty, there is always a kind of paradox:

> While I feel it is my duty to create a safe and open classroom environment, I do feel compelled to tell you that I also feel that it is my job to make you intellectually uncomfortable; it is your discomfort and unease that will educate you. I am a scholar of "queer pedagogy" and my teaching style and method is greatly informed by this field of interest (which we may discuss at various times this semester). By remaining in this course, you agree to spend this semester considering the idea that that which brings you discomfort, that which you might find unthinkable is that which you most need to read, re-imagine and (un)learn. You also agree to treat every member of this class, including yourself, with respect and kindness. We will discuss many difficult and sensitive subjects this semester, and you must be able to remember that it is one another's writing and ideas that are subject to critique—not one another's character or background. As an instructor, I value difficulty and complexity; I value discussion, community, awareness, creativity, rigor and passion. Consequently, I do not

find apathy, disinterest, dismissive-ness or reduction to be of value. This semester, it is my hope that we will learn a great deal from one another and that we will also enjoy one another's input, energy and company. If you feel at all unsure as to whether you will be able to discuss and consider the subject matter of this course in a mature, inquisitive and active way, perhaps this is not the course for you. If you feel up to the challenge and responsibility, then I look forward to the distance we will travel together from now until the end of the semester.

I once heard this instructor's statement described by a first-year graduate student TA (who did not know it was mine) as "the S/M syllabus." This description actually seems quite apt if we consider what this actually means in terms of power and if we consider the ways the writer and queer theorist Kate Bornstein situates the power relation in an S/M "playing" context. Bornstein explains that "most players agree that power is *shared*, with the top in control but only within the bounds agreed upon and often requested by the bottom. Some say there's a sublime moment when top and bottom together and at once have all the power and none of the power" (*Gender* 122). Bornstein goes on to describe S/M play as "safe, sane and consensual," unlike, she says, "gender," which is none of those things (123). Perhaps this is an uncomfortable moment; perhaps a comparison between how power works in S/M playing seems unsettling, "inappropriate" even, however uncanny the resemblance might be to teaching at times. But the connection does help to illuminate the paradox of trying to "create a safe and open classroom" and at the same time demanding of my students a significant amount of risk. In this sense, we must trust one another as players, must, as Bornstein puts it, work "within the bounds agreed upon." This instructor's statement is the beginning of those bounds, which are, in some ways, pushed on and moved and redefined by both my students and myself.

Surprisingly, when dolphins give birth to a newborn dolphin, there is a kind of midwife referred to as an "auntie" dolphin, which may be male or female and assists in the birth. This is usually the only other dolphin, other than parent dolphins, who is allowed near the newborn.

My list of values is very connected to the habits of mind I began with in this chapter. And their relationship to writing is something the course aims to explore and establish. These two documents together, along with the department's list of goals for this course, are essentially the only "rubric" students have. This fact in itself can make them intellectually uncomfortable, especially those students who have come from rubric-centered writing curriculums where they are asked to demonstrate skills and illustrate competence rather than exhibit or practice some abstract "habits of mind," and I am asking them to trust the process, to trust that these changes in orientation will result in new and more complex writing, writing that will presumably earn them academic merit and personal growth. Often students, quite importantly, distrust. They look at me and at the course with the same suspiciousness with which I sometimes look at them. The trusting is always a process. I want to examine what I see as the habits of mind of this writing course as I designed it, through the assignments in sequence and through some of the student writing in response to those assignments. And in order to consider those assignments, it seems useful to begin with the first set of materials of the course: the course texts—that is, the course texts that prompt or invite the more primary course texts of student writing.

In her essay "Unresting the Curriculum: Queer Projects, Queer Imaginings," Marla Morris writes, "A queer sensibility concerns the reception and reading of a text. The text is a site of interpretation. Thus, there is nothing inherently queer about a text, even if one may read a text queerly. As Alan Block (1995) points out, reading constructs the reader as well as the text. Reading creates the reader: reading queerly creates a queer reader" (276–77). It is with this complicated understanding of reading that I begin my thinking about the reading my students will do in a writing course. Morris's claim that "there is nothing inherently queer about a text" may seem at first erroneous. For example, Kate Bornstein's *Gender Outlaw: On Men, Women, and the Rest of Us*, is certainly a "queer" text—it is a book by and about a person who identifies as trans, who interrogates and debunks traditional and stable notions of gender. Certainly, this text is queer in the sense that it is *about* queerness or that it can be found in the LGBTQ section of a bookstore or library. However, Morris is concerned with queering as method, with the idea of reading a text (regardless of its subject or location in the bookstore) queerly. If "reading queerly creates a queer reader," then one of the goals of my course might be to create more queer readers and writers—to shift students' literate orientations, or to value different kinds of reading and writing than may have been valued before. This queer reader is not necessarily *a queer*, but this reader is reading queerly.

A mother dolphin whistles to her newborn for days to help the newborn dolphin identify, with more certainty, its family's call.

Reading queerly requires the habits of mind I try to articulate in my course description, instructor's statement, and in this book. As queer habits of mind, they are, at times, difficult to pin down, but we can do so momentarily, provisionally. If we cannot do so at all, there is little ground on which to stand, or little, really, we are able to say. The habits of mind I want to advocate are, I hope, visible not only as I describe them but also in the very writing of this project—its approach or style. Uncertainty, confusion, fluidity, self-reflexivity, multiplicity, embodiment—all tendencies, positions I ask students to inhabit, even if only temporarily, even if I know that ultimately they (and I) will fail at keeping up, that there requires, for all of us, a moment of stability—a syllabus, an assignment from which to respond, a due date (however movable), or a name we might give to even the most unstable reading. Queer pedagogies cannot extricate themselves from definition, despite the term *queer* being, by definition, a resistance *to* definition. But, I might say that in order to queer *queer*, we must be able to teach and write along with that contradiction—the temporarily stabilized fluidity, the momentarily singular multiplicity. These paradoxes signal a unique relationship between queer theory and composition studies, both "disciplines" that spend a great deal of scholarly time trying to name and rename their histories and trying to decide, or undo, what is included inside them as disciplines.

No two dolphin whistles are the same pitch. Their whistles function as signatures, names. Because of these signatures, dolphins may come to know one another even from great distances.

The intersections between queer studies and composition studies have been explored for two decades. In a 2009 *College Composition and Communication* article, Jonathan Alexander and David Wallace offer a kind of survey of that work in their essay "The Queer Turn in Composition Studies: Reviewing and Assessing an Emerging Scholarship." Alexander and Wallace discuss the important political projects taken on by queer compositionists as they describe what they see as three movements in this area of inquiry: "confronting homophobia, becoming inclusive, and queering the hetero/homo binary" (300). I appreciate and engage the political and activist work of these three movements, yet here I am primarily interested in the creative and intellectual work queer theory offers to the field of composition studies. I do not mean to suggest that the political and the intellectual are separable pursuits (or that my concerns are not political—they surely are), but I do want to explore queer(er) possibilities for *writing*, for teaching *writing*. So far the scholarship in this "queer turn" has largely been about the movements Alexander and Wallace describe—about combating heterosexism, about including LGBTQ voices and students in conversations about identity and composition, and about troubling the gay/straight binary. The course I designed surely demonstrates these movements; however, it is my primary goal to extend queer impacts on composition by bringing queer theorists themselves into the conversation more fully and by investigating the possibilities of queer pedagogies that are not necessarily or always attached to *queer* texts or *queer* people.

Dolphins have a limbic system, and they are said to have emotions and even some levels of consciousness about those emotions. Some have even argued dolphins to be compassionate beings, conscious of even the fear and playfulness of others, humans even.

It is later in the article that Alexander and Wallace talk about queer compositionists developing, along with their students, "a new understanding of what it means to take literate agency in a postmodern world" (301). It is this last gesture forward where I want to intervene, or interfere. I approach composition courses with a concern that students "take literate agency." The course itself might be viewed as an inquiry into what it would mean to do such a thing. And what does this literate agency have to do with queering as a methodology? I would contend that the most celebrated and interesting writers have queer methodologies—nonnormative approaches to body, identity, reading, and writing. My writing courses seek to teach students to do the same—to become provocative, creative, queer, and literate agents "in a postmodern world." Although

Alexander and Wallace discuss this literate agency, they do not focus on what agency might mean in a queer context; it is important to think about how we might understand agency (our own and our students') or what a queer understanding of agency might be. Butler puts it this way: "That my agency is riven with paradox does not mean it is impossible. It means only that paradox is the condition of its possibility" (*Undoing* 3). Butler's understanding of agency here leaves open the possibility that agency is both possible and constrained, empowered and limited—or to put it another way, that limits are the conditions from which agency might emerge, however impossible that may seem.

After all, while I want my students to become the "literate agents" Alexander and Wallace evoke, I also know that paradox is the condition of their agency: limitations designed by me, assignments written by me, habits of mind required by my course, texts chosen by me. I become part of my students' paradoxical agency.

In addition to Bornstein's *Gender Outlaw*, there were other texts for the course: *The Trouble with Normal: Sex, Politics, and the Ethics of Queer Life* (1999), by Michael Warner; *Tootsie* (1982), directed by Sydney Pollack; "The Master's Tools Will Never Dismantle the Master's House" (1977), by Audre Lorde; "White Privilege: Unpacking the Invisible Knapsack" (1989), by Peggy McIntosh; "Girl," by Jamaica Kincaid; and a collection of music. The disc of music texts for the course included some "famous" songs ("Respect," by Aretha Franklin, for example), some popular music of the previous decade ("Cater 2 U," by Destiny's Child, for instance), and several underground tunes ("My I.Q.," by Ani DiFranco, among them). The students also read excerpts from some of the major queer theorists and philosophers of our time—Judith Butler, Michel Foucault, Cornel West, Eve Sedgwick, Martin Buber, Edward Said, Gloria Anzaldúa, and Gayle Rubin, among others. While many of these texts might be said to be "queer" materials, some of them would not likely appear necessarily in a queer theory course. And I was very interested in what might happen with those less than queer (or unlikely to be described as queer) materials once students had learned to engage in the process of queering, to practice queering as a habit of mind.

I began thinking of the sequence of assignments in this course not only as being informed by queer theory and queer materials but also as teaching students new *ways* of thinking, ways of thinking I have been calling "habits of mind," a complicated and queer lens through which to imagine what they see, read, and write. It was my sense that this particular approach might create possibilities for writing, for queering the essay itself as an academic task. I first saw some of the possibilities for this kind of work in *Ways of Reading*, the "textbook" from which I taught my first four composition courses at the University of Pittsburgh in 1999 and a textbook I now coedit with David Bartholomae and Anthony Petrosky. I think of my own teaching project in this course as a hybrid, informed simultaneously and dialectically by composition and queer theory. I would agree with David Bartholomae when he writes that "a sequence of assignments is repetitive. It asks students to write, again, about something they wrote about before. But such a project allows for richness; it allows for the imagination that one thing can lead to another, that the world can give and give. This is an idea hard to pin, difficult to say, and, perhaps, offensive to some" (*Writing* 190). Certainly I would first acknowledge that this course might prove "offensive to some," as it asks students to repeatedly come back to the body and to identity. What I hear Bartholomae saying in this passage is a reframing of revision so that, aside from having students return to the same paper over and over as they try to reshape, revise, and edit that particular piece, revision can also be a return to particular ideas or to particular habits of mind. In my course, students are asked to return to themselves, to identity, to fluidity as kinds of revision. The queerer, the more flexible our thinking becomes, the more we are able to "write, again, about something [we] wrote about before," but this time we write it queerer, rich with new possibilities. The assignments in this course were repetitive in that they ask the students to consider, again and again, the context and contingency of their own thinking, reading, and being; this self-reflexivity is part of the habits of mind that they are asked to inhabit as they read and write. The repetition is not merely the returning again and again to a given subject, but the repetition, more importantly, is a return again and again to these habits of mind.

So as not to die in their sleep, dolphins rest one side of the brain at a time so the side of the brain that is wakeful remembers to breathe.

Becoming Oriented

In high school, I had a job at the local roller rink. It was, for the most, my job to regulate the speed of the skaters during public skating sessions. The worst part of the job was evening skate: this is when each song was designated for a particular group. There was "girls only skate" and "boys only skate." There was "couples only skate" and "athletes only skate." It was my job to blow the whistle and say, "Hey you, off the floor, couples only for this skate."

In her essay "The Question of Social Transformation," Judith Butler argues not only that "theory is itself transformative" but also that "something besides theory must take place, such as interventions at social and political levels that involve actions, sustained labor, and institutionalized practice, which are not quite the same as the exercise of theory" (*Undoing* 204). I want to frame this sequence of assignments as part of the "actions, sustained labor, and institutionalized practice" that are both the effect of and reason for theorizing. What actions, labor, and practices do the assignments value, or even devalue? In what transformative directions do they attempt to lead students?

The assignments I draw from in this chapter were the first five of the shorter writing assignments given to my students during this course. I have not changed any of the language, trying as best I can to preserve my intentions, my theoretical influences, my failures and assumptions. For the purpose of this chapter, I want to try to articulate the logics and various habits of mind and orientations informing the course. I want to make visible what queer values shape my understandings of assignments and of students as writers. After the students read both Audre Lorde's "The Master's Tools Will Never Dismantle the Master's House" and Peggy McIntosh's "Unpacking the Invisible Knapsack" (the first two readings in the course), they were given the following assignment—their first formal writing assignment in the course. The assignment reads,

> Track your responses as you are reading Peggy McIntosh's article on white privilege. How are you responding to the article, and more importantly, why might you be responding the way that you are (here I am looking for something about YOU, not about Peggy McIntosh)? In other words, what about you might be causing you to respond this way? What connections can you make between Peggy McIntosh and Audre Lorde? What do those

connections help you to see? How can you take a "queer" position toward these texts, meaning how can you position yourself in relation to them in a way you consider unusual, maybe uncomfortable? What do these texts say about you? Why should you care about these texts at all?

Looking back, I can read this set of questions as brave, or as brazen—or both. The first questions I ask my students are, in a sense, quite personal ones—ones that ask them to embrace a habit of mind that suggests that their reading practices and interpretations are about *them* and not only about the text itself they are reading. It also asks them to trust that I can listen to and honor their answers. And while I did ask these questions, and while I think I would likely ask them again, I am aware of the parts of this assignment that require a kind of personal disclosure about their responses to notions of privilege. The questions also suggest that what we read is about us. And this suggestion can seem, quite literally, untrue. We might even say that some people read to escape from themselves, or even that we read to find out about things *other* than ourselves. I want to entertain the possibility that both the escape and the search for what is *other* than ourselves is always about us—that even when I myself am completing some sort of required reading for a course, that reading is about me. I do not mean to suggest that the book I am reading is *about* me as if I am *its* subject but that, through my interpretations and responses, my *reading* is always about me.

My mother had been sneaking me to baseball practice for weeks, telling my father she was taking me to what was called, in this particular Catholic suburbia, "religion" (when children gather at a neighborhood house and some volunteer parents tell stories about Jesus). I learned more in the locker rooms than on the field. I was alone in there, the only "girl" on the local baseball team. I'd stand in front of the full-length mirror. My body changing with each batting glove, the black cleats, the blue-and-white jersey. I could make the little girl in me die peacefully, even knowing I would have to revive her. For my mother's sake, I would have to breathe life back into the little girl; I would have to push on her chest until I could hear her heart beat. She would learn a Bible verse on the way home. She would recite it for her father. She would dress up as his daughter.

There are a variety of ways teachers have tried to ask the kinds of questions that dis-orient or shift how a student reads or looks. And many of these questions ask students to think about themselves as they read. Amy E. Winans, in "Queering Pedagogy in the English Classroom: Engaging with the Places Where Thinking Stops," poses these questions: "How do I feel and what do I know about this topic? Where does my knowledge come from? What is unknown to me? What is unthinkable to me and why? Questions like these are central to queer pedagogy because they help students learn both *that* knowledge is created and *how* knowledge is created" (104). It is interesting then to pose these questions with/against other important questions that have been asked in composition assignments. Bartholomae and Petrosky, in *Ways of Reading*, encourage students to ask, "Where am I in this? How can I make my mark? Whose interests are represented? What can I learn by reading with or against the grain?" (282). My first writing prompt asks students to think a lot about themselves reading, to take responsibility for their reactions to a text—noting the ways they are responding that belong to them and *not* to the text itself. To think of oneself as "making a mark" on a text is to think of oneself, in some sense, as relating to a text in one direction. I had hoped my assignment to be dialectical, asking students to consider their relation to the text, to consider who they imagine themselves being or becoming as they are reading it. Both Bartholomae and Petrosky, as well as Winans, are concerned with students finding themselves *in relation* to the text. However, Bartholomae and Petrosky's question *Where am I in this?* is quite a different question from the ones Winans asks. Theirs is an orienting question, one that asks students to find a location, to orient themselves in relation to what they are reading. This is not an unproductive or uninteresting question to ask, but it is a question that asks students to find a location and to "make a mark" on the text from that location. Winans's set of questions, on the other hand, is more overtly epistemological *and* ontological: questions of knowing and being. She begins with an affective question: *How do I feel and what do I know about this topic?* In a sense, this question is quite connected to Bartholomae and Petrosky's *Where am I in this?* It is asking students to think about their response and relation to the text. But Winans's follow-up questions take the inquiry a bit further, asking students to think specifically about their *knowledge*—where it comes from and what it means. She asks students about what they *do not know*, marking this question as being equally as important as, if not more important than, what they *do* know.

Winans uses the term "unthinkable," making the suggestion that there are things that, for each of us, are unthinkable *and*, quite ironically, that we can think of those things that are unthinkable *if* we ask ourselves to do so.

In tenth grade, my social studies teacher, Mr. Gish, breaks it to me not so gently, standing six feet tall in front of the overhead projector, which he uses to say everything. Everything he was going to say glowing in the light of the screen. Christopher Columbus. Bullet point. Was a famous explorer. Bullet point. The Niña *and the* Pinta *and the* Santa Maria. *Bullet point. Is known to have discovered North America. Bullet point. Did not discover North America. Bullet point. Brought disease and assaulted the natives. I'm sick with imagining myself in the first grade. I had drawn pictures of Columbus's boats. I had drawn him beautifully in a green hat, looking like a magical, harmless little leprechaun, standing proudly on the shores of the United States. This is the first time I will know what it feels like to be historically implicated.*

Deborah P. Britzman, in her essay "Is There a Queer Pedagogy?," puts it yet another way: "The question a reader might ask is: who am I becoming through the interpretive claims I make upon another and myself?" (163). This question, of course, is echoed in my above assignment when I ask, "What about you might be causing you to respond this way?" Looking back, I wish I had seen Britzman's language again just before writing the assignment because my question seems a bit more static than I would have liked, suggesting that there is something about a reader, something that is a thing and not a process, which causes that reader to respond in some specific way. Britzman's question is, in this sense, queerer than mine; she marks the interpretative process as a kind of becoming, a moving process.

As the field of queer theory has imagined identity as a constant state of becoming, I want to imagine my students as readers and writers in much the same way. The question that directs students' attention to their reactions and who they are that might shape their reactions is a question of becoming; it is a question that invites an affective as much as intellectual project. I ask my students to assume all texts are saying something about them. *What do these texts say about you?* The question is complicated. It is not a literal question, not a question that means a text about nineteenth-century notions of homosexuality is literally about me, for example. But, of course, as I read this text, and respond to it, my reading becomes about me. I do not assume they should care about what the texts, or their reading, might be saying about them. *Why should you care about these texts at all?* I myself don't always care. This first question tries to signal to students that the course is about them, is somehow about their responses; however, it is not their project to describe their responses. It is their project to contextualize and interrogate their responses, looking closely at the material conditions of their lives that inform their reading and writing practices. I began with the hunch that to see oneself reading, or be asked to see oneself reading, might cultivate the habit of self-reflexivity, one that interferes with reaction, one that calls students' attention to the act of reading itself and disrupts the act of writing. Bartholomae writes, "I think a good assignment teaches by interfering. It interferes with a student and his [sic] writing" (*Writing* 185). He writes this statement in an essay about assignments, one in which he is examining Tolstoy's notions of writing and teaching. I read Bartholomae's notion of "interference" as a kind of interruption; for Bartholomae an assignment that interferes is one that interrupts the student as she experiences "all those available phrases" that turn her "vision into an occasion for cliché" (186). Or, put another way, if composition teachers want students to resist reliance on cliché, to push on the already available ways of thinking and writing about a given matter, it becomes our burden to write assignments that interfere with the processes of reading and writing, assignments that demand something other than what is already available, assignments that ask for the *unthinkable*, assignments that interrupt even students' vision of themselves. Queering is a particular kind of interference, an interference that calls attention to the reader and, in a way, to the text as well, as movements, as kinds of becoming.

In 2012, scientists "discover" a lioness in Botswana who has grown a masculine mane and whose roar is as deep as a lion's. Then they find five more genderqueer lions just like her.

While Lorde's and McIntosh's essays are more explicitly about race than they are about gender or sexuality, the course I designed begins with an attention to normativity and the privilege and abuses associated with normativity. Some students noticed in themselves, for example, feelings of defensiveness, guilt, anger, and even righteousness. Some students noted their refusals and affirmations and did some rather interesting thinking about where those responses came from—citing their own various racial and gendered identifications, and in some cases even their parents' identifications, as reasons for their reactions. Jennifer Bracken writes in her response, "Reading [Peggy McIntosh's] article was hard, but writing about it later is even harder. There are so many things in this article I wish I could deny, but I can't. The article makes me feel very uncomfortable with myself, even now that I have read it through numerous times, because I must look at myself in a perspective I'm sure others have seen that I didn't even know existed" (1).

I read Bracken's response as an attempt to try on the habits of mind of the assignment. Bracken is both aware of her own inclinations ("I wish I could deny") but at the same time able to imagine not only how she sees herself but how "others have seen." This piece of writing is taken from a single-spaced one-page response; it is not "an essay" per se. Part of my goal with the shorter assignments is to take away the notion of the "essay" as something students know or have done, to call it something else for a moment, to give them practice. Another student writes, "I can hear my dad as I read and he's saying stuff like, 'don't listen to that liberal bullshit' and 'this is America, everyone's equal.' And like all daughters, I am part my dad, but I am also part myself" (Anonymous Student D 2). One way to read this student's writing is through the lens of Bartholomae's notion of interference—the student becoming conscious of "all those available phrases" that turn her "vision into an occasion for cliché" or that turn her vision into her father's. What amazes me about my students, time and time again, is their capacity already, here in their first assignment, to become and take on contradiction: the student becomes both her father and herself as she reads. Another student describes her initial "defensiveness" and asks, "[W]ho was [Peggy McIntosh] to tell me that even though I don't perform acts of hatred against people of different races that just by living in the world that I do that I am supporting a form of racism?" (Anonymous Student A 1). She goes on to articulate her feeling of being "tricked"—the sense that no matter what she individually does, "systems make it not matter" (2). I am struck again by another student's capacity to articulate contradictions, to struggle with them on the page—her actions both do and do not matter, she is both not participating in racist acts and part of a racist system. In her reading, she is becoming, as we all are, paradox.

Those reactions and insights about their own becoming through their "interpretive claims" became an element of their second assignment as they moved on to read Bornstein's *Gender Outlaw*—often perceived by students as the most radical of the texts they encountered, not only in its particular theoretical arguments about sexuality and gender but also in its unapologetic explicitness (open discussions of sex acts, pornography, sex change operations, etc.) as a means through which to describe gender itself as a violence done to us. In this assignment students were asked to respond to the following prompt:

> In your syllabus, I make the following claim: "it is your discomfort and unease that will educate you." As you read the first assignment in *Gender Outlaw: On Men, Women, and the Rest of Us*, mark passages where you are having difficulty. Perhaps your difficulty is one of understanding, perhaps one of discomfort, perhaps some other type of difficulty you'd like to address. This assignment asks you to consider your discomfort. What is making you uncomfortable and why? Is it at all connected to what made you uncomfortable about the first two essays we read? I also want to remind you about some of the ways you responded to McIntosh and Lorde. Some of you described your responses as guilty, angry, defensive, enlightened, shameful, etc. How is this reading experience different and why? How do you position yourself in relation to this book? What does the book make of you? Who do you become when you read it? If this book is about gender itself, what (so far) is Bornstein trying to say about gender? How is she saying it or what is her writing style? If what she is saying is true, what does that say about you or your own sense of gender identity? Remember you cannot answer all of these questions. They are here as guiding prompts to help you think through your reading process, the ideas you are coming into contact with, and your responses to those ideas. You should quote from Bornstein during your composition and try to engage with the ideas in the text.

After their first assignment, one of the things that came up as we discussed a few student papers in class was the idea of what it meant to "engage with a text" rather than just quote from it. While this is an idea we worked on repeatedly all semester, I want to focus here on one aspect of "engaging" with a text that this assignment highlights, and that aspect of engagement has to do with difficulty. I cannot read this assignment without noting its indebtedness to the projects of Mariolina Salvatori and her work with students on difficulty—projects that theorize what difficulty means and how a reader and writer might engage with difficulty in ways that make new creative and critical readings possible. In "Conversations with Texts: Reading in the Teaching of Composition," Salvatori describes what she calls a "difficulty paper" in which students are asked to write a one-page description of "any difficulty the text they have been assigned to read might have posed for them" (448). My assignment asks my students to do the same, to describe and think about what is difficult about the text, about the act of reading it. Salvatori discusses this assignment as one on which she "repeatedly relied . . . not as a means to expose my students' inadequacies, but as a reflexive strategy that eventually allows them to recognize that what they perceive as 'difficult' is a feature of the text demanding to be critically engaged rather than ignored" (448). I would also say that what they "perceive as difficult" is a feature not only of the text but also of their own becoming, their process of being themselves that is also "demanding to be critically engaged rather than ignored." The culmination of their attention to the difficulty of the text, the difficulty of becoming the reader of that text, and that difficulty of what both they and the text demand or expect makes for a complicated reading and, ultimately, a more complicated way of writing about that reading and about the readers they are becoming *as they read*.

Sometimes my brothers would allow me, if the teams were not even, to play kickball in the street with all the boys in the neighborhood. And I can remember our unison of little boy voices yelling "car" when a car would approach—all of us scattering to the curb to wait for the driver to pass. I remember our chanting "tree" when the ball was kicked high enough to graze the branches that hung over the street. "Tree" indicated the need for a "do-over," the tree having interfered with the natural arc of the kicked ball.

I thought of this assignment as a kind of fracture and interference—queer interference. To understand what might be the difference, I am reminded of Eve Sedgwick's claim that "something about *queer* is inextinguishable. Queer is a continuing moment, movement, motive—recurrent, eddying, *troublant*. The word 'queer' itself means *across*—it comes from the Indo-European root—*twerkw*, which also yields the German *quer* (transverse), Latin *torquere* (to twist), English *athwart*" (*Tendencies* xii). I want to read Sedgwick's definition of *queer* beside Bartholomae's earlier claim about sequencing assignments as being "repetitive," a kind of recurrence or eddying. I also understand Bartholomae's discussion of interference to be connected with Sedgwick's linking of *queer* to *troublant*. In this sense, I am quite drawn to Bartholomae's sense of what it means to teach a student to write, to think about writing, to move through a repetitive and spiraling set of assignments—assignments that are kinds of eddying movements. Bartholomae even goes on to tell us this idea may be "difficult to say" and even "offensive to some." It is at this moment of possible offense, at this moment of *athwart*—a word in English that is a more aggressive and even perverse notion of obstruction or "interference"—when I want to bring attention to the queerness of this assignment, asking students to reinterpret their understandings of their own genders through the lens of a radical transgendered thinker who has told them, even if rather gently (if this is possible), that their genders are unreal, made up, wild, and elaborate illusions. I am struck, again and again, by the notion of "becoming" in these assignments—something I must admit I had not realized repeating to the extent that I did. *Who do you become when you read it?*

Dolphins and tuna often travel the same sea routes; they agree on the directions, on the cartography of the ocean. But the dolphins, despite their sonar senses, can get caught in the tuna nets. The struggle can cut them fatally, or if they struggle too long, the entangling nets can suffocate them.

In *Judith Butler: From Norms to Politics*, Moya Lloyd offers her reading of Butler's sense of "becoming." She writes,

> One of the merits of the idea of becoming a gender is that it suggests that gender is not to be thought of as imposed on subjects, as it is sometimes characterized within feminism (as when authors talk of women being "culturally constructed"). Consequently, as a way of thinking, the idea of becoming a gender poses a challenge to the idea that gender is passively produced by patriarchy or forced on subjects by the phallogocentric symbolic. Becoming implies, rather, that gendering is an achievement of some kind that gendered subjects themselves engage in . . . gendering the

self involves a "purposive and appropriate set of acts, the acquisition of a skill." It is "a project, a skill, a pursuit, an enterprise, even an industry." For these reasons, the concept of gender as becoming introduces the idea that gendering, in part at least, is a self-reflexive process. (38–39)

In this sense, I want to read my assignments, and to propose a theory of reading and writing, as a similar kind of *becoming*. After all, writing has long been, problematically and otherwise, described as an achievement, a set of skills. And compositionists have long been engaging with what those skills are, how to teach them, whether they can be taught, whether they can be called skills at all. Becoming, however, is a contradictory kind of project—one in which one is at once both a constructed subject and an agent of one's own construction. My question to my students about who they become when they read is an attempt to get at the heart of this contradiction—that they are at once constructing a text and being constructed by that text, that they are at once constructing a self and being constructed by whatever self they had constructed before. Becoming is a constant statement of movement, of transformation. It is, as Lloyd notes, a "self-reflexive process." I ask my students in the course description to think of themselves not as students completing assignments but as composers, makers, agents of their own making even in their constructedness. In this sense, one of the shifts in orientations and primary habits of mind I want to give precedence to is for the course to be "becoming oriented"—oriented toward becoming, in Butler's sense of what that becoming means.

As for students, very few of them answered the question "who do you become when you read it?" directly. But we spent some time in class talking about how the responses they did write were already an answer to this question. For example, one student began her response like this: "The source of most of my discomfort is the inability to know how to respond to this book. I was taught how to multiply numbers, how to write formal essays, how to set up an experiment or an equation—but nothing I have learned thus far could have possibly prepared me for how to react to the things Kate Bornstein is saying" (Anonymous Student D 1). This student volunteered to share her opening with the class and wrote this, her first sentence, for us on the board. I begin by asking, *Who is this writer becoming in this sentence?* There is some silence. Perhaps because the question is difficult, perhaps because it feels strange to draw conclusions about who a student is becoming when the student is sitting in the room. After a few minutes, Danielle says, "Uh, she's becoming a person attached to form?" This is not an answer I expected, but its possibilities seemed promising. I ask, *What do you mean?* Danielle explains, "Equations, setups, numbers, essays, all that stuff is things fitting into forms." We spend some time in a class discussion about what features (using Salvatori's understanding) of Bornstein's text might lead us to become attached to form, to become a person clinging to forms. This discussion concluded with Johnnie Hart noting, as students packed up belongings, "It's a lot easier when you think about who the writer is becoming as temporary, like we're not actually saying who she is." Of course, we are not positioned to say who someone else is, or even who she might be becoming, but we may be able to describe her becoming as it is reflected in her reading. And the student who wrote the response says, walking out, "It was cool to hear what I was doing." Becoming, after all, is also a kind of doing. Certainly, this sense of becoming also reflects my understanding of revision. In the next assignment, I ask students,

> Look carefully at your first composition assignment. This assignment asks you to close read your own writing. Pick a passage where you feel you can interrogate or question yourself in some of the ways we were questioning passages today in class. What more did you need to define or say? What could you have said instead? What's more complicated the second time around, looking at it now? You may use my comments in the margins to help you do this, or you may choose to address parts of your writing that I didn't address. It's up to you. This assignment is not "tell Stacey what's wrong with your paper." It is a chance for you to push your own thinking and writing further, for you to try to give your writing the precision and attention it deserves. Ultimately, you need to try to answer the questions, *What do I sound like? What kinds of things do I say? Why do I say them? Who do I become when I write one way or another, or when I read one way or another? What advice do I have for myself after these first few weeks of class?*

I want to ask students to see revision not only as a process of looking back at their own writing but also as a process of looking back at themselves in order to make self-reflexive moves explicitly *about* their own becoming—becoming a gender, becoming a reader, becoming a writer.

One way to think about becoming in the context of this prompt is to think about how language might be said to reflect, contain (or, mostly, to fail to reflect and contain) our becoming. Asking students to see their writing and interpretative moves as a kind of becoming is also asking them to think about the connection between language and ontology, a connection quite embedded in the work of queer theory as a discipline. It is important to queer understandings of pedagogy that students see themselves as a becoming, a contingent arising. If students begin their reading or writing by valuing only fixity and certainty, it becomes increasingly difficult for them to compose engaging prose. They will write five-paragraph essays giving very solid evidence about what appear to be very solid things. This is not a becoming; it is, rather, an *already became*. The next assignment in the course, then, asks students to *become* on several levels by both imitating the style of another writer and by inhabiting some of the voices that may have contributed, or tried to contribute, to their own becoming. The assignment is in response Jamaica Kincaid's short fiction work titled "Girl." The assignment reads,

> After reading Jamaica Kincaid's "Girl," try to write a short single-spaced page essay that imitates hers. Hers is a list of instructions (that seem to be in the voice of a mother or an authority figure) about what it means to be a girl. You can choose any identity category you like. So you could call the piece "Girl" or "Boy" or "Gay Man" or "White Girl" or "Christian Boy" or whatever. Then try to give a list (like Kincaid's) of instructions one might get on how to be this identity. You can get creative and specific with it. Notice the images in Kincaid's piece. Notice the detail. Try to imitate the style and specificity of her short essay. Try to have fun with it.

Students, by this point, had been writing about their becoming as something happening in the present, for the most part. They had been writing about the selves in my class who were reading, and they were thus thinking less about the events, experiences, and ideas leading up to that self. If we take to heart Susanne Luhmann's description of queer pedagogy (which appears as the epigraph to this chapter), anyone interested in queer pedagogies would have to ask certain epistemological questions about how we come to know. Luhmann asks, "If subversiveness is not a new form of knowledge but lies in the capacity to raise questions about the detours of coming to know and make sense, then what does this mean for a pedagogy that imagines itself as queer?" (125). My assignment above is one way of answering that question, and it was my hope that many of the assignments in this course would help answer that question. Subversiveness may, at first glance, seem like a political goal (and of course I do not want to try to argue that it is not or that I don't have political concerns about reading, writing, and the literal circumstances of our world), but I want to read this notion of the subversive as a significant habit of mind, an orientation that can lead to compelling and complicated writing in the context of this course and other writing courses. And if we take Luhmann at her word that subversiveness "lies in the capacity to raise questions about the detours of coming to know and make sense," then this assignment tries to call attention to those "detours" of coming to know, tries to (through the imitative form of the assignments) ask students to "raise questions" about these detours. Students seemed, after the last assignment that was geared toward revision, to see this assignment as a revision as well. One student, Andrew "Iggy" Kelly, said in class, "It's like we revised our papers, and then after doing this Kincaid thing, we had to revise ourselves—or at least face how we became ourselves. Something like that." I do want to include here Iggy Kelly's piece entitled "White Roman Catholic Boy." Kelly, in his imitation of Kincaid, writes,

> Take Communion: This is his body, this is his blood; no this is not cannibalism, it's figurative and sacred; Go to Confession; Do not lie in Confession; Do not bring action figures into Confession; No, I will not be Shredder from Teenage Mutant Turtles®; Barbies® dressed as nuns are not appropriate either; No I will not be holy Ken®, either; Where did you even get the priest garments that small? You sew? What are you, a pussy? I do not wear a dress! Do not call what I wear a dress, dresses are for women; There are no women priests; The brides of God are nuns; No, you cannot marry one; No, you cannot be one; No, they cannot divorce God; Yes, divorce is allowed; No, baby priests are not made by priests and nuns; Stop asking stupid questions! Listen to my sermons; Do not sleep during my sermons; No, that is not the reason the seats are so hard; this is not a black church, we do not clap to the hymns; No that does not mean we do not have fun; Well, not that kind of fun; Fine, no fun in church; You worship in church; Worship is not fun, it's necessary; many things

in life are necessary, few things are fun; Sin is not for fun; Sex is not for fun; Sex is for procreation; Do not masturbate; You cannot procreate with a tissue; Do not even try; God creates life; God is not going to create a tissue man; God created man out of clay, yes, but that does not mean he might do it with a tissue; It just doesn't work like that; Yes, God can do anything; he is the creator of heaven and earth; He is the Almighty Father; no, I am just "father"; Well, you should respect God more than you respect me; You must respect me; You must honor me; Yes, you must honor your mother and father; No, I am not your actual father; God is not your father, either; You are a child of god; No, that does not mean he is your father; He is the Father, and the Holy Spirit, and the Son at the same time; You cannot be more than one thing at a time; You cannot be more than one thing, you are only as God made you; Do not wear a dress, that is not how God made you; Abortion is wrong; War is wrong except sometimes; Abortion is always wrong; Love thy neighbor is right; Loving thy neighbor like that is a sin; Prostitution is wrong; I don't care what the Popes did with prostitutes; the Pope knows the will of God; Okay, so he doesn't always listen; You need to listen more; Boys do not wear make-up; Christ is not wearing makeup in that picture. Altar boys do not wear dresses; Altar girls do not wear dresses, either, unless that's what they have on underneath; No, you may not wear a dress underneath; I will know and God will know; God is not Santa Claus; Yes, he sees you when you are sleeping, yes he knows when you've been bad or good; No, that still does not make him Santa Claus; No, Jesus is not wearing a dress; What is it with you and dresses? I don't care if Jesus was black, God is not black; After Confession, pray the Hail Mary prayer; Do not pray to Mary, pray to God; Go to mass on Sunday and Holidays; Do not eat before you go to mass if you want to receive Communion; No, you may not have seconds on the body of Christ; No, you may not pop out for a bite to eat in the middle of mass; If you don't die right after Confession, you are probably going to burn in Hell.

Of course one of the first things to note about Iggy's prose is the ironic, sharp, and elegant writing of this student. Iggy is a talented writer. Iggy has an interesting sense of "becoming," enacting for his reader the contradictions of all becomings: *You cannot be more than one thing.* This message about fixity and singularity is one that came up for all of the students—

whether they were writing about being a part of a marginalized identity or being a part of a privileged category. Many of the students seem to recognize and offer commentary on the contradictions, paradoxes, and impossibilities of being what they were expected to become, given the names and identities they had been given; some wrote about gendered expectations, religious expectations, class status. I read each student as having, like Iggy, a sense that these categories had failed, even when they themselves succeeded. Queer interference seemed to offer students a way of contending with those contradictions, so that instead of focusing on the parts of their becoming that seemed solid, they *raised questions about the detours*. They challenged even their own assumptions or exposed even their own confusions about "coming to know and make sense." Following this assignment, we considered for an entire class period a quote (a passage I refer to in this chapter itself) from Judith Butler's *Undoing Gender*. I wrote it on the board: *That my agency is riven with paradox does not mean it is impossible. It means only that paradox is the condition of its possibility*. This is largely the way queer theory texts appeared in the course—as brief and excerpted materials up for discussion on any given day. These appearances not only gave students a chance to practice close reading as a group but also gave them the opportunity to consider the grammar and logic of queer theory in relation to what might be possible in their own writing. The "close reading" I refer to in the context of my class is a way of referring to a sustained attention to the moves and language of sentences or short passages of sentences, as well as a way for students to see, in one sentence, the shifting possibilities of what is there in the text and what it might *mean*. Ann Berthoff puts it this way:

> Close reading teaches that the transactions with the text are always tentative and subject to the pragmatic maxim: "If we take it—metaphor, syntax, word, line—this way, what difference would it make to the way we read the rest of the poem? the opus? the age?" Close reading is entailed in critical reading. It is not an elitist, nose-to-the-text, words-on-the-page pedantry but the way of attending to the interplay of saying and meaning. ("Reclaiming" 677)

This passage from Berthoff's essay "Reclaiming the Active Mind" helps me to think about this "interplay of saying and meaning." Her attention to reading that is "tentative" is also part of my understanding of close

ALTERNATIVE ORIENTATIONS

reading. To be clear, the passages I offer students on the board, which are often short but complicated and layered passages, are not close reading because they are out of context; it's merely that the context in which we read them is the course itself. Shifting the context is not necessarily part of Berthoff's or even of my understanding of close reading, but I think it could be—*the opus, the age*. We look at Butler's sentence about agency closely, grammatically, and semantically. We try to find out what she *could* mean and what that meaning would then *mean* for the course, for writing, for gender, for our lives. Another way worth thinking about close reading in the context of the course I describe is connected to Joseph Allen Boone's conception in *Libidinal Currents*, where he writes that both the act of sex and the art of writing "are not only overpowering but expressions of absolute powerlessness, enacting the intense human desire to let go—to be released, to yield to an 'other' (a lover, a text) that ceases to remain other in the imaginary intercourse that is constitutive of sexual and fictional exchanges alike" (1–2). While I don't think Boone's sense of sex and reading is the only way to conceptualize their relationship, I do find his claim fascinating. He agrees with Berthoff and with Salvatori, in fact, that reading is an exchange, a kind of conversation, but Boone layers the understanding, linking reading itself to sexuality, which inevitably takes reading back to power.

In North Carolina, it is law that a person must use the bathroom that corresponds to their "birth gender." This means there is no public bathroom in the entire state of North Carolina that can be used by a person like me—someone whose "birth gender" is both genders, someone for whom the body and its chromosomal composition do not line up. In North Carolina, it is only on the shoulders of highways and in the deep woods where the waste of queers can legally rest.

The writing assignments that are the focus of this chapter try to follow the habits of mind and orientations I value—contradiction, interference, repetition, becoming, self-reflexivity, sustained and returning inquiry. At this point in the course the students were to view the film *Tootsie*, a comedy classic 1980s gender-bending film starring Dustin Hoffman. It is at this point in the semester that something troubling, and quite interesting, happened. As students moved from the texts we were discussing—their own and those of the authors we were reading—

something changed in their reading when the film was put in view. The discussions surrounding the film seemed reductive. Students were interested in seeing the film as "groundbreaking" and "troubling the norms," as Kelsey Fagan put it in her response. In watching the film, what became apparent was that there seemed no moment when students wanted to trouble the ways normativity was reaffirmed or perpetuated even as it was seemingly disrupted. It seemed that as I turned the students' gaze from the more "intellectual" texts of the course to the more popular representations they see everyday, it became more difficult for them to find moments to disrupt, or interfere, in the film's logic. I don't mean to suggest that a student needs to find this film troubling in order to write about it, but I am suggesting that if the troubling aspects are not visible, then it will be difficult for the students to write papers that are nuanced and complicated. If the only thing to say about *Tootsie* is how wonderfully it shows the breaking of gender norms, the essays that writers could write are minimally uncertain, and surely those essays would not be raising questions about knowledge or exercising the kinds of habits of mind I have outlined here. It is at this moment that I would write what would prove to be the most troubling assignment of the semester—perhaps the one I most wish I could take back. I gave students the following prompt:

> The following quote is from the TeachWithMovies.com website, which is geared toward teaching students probably a little bit younger than you. The website says:
>
>> *Tootsie* is about a man becoming a better man by experiencing what it's like to be a woman. The film explores the different ways in which people conduct themselves and perceive life, based on their gender. It also leads viewers to think about some of the differences and similarities between men and women.
>>
>> The TeachWithMovies.com Learning Guide will show teachers and parents how to use this hilarious film to teach boys not to mistreat girls and to teach girls to be less tolerant of male misbehavior.
>
> Write a response to this website in which you tell the authors of the above passage why the film is more complicated than the portrait they have

painted above. You might do this by having an argument with the quote (both what it says and how it is written), by pointing out other things (having to do with gender and sexuality) in the film that the un-critical eye might not see, or by close reading the above quote to provide an interpretation of what it would mean for girls and boys to use the film as "instructions." You might think back to your own work with instructions (in your longer essay or in your shorter imitation of Jamaica Kincaid). What is contradictory, complex or even dangerous about the film's "instructions" about how to be a "man" or a "woman"?

I would not be so naïve to say that the assignments prior to this one were not leading assignments, but I would also say that this assignment is the most leading of the group I have offered so far, asking students to take an already established position in relation to a text written about the film, a text that had, in some ways, taken the positions many of the students had taken in class. My intentions seemed good enough—that I wanted the students to see the film in a more complicated way than they had upon first viewing, that I knew (or thought I knew) their first readings of the film were not going to produce compelling and creative essays about the film. However, the assignment seemed, ultimately, to fail to follow my own orientations of uncertainty and my assumptions about the students having self-awareness about their own readings. I did not, for example, ask them who they were *becoming* while they watched or who the film supposed them to be. I did not ask them what the film wanted or how it might shape both conventional *and* subversive notions of gender. I noticed, through this assignment and through some of the other work in the course I want to discuss, how difficult it is to cultivate the habits of mind I am asking students to adopt or consider. I notice, again and again, that these habits are a process, a continual reinvention of what seems to be right in front of you. In this sense, my teaching is no different from this scholarship on teaching you are reading. I try, with earnestness and intention, to keep the ideas moving, keep them from slipping from my grasp as I reach for them. But there are moments the ground does become solid, even if this solidness is fleeting. Both the course and the theoretical tenets of queer pedagogies call attention to both the vital need to disrupt normativity *and* the essential need to develop and understand norms—even if only to disrupt the norms again in the end. Perhaps Judith Butler says this best when she writes, "My difficulty will emerge not out of stubbornness or a will to be obscure. It emerges simply out of the doubled truth that although we need norms in order to live, and to live well, and to know in what direction to transform our social world, we are also constrained by norms in ways that sometimes do violence to us and which, for reasons of social justice, we must oppose" (*Undoing* 205–6).

Of course it is at these moments that I return again to my own investments in this particular course and in teaching in general. I know, always, that there is a part of these queer methodologies and pedagogies that belong to my own desires—my desires to *queer* understandings of this world so that I might live more safely inside it. My assignments, then, are not objective, not merely a set of intellectual practices I believe in as ways of teaching writing, though I do believe in these intellectual practices; my assignments reveal themselves, perhaps most especially in this fifth one, as trying to orient students in the direction of what might be a more "livable world," as Butler would call it, for a great number of people. In this sense, the course is highly politicized and quite connected to the very roots Alexander and Wallace describe in their essay. I say this not as the confession of a queer teacher who is invested in queer subjects or queer lives; after all, all teachers are invested in their version of what makes a livable world and their version of what makes a productive thinker, a compelling writer. I say this to keep in my mind, as I try to write about and think about my teaching and my students, the ways a particular lived body frames an understanding of pedagogy. I say this to offer the same self-reflexivity I ask of my students. I talked about this assignment with my students. I asked them, *Did you notice anything different about this one?* And Danielle offered an interesting answer: *I don't know about the question*, she said, *but when I started answering the assignment, it felt like there was nowhere to go.* Nowhere to go. No movement. No opportunity for movement. The question that already positions the students (however much time or however many revisions it might save them on some particular essay) sets the students up to stand fixed and solid far longer than a queer pedagogy would aspire to and far longer than a compelling and complicated essay would allow. Uncertainty, like the dolphin's breathing, is not a reflex. We can, as it were, forget to do it. But it is imperative that we do.

Queer(er) Methodologies

Asking students to think queerly, in order to read queerly, and finally to write queerly is, in a sense, asking them to try on a new identity, a queerer reading and writing self. And as is often the case in queer theory and in the study of identity, none of these categories of thinking, reading, and writing can be separated out from one another. There is no such course that *only teaches writing*, whether a person might claim a course to be so or not. Even if there are no texts in a course other than the texts students themselves produce, this course is still about reading, about thinking and interpretation. And in the first-year writing courses that are the subject of this book, students are asked to inhabit and engage with queer ways of doing these seemingly familiar practices. In the foreword to Susan Talburt and Shirley R. Steinberg's book *Thinking Queer: Sexuality, Culture, and Education*, William Pinar, the editor of *Queer Theory in Education*, tells us, "The appearance of 'queer thinking' in the field of education is recent, its formulation in an early stage, even as the political hour feels late" (x). While Talburt and Steinberg's book was published more than a decade before my writing of this book, the formulations of queer pedagogies and queer thinking can still be said to be in these early stages. Part of the reason for this lies in how Alexander and Wallace describe the movements in this queer turn in composition, and I take as part of the project of this work to move from queer subjects and queer materials to queer methodologies—queer ways of knowing that I want to argue can ignite and inspire queer ways of writing.

Why would we want to write queerly? We need only imagine the queerness of those texts we most celebrate—their contradictions and complexities, their refusal to signal, monolithically, their violations of form, their at times even perverse disruption of what it means to write a novel, an essay, a poem. We respect writers who write queerly. It puzzles me why the editors of so many course readers and syllabi ask students to write in ways those editors, I'd bet, would never want to read. And as I think about this approach as a methodology, as a way of teaching writing, I am reminded of Ann Berthoff, who says in her book *The Making of Meaning*, "Although a method can take the form of a list of steps, such a list is not necessarily a method. Like language itself, method is reflexive; it is dialectical by definition: *meta + hodos, about the way.* . . . Without an understanding of dialectic as the heart of a method, we are doomed to see one after another promising technique disappear without ever having been given a fair chance" (51).

I cannot, or perhaps I would not, offer a bullet point list of the steps one takes in order to perform the promising techniques of queer pedagogies. To make such a list would be to make linear what is not linear; it would be to suggest as whole what is already incomplete; it would be to formulate notions that slip through my fingers as they take form. The nature of writing means that one writes with a deliberate, conscious intention to disrupt oneself, one's reading, one's teaching and text. I can say that I hope to shift my students' orientations, to scandalously encourage them to be queerer than they are—queerer thinkers, queerer readers, queerer writers. It is my contention that queering as a method holds a very important and powerful place in composition studies, adding to an already layered and complex discussion of how and what we teach when we teach writing. As Berthoff says, "method is reflexive," and that "dialectic" is at its heart. When queer theory becomes more integral to composition studies, when queer theory's relationship to writing is dialectic and dialogic, what our students say and write may surprise us in new ways.

CHAPTER 4

BECOMING LIQUID

Queer Interpretations

The highest motive is to be like water.
Water is necessary to all living things.
It asks nothing in return.
Rather it flows humbly to the lowest level.

Nothing is weaker than water,
yet against those things which are strong and hard,
nothing can surpass it, nor stand in its way.
May we all learn the way of water.

From the Buddhist "Dedication of Merit"

Queer Literacies

Without the ability to develop and cultivate alternative ways of reading and composing, I might be dead. I grew up with the sense that there was something strange about the ways I interpreted the world. "There's something wrong with that kid," my father would say to my mother when I'd curl up under the basement stairway, snug-safe in my Yankees cap and my brother's jeans, reading biographies of great baseball players, or reading the Three Investigators detective series. In these books, I saw the boys and men I wanted to be: Jupiter Jones, the kid detective, was chubby and smart, with an inability to stay away from mysteries and unanswerable questions. I'm not sure what my father meant, whether his "something wrong" with me was referring to my reading habits or my gender disobedient behavior. But I knew one thing for sure: my father and I were very different readers.

Without queer interventions in sets of dominant discourses—about gender, about philosophy, about sexuality, about identity, and about teaching—many of us, and our students, might be living lives we do not recognize or cannot articulate. I begin with gender, as we all do, as one possible line of inquiry in thinking about queer interventions in writing pedagogies and about how students might develop sexual literacies that have the potential to offer alternative ways of looking at the world and their writing within it. As Jonathan Alexander tells us in *Literacy, Sexuality, Pedagogy: Theory and Practice for Composition Studies*, "Learning how to talk fluently and critically about sex and sexuality composes a significant part of becoming literate in our society" (2). Alexander's book focuses on what it means for students to have or enact sexual literacy. I read his discussion of literacy as a layered one—one where to "talk" about or look at, say, an advertisement or film, is a particular act that makes up the layers of literacy. Like Alexander, as a teacher of composition I believe that this "talking about" and "looking at" are part of a continuous literacy process. For the focus of this chapter, I want to consider literacy as bound to notions of thinkability. I am interested in exploring the ways that what is thinkable, or imaginable, is part of the process of reading and writing. For the purposes of the courses I design, we might say that I am asking students to consider their own gender literacy, one of the first literacies most of us learn. We accumulate gender literacy as children, as we practice telling the *difference* between boys and girls and as we study the rules and markers of this seemingly sacred difference.

In tai chi practice, there is both philosophy of movement and movement itself—not to be misunderstood as separate. We practice, in our movement and in the world, the principle of nondualism. This refers to things that appear distinct while not being separate. It is inseparability, inextricability. The body stays balanced through this principle after learning to root. The body is simultaneously one whole and its parts. When I block, I block with my whole body, though it may appear that the arm or hand is doing the blocking on its own.

For a first essay assignment in one of my composition classes, I asked students to write a history of one of their identities. I asked them to talk about how they learned what it meant to *become* this identity. They responded to this assignment after reading Kate Bornstein's *Gender Outlaw*; this essay assignment was done after the shorter writing assignment I discuss in chapter three. The assignment grew out of my interest in queering culturally valued binaries by investigating very taken-for-granted gender literacies. In a sense, the assignment asks students to tell a story they may not have thought of *as a story* before. The stories of our genders can seem obvious, invisible even, to many students—except for those who have not had this luxury, students whose gender has not been taken for granted by others, students who have visibly and perceptively *failed* at their genders in the view of others and have known that this particular sense of failure was indeed connected to notions of gender. I point to the importance of this failure being *visible* to others because, in the end, I believe we all fail at our genders—that gender is set up, in fact, *so that we fail*. No one, after all, can be a complete and perfect man, or a complete and perfect woman—at least no one I have ever seen. But if the failures of gender are not visible *as* failures, then gender is not a story, gender is an *is*. In other words, gender is imagined as specifically *not* a story, not a becoming; it is thought to be an *is*—to be, rather than become. If students can become curious about this invisible story of how one *becomes* a man, or a woman, or some other identity, they can perhaps begin to understand something about the ways identity and knowledge are made—not merely to expose identity *as* made but to see and articulate *how* it is made. Part of the project of any teacher interested in queer pedagogies is to first call attention to the literacy practices that have been taken for granted as natural (so much so that these ways go without question) without our full knowledge, consent, or even conscious participation. I am interested in the ways my composition courses engage with queer theory, which in turn seems to invite queer theory to speak back to the work of teaching composition and even to the work of writing itself. I take the work of composition to be the work of fluid, nuanced, embodied, and conscious readings and interpretations. This work embraces bodily, readerly, and writerly contradictions as moments of productivity rather than problems. And I take writing to be a reading. In other words, in the act of writing, students are reading—both offering a reading and *doing* a reading.

Several doctors have told me they can "fix my voice" or "thin out my hair follicles" with female hormones. There is, of course, no medical reason for this, though it seems to make them feel better to offer me a gender consolation prize. I am hard for them to look at. They wish I would shave my legs, or grow the back of my hair at least down to my shoulders. They do not know why they feel this way. They know not what they do.

In the first longer essay assignment in a first-year writing course, I ask students to consider the following prompt:

> We have talked extensively thus far about the makings and complexities of identity in terms of race and gender, specifically. We have heard from McIntosh about the category of privilege, from Bornstein about the socially constructed nature of identities. Begin to think about how your race and/or gender identity has been made, constructed—by yourself and others. This assignment asks you to tell the story of your own making: for example, how you became a "man," or how you became a "woman" or "neither" or "white" or . . . the list could, of course, go on and on. You should seek out the origins, instructions, influences, decisions, forces, and complexities of the makings of whatever identity you choose to write about. You should quote from at least one of the relevant texts from class at various moments in your paper in order to try to put the story of your gender-making, for example, in conversation with Bornstein's. This assignment, please understand, is not: how did you become the great woman you are today? This is not a success story, or a tragedy, or a tear-jerker film about your destiny; this paper is a careful analysis, study, and reflection on the way you have come to know about some aspect of your identity—the epistemology (remember this word?) of your identity. The titles might be something like "The History of My Woman-ness" or "A Long White Journey," etc., etc. Your writing should illustrate: your understanding of the texts from the course you are working with, your ability to quote from and close-read passages from at least one of the texts we are working with, your willingness to ask critical questions of yourself, your level of consciousness while you write, your ability to write in a "voice" that is NOT generic or spoken by the infamous "Paper God," and your composition of creative and complicated prose. Good luck. And try, as much as you can, to get something out of this process. As Amanda reminded us in class, writing may be able to lead somewhere else, somewhere we might not have thought it could lead. Remember what Annie Dillard said: it's "a surgeon's probe," not a scalpel.

In reading this assignment again now, I notice first the language of the course itself—the terms my students and I, together, develop in order to talk about writing. While I often choose most of the readings and assignment due dates prior to teaching a composition class, I do write most of my assignments *during* the semester. My students write, and I, in turn, write back. I am drawn to writing assignments in this way because it allows a kind of movement and conversation during the semester. Different sets of students develop different vocabularies, and I find it useful to use the vocabulary of the class, rather than only a vocabulary *I* might give to *them*—though, of course, there is some of that going on as well. For example, I offered them the term "epistemology" as something worth talking about and thinking through as a writer. But my students gave me the term "paper god" as a way of describing a "voice" they often hear, or a voice they sometimes believe a paper for a course should "sound like."

In many places, and for centuries, tai chi has been learned by observation. A student shows up and begins to watch the sifu practice—imitating or tracing the teacher's movements. The student may do this for a long time without knowing the names of the moves they are doing, without knowing their martial applications, and without an understanding of breath or energy work. All of these layers of knowledge are essential to the practice of tai chi. As beginners (and this learning period could last as many as twenty-five years), students imitate tai chi.

There are things I wish for this assignment now. While, for instance, I use the word "become" when asking students to tell the story of their identities, I see now that this "become" could signal a finality—as in, you "become" some identity and now you *are* that identity. I wish, in retrospect now, that *I* had written even more reflectively of the ways I was asking *them* to write. I am aware, especially now, after having taught the course, of how complicated what I am asking students to try to do actually is; it's difficult, not just because writing is difficult, but because it is hard to remember, to remind oneself again and again, to undo stability—or at least to mark it as momentary. Despite the various ways I see myself struggling to write an assignment in some of the same ways students struggle to respond to them, my students always surprise me, always destabilize my assignment further, and respond as, in many ways, my teachers. Part of the follow-up work to this assignment was for students to write a reflection in which they thought through what it was actually like to write this essay and why it was difficult. I asked them, after they turned in these papers and expressed some struggle in writing them, to write a response to the following:

> Many of you expressed difficulties in writing your first paper. Some of you talked about the specific challenges of trying to recall or remember things from your past that might have constructed the various identities you wrote about. Write a one-page reflection in which you discuss your difficulties with the assignment. What was most difficult and why? What does the difficulty reveal to you about the identity you chose to write about? Can you imagine ways to deal with those difficulties as a writer? Was the assignment even possible? What is missing from what you wrote? What do those absences mean?

One student, Amanda Cardo, responds,

> I knew Bornstein was right to say that gender is non-consensual. I know that no one ever asked me if I wanted to be or liked to be a girl, but I think the paper was so hard because *I had never even thought to even ever ask the question* if I liked it or not. And it was hard to write a "history" of how I learned to be a girl when *I don't know how I learned to be.* I just *never really thought about it.* It just was. Which is weird because kids ask questions about everything like why is the sky blue and where do babies come from and all of that, but what kid asks what being a woman means? She doesn't ask, she just watches and learns. *But I don't think that makes being a woman a made up story that isn't real.* (Emphasis added)

There are several interesting and valuable things happening (or perhaps beginning to happen) in Cardo's thinking/reading/writing that seem to highlight the relationships between queer theory and composition pedagogy. Cardo calls our attention to reading practices and strategies of interpretation that *prevent* her literacy even as she is trying to enact it. Cardo notices that her strategy for reading her own gender has been one of acceptance, absorption, and unconsciousness. *It just was.* These strategies are *one* way of reading, one way of reading that prevents the kind of critical and inquisitive reading practices that help to shape articulate and complicated writers.

There are possibilities rising out of the above student text that queer theory calls our attention to in a particular way. I want to consider first the notion of "thinkability." Cardo seems interested in the fact that she had "never even thought to even ever ask the question" and that she "never really thought about it." I want to first suggest that Cardo's response is not casual but is a serious interpretation of her difficulties with the assignment. Cardo observes something about Bornstein's text (that the claim that gender is nonconsensual is true in some way) *and* something about her response to the text (that she had never considered this possibility before). She notices the ways in which the process of gender-making has been invisible, and she begins to articulate some of the conditions of its "invisibility." Queer theorists have long been interested in ideas of thinkability, legibility, and possibility—as have writers; after all, what kind of writers would we be if we could not imagine what seems unlikely, disparate, even impossible? Part of what I consider to be my job as a teacher of composition is to disrupt the terms of possibility and thinkability and to ask students to participate in practices of reading and writing that question the stories we all tell ourselves about identity, stories in which we craft our identities (or the identities of others) as thinkable or unthinkable. Literacy, for me, means that more must become thinkable, readable—including the idea that what is unthinkable is not there. Certainly the feasibility of any given identity is connected to whether that identity can be imagined and by whom, to whether the identity is recognizable, and of course whether such identity is even possible (to say, to name, to think).

To practice tai chi is to transform the body into the water it already is. This cannot necessarily be taught. Its layers are felt and experienced by the student. Sometimes this understanding is fleeting.

Judith Butler has deep concern about these connections. She writes, in *Undoing Gender*, that "the articulation of the possible . . . moves us beyond what is merely actual and present into a realm of possibility, the not yet actualized or the not actualizable" (28). If we think about Cardo's response to the assignment as trying to "move beyond what is actual and present into a realm of possibility," what good does that do us as teachers of writing? What good does it do Amanda Cardo for me to think about her work in this way, or respond to it with these concerns in mind? I would like to suggest that these questions are deeply connected to questions of imagination. I think of literacy as inextricably linked to imagination in that what can *be* imagined is what one is able to consider or question. If we cannot even imagine ourselves asking a certain kind of question about ourselves, or the world, this lack of imagination can become a lack of literacy, can become the prevention of the very literacy I want to foster in my students' work. What I am trying to describe is quite cyclical. One needs an ability to imagine possibilities beyond what one already knows, but in order to learn to do this, one needs to imagine possibilities beyond or outside of what one already knows. What is Cardo able to imagine and why? How can I facilitate what she is able to imagine? How and why would I want to encourage her to not only ask the questions she had "never even thought to ask" (an issue of interpretation, of being taught which questions to ask of a text) but also to encourage her to explore the *reasons* she "never even thought to ask" (a question, perhaps, of epistemology)? Karen Kopelson puts it this way: "*Queer* is a term that offers to us and our students an epistemological position—a way of knowing rather than something to be known" ("Dis/Integrating" 25).

What queer theory and sexual literacy (or perhaps, in the context in which my student writes, we might call it gender literacy) offer to the teacher in this composing moment is a way of thinking about and responding to Cardo's writing, a way that highlights and values how she has come to *know*, or even how she has come to fail to *know*. It is common practice to think of literacy as resulting in a gaining of knowledge or forming new knowledge, but we must also consider the possibility, as Cardo calls us to do, that being literate in gendered cultural norms (or other types of often unquestioned versions of normativity) means learning how to *not know*, how to *not ask*. Or, put another way, it means to practice a literacy that precludes other possibilities for knowing and being. This is *a* literacy, but it is not queer literacy, not literacy that leads to the unthinkable, the unimaginable. It's not, then, that many of us are sexually "illiterate"; it's that the literacy practices we have learned (however invisibly) when it comes to our bodies, when it comes to identity and gender and sex, are practices of *not knowing*, practices where to know *means* quite literally *to not notice*, to accept without question the conditions given to us, the conditions of our very possibility. For some of us, particularly those of us who are queer or who live outside the terms of these conditions of possibility, teaching students to become more conscious about these invisible literacy practices is not merely a matter of stronger and more complicated papers (though it can help to produce or encourage those); it is a matter of survival.

I was in love with my father's secretary. I was eight years old. Lori would let me sit in her desk chair and answer the phones. I drew pictures of Lori and me going to the beach and to sporting events. But I would code the drawings, placing hidden images in them the way I'd seen done in Highlights Magazine. *I knew to hide the images of my love for Lori because I once heard her express disgust for the UPS woman, Charlie, who looked like I could imagine myself looking as a grown-up—uniformed neatly, with short, spiky hair, a voice as deep as my father's, a tattoo on her forearm. Charlie walked like a soldier. But Lori said she was a "weird dyke," and I figured I was one of those too. So I drew pictures of Lori and me at the beach; I hid some wedding bells in the sun, violins in the trees, and sometimes I drew on the handle of Lori's purse the bow tie I'd be wearing. Sometimes I'd take my shirt off while washing the cars in the driveway with my brothers, who were kind enough to leave me be as I'd lie down on the wet blacktop, my shoulder blades cooling in the swirl of water. I'd close my eyes and imagine other worlds, other genders, other galaxies where Charlie and I were adored—baseball players, or detectives, or even president and vice president. When you're eight years old and queer, you have to compose the world as you wish it were; you have to be an inventive reader. You have to fantasize more wildly.*

Liquid Interpretations

One way of thinking of the kind of literacy I am arguing for is by thinking about literacy practices that approach the world as a solid (something fixed, stable, simple) and thinking of practices that approach the world as a liquid (something fluid, mutable, difficult to pin down). While I understand the process of reading and writing as always *both* solid and liquid at once, for the purposes of my teaching I focus my attention on fluidity. If this particular culture has taught us that gender belongs to the solid category, then it need not be read or interpreted. We might hear Amanda Cardo again: *it just was.* But becoming literate in the current moment might have more to do with fluidity; it might have more to do with coming to terms with the idea that nothing, even that which appears so convincingly solid (like gender), is solid. It is all a kind of fluid, and to see the world as a moving force, to see a text this way, to see ourselves and our writing this way is to engage in a kind of reflective literacy. Hans-Georg Gadamer puts it this way: "The real question is whether one sees the function of reflection as bringing something to awareness in order to confront what is in fact accepted with other possibilities—so that one can either throw it out or reject the other possibilities and accept what tradition de facto is presenting—or whether bringing something to awareness *always dissolves what one has previously accepted*" (*Philosophical* 34, original emphasis).

While I am resistant to Gadamer's notion that we might "either throw out or reject," because this seems to be a pretty limited way of understanding what might happen at the moment we encounter a text, I am interested in the moment we come into contact with what challenges, affirms, resists, or does not fit in with our prior knowledge of ourselves or others. Certainly both Bornstein's text and my assignment seem to call up this moment in Amanda Cardo—the moment when "bringing something to awareness" begins to disrupt her view of gender. This moment of disruption is a crucial one in which Cardo begins to see what she reads, even if she reads herself, as difficult to pin down. However, Gadamer questions whether what we ultimately "decide" (for example, whether Cardo decides that gender is a nonconsensual sham or whether it is still "real" or some version of both or neither) even matters. Can we be in the act of literate understanding if this act has *not dissolved what one has previously accepted*? In other words, if students don't end up subscribing to some different notion of the world, then have they done any real interpretative or writing work at all? In thinking about queer theory and the possibilities of queer pedagogy, I am most interested in this verb *dissolved*—to cause to disappear or disperse. And I think if we are defining *dissolve* in this way, then Gadamer is correct in saying that we are reflecting, even if our previous understandings have not been "dissolved"; I do not want to *dissolve* my students or to repeatedly ask them to adopt the worldviews of the texts they might read. For me, this kind of dissolving is never even possible; the former understanding of world or self never dissolves in this way, never disappears to be replaced by another. However, if we understand the definition of *dissolve* as to make or turn into liquid, suddenly I find myself convinced that interpretation always involves this "dissolving," always involves movement—the kind of movement solids are not capable of. Our former understandings (for example, Cardo's understanding that being a woman was something that "just was") will never, ultimately, disappear, but when they become liquid and fluid as opposed to solid, it makes them movable; it makes them open to evaporation (which is *not* a disappearance but a change in form). They are, then, in however small a way, transformed in the various ways that something which is not solid might be transformed. It can make it nearly impossible to interpret or understand if our previous understandings are solid and thus unable to be moved or reshaped. The act of writing is a liquid act, a fluid act. Queer pedagogies have the potential to address and enact this very fluidity. And if students begin with some of the most "sacred" solids we are—bodies—other transformations might seem almost obvious. But how do our perceptions or ideas or identities become liquid? Is it a predisposition? Something learned? Something suffered? Something that can be taught? I am arguing here that it is possible to teach students (and teach ourselves) to "become liquid," to approach literacy as a fluid process.

Bornstein posits a complicated argument for gender *fluidity*: "the culture may not simply be creating roles for naturally-gendered people, the culture may in fact be creating the gendered people" (*Gender* 12). While the notion that there are gender *roles* is one I find most of my students to be familiar with, the suggestion that biological gender may also be "created" is a more complicated claim, one that can begin to dissolve scientific truths that now feel so self-evident. So if Gadamer encourages us to think of reading as an exercise in "dissolving," what better way to do that than through an argument that attempts to make liquid one of the things many of us find most solid and obviously solid: gender. There are men and there are women. End of story.

I remember only a few class discussions from high school, but I defended Holden Caulfield with certain passion—despite his obvious sexism, his arrogance, and his all-around bad attitude. "He lies all the time," many students said. But I remember not reading the lying as lying. I remember reading Holden saying, "It's partly true, too, but it isn't all true. People always think something's all true."

But when students read Bornstein, or if they allow themselves to *read* Bornstein, the body itself can seem at risk, understanding is at risk, the notion of self is at risk. Readers can become disrupted—personally, politically, educationally, even physically—by Bornstein's assaults on the meanings of bodies. *Gender Outlaw* requires its readers to do a great deal of work in order to question, interrogate, and explain some of our most cherished assumptions; the text itself moves queerly on the page—the sections moving (as this text I am writing moves) from interviews to quotations from others to scenes from comic books to photos to lists of elaborate sexual ribbon systems to descriptions of Bornstein's own life. The text itself can make visible the act of reading; the strategies of interpretation we are used to using as we read may not work—formally or otherwise. Students are often jolted by the text, surprised, even offended—perhaps at the crux of what is thinkable and what is unthinkable, with the very paradox of what it is possible to think about, and therefore write. And it does seem to me that much more needs to be written about the risks, limits, *and* possibilities of teaching right at the crux of what is imaginable. Imagination, after all, is also something most of us who teach writing hope to see rising up in our students' work. But we cannot talk about imagination as some sort of artistic or creative movement without grappling with the radical political promise of imagination.

I want to highlight that what I am describing as *fluid* literacy is not merely me wanting my students to arrive at the conclusion that gender is constructed, though this might happen. The constructed is not the opposite of "authentic" or real, though the constructed is unavoidable (Amanda Cardo seems to recognize this to some extent); it is the constructed's "how" that I must teach in order to encourage the kinds of writers/readers/thinkers who will move into a world understanding both the power and paradox of their own agency and who will become agents of queerer, more deliberately disruptive literacies. Queer pedagogy offers a particular epistemology, illuminating both an introduction to and an example of the kind of methodologies that expose the "how" of knowledge-making, identity-making, even literacy-making. To guide Cardo toward revising the assignment she is reflecting upon, I might try to pose questions that help her to imagine the "how" of her "I don't know how I learned to be." Students sometimes learn how to address the question of how they come to know through *evidence* or *support*, but Cardo's search for evidence of how one *becomes* a woman is not a simple search. It's not matter of finding the passage to quote, it's not a matter of research; it is a matter of contingent arising, a matter of positioning and understanding the writer as one involved in the act of making possible what seems impossible.

To learn tai chi is also to learn to be present—to be entirely and concentrated in one moment. To be a mirror to yourself, or a window. I have heard poetry described in this way.

Queer literacy, then, involves understanding literacy as bound to seeing and articulating possibility, even when there seems little room to do so; it involves troubling the very binaries on which our first experiences with literacy are based. Cardo, after all, does write the assignment that tells the history she fears she cannot find. She enacts the very literacy she fears she cannot describe, though she enacts it in a surprising way. Here is a longer excerpt from Cardo's essay. She titles the essay "All About Them Words" and writes extensively about what words *do*. For me, the essay in many ways reimagines my assignment, responding in ways I had not anticipated:

> To be transgendered is to decide consciously to not subscribe to one side or the other of the "bi-polar gender system," as Bornstein affectionately dubs it. This is looked upon by the dominant culture as "queer" because transgendered is neither of the two acceptable genders. "People are genuinely afraid of being without a gender," says Bornstein (58), but transgendered people take that fear and transmute it into an action that pushes past borders of definitions. People are afraid because to not have a gender identity is not to be recognizable by the dominant culture, and to not be recognizable by the dominant culture can have consequences of not being accepted, of not being wanted. This fear is real for many, I know it is for me. So I, like many others, crawl into the box-like definition of gender and holed myself up there for a long time, cramped but happy because I had the company of others who did the same. I considered myself a "tomboy" at times, but never a boy or man. Here language and words fooled me by convincing me that there is a very solid, impervious line between man and woman, and one could not be a little bit of each. No one could be a man *and* a woman at the same time.
>
> But everyone *is* a little transgendered. Everyone does something that can be seen as a little queer, a little different from what is expected of their gender. There is absolutely no denying it. Girls burp loudly at

dinner or get in fist fights, which falls under the definition of "man" or "manly." Some guys wear perfume and style their hair and enjoy babysitting, which I've found seem to be covered by the umbrella definition of "womanly." These little aberrations tend to be overlooked or classified as just little "slip ups" and not considered important to the identity that lies below them, but what does this say about language? That the terms "manly" and "womanly" aren't all-inclusive or exclusive, because someone who is "womanly" by definition can commit something "manly" and still be considered "womanly" or a woman. Language fails us here because it denies the fact that even with a solidified definition of woman or man, deviations in actions or notion can change the definition. This then makes definition obsolete, doesn't it? How can something have a solid, reliable definition that is constantly changing? It can't, which begs the question: why rely on language and words so much?

So where does that put me? What influenced me to be who I am today? Words did. I pledged, we all pledged, our lives to them, to definitions that keep us confined, and within those confines I belonged to a group that made me feel welcome and cared about. In feeling cared about, accepted, I didn't question the box I was in; rather, I enjoyed the company I kept. My family made of a word. At the same time, though, I did question the borders of the box by being a tomboy, by playing ice hockey, by getting in fist fights and by partaking in more "masculine" activities because I was bored with the activities that were limited to women. Language changes because we change, ideas change, morals change, and words' meanings change. So, gender can change, apparently literally as well as gender as a concept. I was made into a woman by words, words of my parents, of the television, of books, of my friends and foes, fellow women and opposing men.

Now, I am Amanda, inevitably influenced by words because they are our only means of describing what is truly going on in our heads. . . . [W]ords are all we have, but they can only do so much to say what we really mean.

I am struck by Cardo's turn to language, and as I read through the papers that responded to this assignment, her explicitness about how language shapes identity is unique. And, at first, I wondered if her philosophical inquiries were also a way of avoiding the *story* of her gender as the question puts it. But rather than imagine her as not telling that story, I begin to see the ways in which her paper explains why it is a hard story to tell using the language available and the ways in which her paper gets to the heart of the question. When I say that responding to this assignment, or writing itself, is a matter of contingent arising, I have in mind some of the moves Cardo makes in this paper. She struggles to hold many aspects of the self in mind as she writes, acknowledging her fear ("I know it is for me") and her "cramped but happy" position inside the "box" of a gendered life. One way to read Cardo's essay is as a kind of response to this "being cramped" and as a way for her to write her way out of the box—not to become something other than herself, but more to continually become herself: "Now, I am Amanda." I read her saying of her name at the end of the piece as a kind of contingent arising. She is Amanda "now," and Amanda is an identity that more easily moves and shifts. Amanda is a writer who moves and shifts. This paper thinks not only about how gender is made but also about how a world is constituted through language—an idea that I take to be one of queer theory's primary pathways of inquiry, a pathway that is always complicated by queer theory's imperative to contend with the body as it expresses our genders, desires, and renderings.

I must admit to flinching as I read, "But everyone *is* a little transgendered. Everyone does something that can be seen as a little queer, a little different from what is expected of their gender." I flinch because this moment happens frequently in my courses—the moment where many students decide that everything and everyone is queer. And my response itself is a contradiction: I am both interested in their finding the queers in themselves (and everywhere), especially as readers and writers, but I am also conscious of the collective anxiety that *queer* loses its meaning once it points to everything, even though Cardo is not wrong—it does point to everything, to all of us. But still, that "everyone is a little transgendered" seems reductive, solid in a sense, even as it describes us all as *not* solid, not solid genders. I read Cardo's final sentence as grappling with this paradox when she explains that words "can only do so much to say what we really mean."

As we were growing up, I watched my brothers intently, wondering if their boy lives had answers about what or who I might become. But we were not the same kind of boys. My brothers listened to Van Halen, and they listened to cassette tapes of Andrew Dice Clay when our parents weren't around. They thought this guy was hilarious. And they kept repeating his nursery rhyme jokes in their heaviest versions of our New York accents. Jack and Jill went up the hill, each with a buck and a quarter. Jill came down with $2.50. Ohhhhh! And they would laugh and punch each other in the arm. I wasn't stupid, so I got the joke, like Jill was some sort of hooker or something. But I thought it more likely that Jill kicked Jack's ass and took his money to buy her girlfriend a charm bracelet, or Jill won a bet about who could spit farther down the hill. It occurred to me already that jokes were usually only funny if you shared their assumptions, and if you didn't think of your assumptions as assumptions, and if you couldn't imagine alternative ways of reading the text of the joke.

I want to help my students extend the reach of words, to help them say what seems unsayable. I want to consider that when Amanda Cardo writes about "what we mean" that she suggests not only what we mean *to say* but also what *we* mean, how we come to mean. Just in Cardo's asking "how can something have a solid, reliable definition that is constantly changing?" I hear the questions of the course, the questions of *my* life echoing in her essay. Yet, her paper, in a sense, answers this question, struggling to find the language to describe definitions that can change, solids that can transform to liquids, a once woman who is becoming Amanda, who is both tomboy (boy) and woman. I think this articulation of possibility, this doubled truth makes her paper a *queerer* piece of writing, a piece of writing that engages with the complex work of being present *as a becoming* as one writes, keeping the self in view as she writes. William Spurlin explains that *queer* "functions as a mode of analysis and as a strategy of opposition that circulates in culture and disrupts not only normative ideologies pertaining to sexuality, but . . . the family, childcare, the body, health care, censorship, health and reproductive politics, citizenship, national affiliation and neo-imperialism" (10). Spurlin's extensive list highlights the ways in which "queering" becomes a "mode," a way of looking at the world—and perhaps also a way of reading and composing a world. Cardo, I believe, enacts this composing in her text quoted above, trying to work inside the contradictions of language and being. Spurlin connects this mode to "opposition" and "disruption." Queer pedagogy offers some alternative ways to understand opposition (resistance) and disruption (a kind of liberation from what has been thought before) as I have tried to begin outlining here—ways of understanding these terms as situated and complicated. Literacy, then, if we understand it as connected to interpretation, must contain some aspect of interruption. I am reminded of David Bartholomae's statement, which I also quote in chapter three: "a good assignment teaches by interfering. It interferes with a student and [with] writing" (*Writing* 185). I want to offer an understanding of literacy that hinges on this interference and bring Bartholomae's significant assertion into contact with the particularly queer understanding of gender and interpretation I have offered here. Queer literacy might mean to interfere with readers' understandings of gender and, consequently, interfering with readers' understandings of themselves—their bodies, their interpretations, their reading, and their writing. My assignment tries to interfere with Cardo's understanding (of writing, of gender, of herself). Cardo's response also interferes with my understanding (of story, of queerness, of my own affective and embodied investments in my courses). In this sense, my students and I, ideally, interfere with one another. I understand strong writing as writing that disrupts normative understandings, that calls into question something that seemed not a question at all, writing that, grammatically and structurally, struggles to articulate its own ideas.

I want to understand more about how to ask students to engage with what they have not yet thought, to try to compose what seems uncomposable, to say those things they cannot say, to see (of themselves and of the world) what has thus far been invisible, to see, as Cardo does, womanhood in some new and not-before-imaginable way. Doing so, I believe, can *teach* not only the ability to imagine possibilities or the ability to *dissolve* into liquid what we see, but also situatedness, positioning, a particular kind of questioning that enables students to read, interpret, and write in more creative *and* critically conscious ways. Through this process, students (queer identified or not) can enact queerer literacies.

The Queer Art of Difficulty

In "Queer Pedagogy and Its Strange Techniques," Deborah Britzman asks, "What if one thought about reading practices as problems of opening identifications, of working the capacity to imagine oneself differently precisely with respect to how one encounters another, and in how one encounters the self? What if how one reads the world turned upon the interest in thinking against one's thoughts, of creating a queer space where one's old certainties made no sense?" (55). Certainly we can imagine Britzman's questions here to be deeply connected to how I have tried to explore Gadamer's use of the term "dissolving." Britzman suggests that queer pedagogy has something to do with "thinking against one's thoughts." So, the first step, then, is to create a situation in which it might be possible for students to see, read, or witness something that puts their "old certainties" into question. I am interested in the kind of thinking such a situation might prompt—thinking that enables students to provoke, locate, and discuss moments of "thinking against one's thoughts" in their writing. Does Cardo, in the short excerpt I have used to try to ground this chapter, have any moment of thinking against her own thoughts? In a sense, we might look at her entire response in this way. Cardo struggles in "thinking against her own thought" that *woman* is not "a made up story that isn't real." The assignment does ask her to think against that thought, to imagine that her way of thinking about gender (something real, stable, not "a made up story") is a way of thinking that exposes those "old certainties" to which Britzman refers.

My relatives were always trying to give me my gender in the form of dollhouses, Hello Kitty blankets, pink things, yellow things, Barbies, the beloved Cabbage Patch dolls. I wanted them to give me another version of gender, and sometimes, usually in private, someone would. My mother: a batting glove. My grandfather: a baseball hat. My brother: advice. "This is how you punch back," he says. "Right. Like this. This is how."

Halberstam suggests that a queer theorized teaching practice might start by "refusing the schemata of identitarian institutional positions (lesbian teacher, heterosexual students, for example) and proceeding eccentrically. By this I mean that the queer teacher may take up an *eccentric* position in relation to queer material and position herself as always implicated in *and* outside the topics she is teaching" ("Reflections" 271, emphasis added). Geometrically, *eccentric* can imply two circles or spheres, at least one of which contains the centers of both. But the word *always* implies that the center is in question (the center of one circle is within another but not necessarily the center of that other circle)—hence the term's use as a way of saying someone or something is unusual, strangely paired, or peculiar. For Halberstam to suggest that the queer pedagogue position itself is decentered, as being both "in and outside" the materials one teaches, means that a queer theorized teaching practice is the practice of decentering.

Along with decentering we take into account "how deeply and intimately *rhetorical* queer theory is, for queer theory asks us to question, at the most fundamental levels and in the most essential ways, the nature of authorship, representation, and the process of coming into being through language" (Alexander and Gibson 8). I think our teaching of composition asks us to do the same. It asks us to "strain against and celebrate our double binds" (Monson and Rhodes 90); it asks us to engage with paradox, with difficulty, with the ambiguous blurs of articulation; it asks us to bring questions of the body back to writing. This engagement is a pathway through which teachers of composition can move toward goals I actually think those of us in composition do, generally speaking, agree about, goals of teaching embodied, reflexive, complicated, nuanced, and fluid writers—writers who exercise habits of mind that might more likely lead to more imaginative, bolder, queerer compositions, and queerer notions of literacy itself. After all, as Mike Rose aptly puts it, "To acknowledge our collective capacity is to take the concept of variability seriously. Not as slots along a simplified cognitive continuum or as a neat high-low distribution, but as a bountiful and layered field, where many processes and domains of knowledge interact. Such a model demands more not less from *those of us who teach*, or who organize work, or who develop social policy" (216, emphasis added). To take "variability seriously," to take difference and how we think about difference seriously, then, is to understand variability as existing in this moving field; it is to understand literacy as fluid, as a series of variable moving processes that exist in this layered field. This is what makes it possible for us to continuously define and redefine what literacy means. Without this movement, this revision of understanding, we would be left with the kind of reduction and simplification Rose continuously warns us against. And of course there is great responsibility that falls on "those of us who teach" if we are to accept this complicated, fluid, and variable notion of literacy and try to teach in ways that embody it, and do so with a kind of queer and conscious abandon.

I am eating lunch at a small sandwich shop in Rockland, Maine, where a young boy has been reading over my body with his eyes. He looks inquisitively at my face, then chest, then legs. I keep looking down at the wheat grains, crumbling into small traces of bread-dust across my lap. Finally, he turns to the resident interpreter of environment for clarification: "Is that a boy or a girl, Mom?" His mother dutifully replies, "It's none of your business. Eat." He does eat, but only after saying, "I think it's a boy." I cannot say for certain whether I classify this child's reading of the text of my body as a mis-reading; I know only slightly more than he does about how to interpret my own gender performance (the text of myself). I do know that these scenarios (which are repeated in one way or another every time a body is seen or even heard) mark quite clearly the ways we might construct processes of interpretation. The tools the young boy has to guide his interpretation, in a sense, fail him. He has sets of rules that lead him to interpret a body in either one way or another.

When readers come into contact with bodies, the process of gender interpretation is usually, for the most part, invisible. We seemingly interpret gender with subtle ease and move on to treating that person in congruence with the gender interpretation; however, when the ease of that interpretation disappears, we might move on to a more serious method of analysis. Richard Palmer, in his book *Hermeneutics*, writes, "Analysis is interpretation; feeling the need for analysis is also an interpretation" (23). The fact that the young child feels the need for further analysis reveals a great deal about what our primary interpretative tool is for "analyzing" the body. Gender is first and foremost, and it often frames and therefore appears to explain, readings of that body. Our method of interpretation for gender, however, is limited, and, as Palmer also suggests, sometimes our method of interpretation "delimits what we shall see" (156). The child in the sandwich shop has a specific interpretative method—using a strategy that will help him say, explain, and translate the bodies he sees. In this case, we might call this traditional perception of gender interpretation a kind of pre-understanding of the body. In my own pedagogical work and thinking with my own students, I think both queer theory and my experience as a queer person offer particular ways of thinking about the notion of pre-understanding. One of the first challenges for a writing teacher, and perhaps for many teachers, is asking students to learn to sit with, or even relish in, challenging their own pre-understandings. It is my contention that to be able to enact this consciousness, to write as a writer aware of her interpretative limits and as a writer who pushes on her own limits is to enact composition—to enact, as Jacqueline Rhodes and Jonathan Alexander put it in *Techne*, "a composing that is not a composing, a call in many ways to acts of de- and un- and re-composition." I agree with James Slevin when he writes, "I understand composition as a response to the difficulty of writing" (13). Slevin describes, in this one sentence, a particularly interesting way of thinking about how composition got here in the first place, and he cites its origins as a "response to the difficulty of writing," which is to acknowledge not only the struggle for ourselves and our students as we try to compose but also the ways that reading and writing are difficulties, are already problematic. Mariolina Rizzi Salvatori and Patricia Donahue offer a compelling way for students to put pressure on the field of constraints in which they read and compose, to push on their interpretative *methods*. In *The Elements (and Pleasures) of Difficulty*, they examine the relationship between a student's difficulty and "a possible rule and strategy of interpretation" (xxvi). This relationship suggests not only that the student be aware of when their reading might be a way of making their limits visible but also how those limits call up a "strategy of interpretation" that also has limits and constraints.

Even in college, my readings were perceived as the "wrong readings." When I was in a college poetry seminar, we were reading Emily Dickinson's "Wild Nights—Wild Nights!" The class was discussing the poem as a love poem to a man. I read the poem again and again silently as they talked. I reread the ending:

> *Rowing in Eden—Ah—the Sea!*
> *Might I but moor—tonight—In thee!*

So I commented, out loud to the class, that the verb "moor" felt far more like she was talking about a woman—that the idea of Dickinson anchoring herself in a lover seemed pretty gay to me. The queer English professor, of course, laughed and gave us some background on some "debates" about Emily Dickinson's sexuality. But the class was not amused, and one student says to me: you make everything about being gay all the time. This wasn't the first or the last time I would hear this accusation, but the world is a queer place and as I grew up and left home it became a kind of mission to illuminate its queerness, to ask that others see the queerness in this world, and even imagine the possibilities of queerer worlds.

Gender and Other Failed Binaries

Johnnie Hart, a student in the composition course I draw from throughout this project, writes in response to a question about Kate Bornstein's *Gender Outlaw*, "Kate Bornstein's book threatens what I know about my gender identity because the book makes me feel like my gender doesn't exist. Like I have put my money in a fake bank of what Bornstein calls 'either/or'" (1). I distributed these two sentences as the basis for a class discussion during the fourth week of the semester. I chose Hart's passage because of what I saw as a productive site of discussion—his use of metaphor, his verb choices, his reference to Bornstein's notion of "either/or."

I began the class with one question, not knowing exactly where the question might lead. I asked my students, *What kind of bank is this that Johnnie refers to in his response?* I record their answers on the board: *The kind where your money's not there when you go to get it*, says Amanda. *The building is not even there*, answers Iggy. The class goes on to imagine the various ways a bank might be fake. Many of their reasons have to do with the idea of investment. I write the word on the board: investment. *What is Johnnie afraid he has invested in?* I ask them. *Either/or*, several students in the front row point out. *What's "either/or"?* I answer with another question. Danielle says, *It's like you had a choice of two accounts at the fake bank, and neither one of them is an actual account. Your money is gone.* I ask them what kind of accounts Bornstein might be putting pressure on, not only for Johnnie but for all of us really. They dutifully answer my most reading-comprehensionlike question. Johnnie says, *The man and woman accounts, the gender binary.* I write the words on the board: *Binaries*. Underneath that, I write *man woman*. I ask them for more binaries. They play along. This, our final list:

man	woman
gay	straight
pro-life	pro-choice
Republican	Democrat
urban	rural
wealth	poverty
good	bad
beautiful	ugly
soldier	pacifist

What do you notice about the list? Here, the class erupts with ideas. It is difficult from the transcript (taken by one of my students) to tell who is speaking. But, collectively, they do notice first that the opposites are not really opposites—that, for example, some soldiers might *be* pacifists or that the definitions of what is considered wealth are "subjective." They say the list "does not leave room for the in-betweens." They find fault, in a sense, with binary thinking. And finally, it's Amanda who calls out what she sees as the culprit. *It's a trick of language, she says.* The room sort of pauses. No one seems quite sure what she means, but they seem interested in what it might be. She notices the construction of "pro-life" and "pro-choice" as reducing to two things no one would disagree with. *Who doesn't like life and choices? she astutely asks. Are those the only ways to think about abortions?* Finally, Kelsey chimes in, jokingly, pen in hand, pretending to record my answer: *So, binaries are bad?* I ask them to keep the list somewhere they can see it for the rest of the semester.

Of course, to say merely that binaries are "bad" might be to offer to Kelsey, and to all my students, a new binary, replacing their binary way of thinking with thinking in binary terms *about* binaries. In other words, it would offer them only a new kind of knowledge to replace the old. And as Patricia Hill Collins writes in *Black Feminist Thought*, "Alternative knowledge claims in and of themselves are rarely threatening to conventional knowledge. Such claims are routinely ignored, discredited, or simply absorbed and marginalized in existing paradigms. Much more threatening is the challenge that alternative epistemologies offer to the basic process used by the powerful to legitimate their knowledge claims" (219). If we take those words to heart, which I do, telling my students that binaries are "bad" or problematic, or whatever nuanced academic way I might say it, is not enough. What a queer pedagogy needs to imagine, hope for, create a space for are ways of knowing that "challenge . . . the basic process used by the powerful to legitimate their knowledge claims." These knowledge claims are then not only used by the powerful but reinforced by all of us, tacitly, unless we can find ways to intervene in this inheritance of hegemony. In this case, the knowledge claim is: there are men, and there are women. It is not enough to say this is not true, or even to show the scientific "evidence" Bornstein provides of it not being true. Together, we must find another way to know gender, an alternative way to write about gender, a more complicated way to write about anything. My students bring up this list numerous times during the semester. In a sense, it both grounds and unsettles them.

Robert Frost writes, "What I am pointing out is that unless you are home in the metaphor, unless you have had your proper poetical education in metaphor, you are not safe anywhere. Because you are not at ease with figurative values: you don't know the metaphor in its strength and its weakness. You don't know how far you may expect to ride it and when it may break down with you. You are not safe in science; you are not safe in history."

As an instructor of composition, I see both my students' (and my own) binary interpretations fail. Some of the least productive workshops I have ever led as a teacher of writing have begun with my own binary askings, for example, *What are this paper's strengths and weaknesses?* A question I remember having asked quite a few times in my first year as a writing teacher, one I had heard my own teachers ask in the past. This is a question that only leads to its own failure *as* a question. Either my students and I make false binary categories of strong writing and weak writing, or we end up circling back to the fact that the question itself is a trick, a shortcut, a reduction of complexity. But if a teacher of writing cannot say what the strengths and weaknesses of a given paper are, what can this instructor do? If we cannot say that some given person is either a man or a woman, what can we say about this person? If we begin with the assumption that a binary question produces binary answers, or that a binary argument leads to problems for its composer, what then can we teach students to do if we do not teach them to take one side of a "yes-or-no" argument, if we do not teach them to say whether their writing, their bodies, their ideas are either *this thing* or *that thing*? It is often my own body that teaches me what I might do instead.

I spent the first year of my tai chi practice learning to stand. In tai chi, it is called rooting—the process by which one learns to imagine the roots of trees growing out of the bottoms of the feet and deep into the ground. The body then bends and sways; its branches move in response to wind or force. But the feet are rooted, positioned, firm in their standing. The body bends as it roots.

Teaching students to write, in one way or another, does lead to a discussion of teaching them what an argument is, what taking a position means—a kind of rooting. This is not easy, nor is it a simple thing to articulate. Many of us have thought to think of this teaching in terms of academic discourse—imagining ourselves trying to lead our students to participate in the conversations of the university. David Bartholomae, in "Inventing the University," writes, "The student has to learn to speak our language, to speak as we do, to try on the peculiar ways of knowing, selecting, evaluating, reporting, concluding, and arguing that define the discourse of our community" (*Writing* 60). I think it is a misreading to understand Bartholomae's assertion as a conservative or elitist academic assertion. And I am interested in the idea that learning to write is a "trying on" of what may at first seem queer or unwearable. The larger project for me becomes, What are these "peculiar ways of knowing"? Which ones of them are most valuable? Why do these ways of knowing even matter? Who gets to say? What are these languages in which we write? These questions can be answered indefinitely by an infinite number of students and scholars both in and outside the institution of the university. Bartholomae's list does not end with "knowing"; he also suggests students of composition try on ways of "selecting, evaluating, reporting, concluding, and arguing that define the discourse of our community." I do not understand "our community" to mean some institutional location only, but I take Bartholomae to mean a community of critically thinking persons who care about complexity and intellectual curiosity and who see writing as a means to discover these processes. Bartholomae's list, to me, calls my attention to just some of the layered components of writing. And if part of the goal of my composition courses is to mobilize queer as a kind of knowing, then following Bartholomae's suggestion, I must try, with my students, to imagine queer kinds of selection, evaluation, research, conclusions, and arguments. This is something I deeply value. Something I want to teach students to do. Something we need to do more of as scholars in our field.

Like Butler says of gender, it is "a practice of improvisation within a scene of constraint" (*Undoing* 1). I believe writing is also this practice. For who is ever prepared to write? We offer students outlines, brainstorming, writing moves, but those of us who write know that writing is still improvisation, still an invention, an impromptu composition that begins in the middle of something else. The constraint comes in on us from all around—the context for the writing, the expectations about what writing is and what kinds of writing matter, even our ideas of who we are—identity itself. We are no different from our students. However, I do think Bartholomae is right that there is something about critical engagement and intellectual thought that we are asking students "to try on." To pretend otherwise would be dishonest, would be to ignore the constraints that are always there. The mistake I think we make (and I know I have made it) is to assume we know what ways of reading and writing actually do "define the discourse of our community." We might do best to begin thinking about the teaching of writing the way the poet Richard Hugo does. He says, in an address to his students, "Every moment, I am, without wanting or trying to, telling you to write like me. But I hope you learn to write like you. In a sense, I hope I don't teach you how to write but how to teach yourself how to write" (3). I quote Hugo here not to align myself with expressivist notions of what it means to teach writing (though I do value many of those notions) but to be clear about my own anxieties about teaching writing from a queer perspective, about teaching students to value the moves of queer theory or to value queerness itself as part of learning to write and to think interpretatively about the writing of others. Am I teaching them to "write like me"? Is that what all writing teachers are doing?

Once a student of tai chi has learned to stand, and has learned to bend and move with the feet rooted in the ground, the student may begin to learn what is called "push hands"—tai chi's version of sparring. One student places her hands against the teacher's hands. They move slowly together. The teacher will pull on the student's hand should she lean forward, should she pull up the roots from her feet. The teacher will push on the student's body should she lean back. The push and pull is a tender reminder; it calls the student's attention back to rooting, to their position of balance.

There are some who believe that to teach the "peculiar ways of knowing" to which Bartholomae refers is to teach students to make certain discursive and rhetorical moves. For instance, Gerald Graff has suggested in *Clueless in Academe: How Schooling Obscures the Life of the Mind* and elsewhere that students are kept in the dark about participating in academic discourse at the university. He writes,

> One of the most closely guarded secrets that academia unwittingly keeps from students and everybody else is that all academics, despite their many differences, play a version of the same game of persuasive argument. . . . The first step toward demystifying academia is to start being more explicit about the academic centrality of persuasive argument, as did a high school

teacher with whom I work, Hillel Crandus, and his students, who coined a useful shorthand term for it: "Arguespeak." (22)

While I would agree with Graff that, as teachers of writing, we should (where it is possible to do so) be explicit with students about moves that are valued in our courses, I am unconvinced that "the centrality of persuasive argument" or "Arguespeak" actually does the work of helping students understand what thoughtful, nuanced, complicated, and engaging prose might look like (or how it is made). I am not, despite how complicated and fluid I conceive of my teaching project, interested in mystifying my students, in making them believe writing is a kind of magic and that I cannot tell them how to do it. I can tell them many things. No matter how queer my classroom is or my assignments are, I can still teach my students *things*, rules, skills—how to cite in MLA style, how one might work a quotation into the text, how to use dashes and semicolons. There are things about writing we can, quite explicitly, teach. However, some aspects of teaching writing are necessarily implicit, process-oriented, so connected to reading that one cannot simply *show* a student how to write sophisticated, questioning, complex prose that is compelling. This knowing is always an idiosyncratic doing.

Gerald Graff and Cathy Birkenstein have published a composition textbook that suggests ways to implement strategies one might follow should one subscribe to the above claim. The widely used book is called *They Say/I Say: The Moves That Matter in Persuasive Writing* (2007), and it provides formulaic sentence structures and templates for students to follow. The textbook frames these templates as representative of how moves are made in academic writing. In the chapter entitled "Yes / No / Okay, But," Graff and Birkenstein provide some sentence structures for students to fill in or complete while telling students that "whether you are agreeing, disagreeing, or both agreeing and disagreeing, you need to be as clear as possible" (61). There is a part of this kind of writing instruction I really value—the part where we, as teachers of writing, try to become more explicit with students about the moves of a complicated writer and also the part where students try to imitate the writing they see. However, I find that the notion of disagreeing and agreeing can often set up a binary for students, and I would contend that this binary is still set up even if students take Graff and Birkenstein's option of "both agreeing and disagreeing." Are these the options: agree, disagree, or both? After all, even the book's title is a kind of binary: *they say, I say*. Of course this is not the only kind of writing in the book, but there is either explicit or subtle dependence on binaries to explain or demonstrate how to write. The book also values and demonstrates a kind of clarity that may be valuable in many writing contexts but not necessarily in all. I am skeptical that binary choices and clarity are at the nexus of introducing students to writing that imagines alternative worlds, new ways of thinking—queer writing, sometimes queer theory. In working with students to understand, for example, the work of Judith Butler or Michel Foucault, I often find myself talking with students about the circular nature of their arguments, about the rhetorical contradictions and movements that make reading social theory so difficult to do. But Birkenstein seems interested in reducing these queer moves to the already available normative understandings of argument that *They Say/I Say* suggests are the "moves that matter."

In an article in *College English*, Cathy Birkenstein takes up this very question of Butler's prose. The article, "We Got the Wrong Gal: Rethinking the 'Bad' Academic Writing of Judith Butler," makes the argument that, far from being incomprehensible, Butler's writing carries a commendable "lucidity" and "rhetorical adeptness" (273). I'm not sure how Butler would respond, given her work, to being positioned as "gal," but I do think Birkenstein is onto something when she provides us some really detailed and accessible readings of Butler, illuminating, she claims, for the readers of the article how traditionally rhetorical and academic Butler's writing really is. The trouble here, of course, is in the ways Birkenstein positions Butler's radical ideas as containable in already existing forms. Birkenstein "challenges the idea that difficult academic writing must adopt a form that is, itself, difficult or impenetrable—or, more precisely, that challenging complex academic contents can be conveyed only through writing that itself avoids simple or conventional rhetorical forms" (281). Birkenstein's analysis is fascinating in the ways it reads Butler's sentences closely—something my students and I do as well. But it is also hard not to hear the article as an argument for Graff and Birkenstein's textbook, an argument that explains how to "demystify," as Graff and Birkenstein put it, the "basic moves" of academic writing (1). In this spirit, Birkenstein is more interested in the ways Butler *conforms* to rhetorical canonicity than she is in the ways the shape of her writing might not conform, might prove less linear and tidy than Birkenstein's reading allows. To be clear, I am not (nor do I want my students to be) uninterested in conventional rhetorical moves, but I am more interested in students renaming those forms and inventing new forms as acts of creative and complex cultivation rather than learning to repeat them as basic, repeatable writing formulas and skills.

Sometimes my father let me be his son, let me pour the concrete for the basketball court in the yard, spent all afternoon showing me how to shoot a layup. First, from the right side, which took months. Left right left shoot. Then from the left side, which took years. Right left right shoot. I still can't go to my left in a full-court game.

What I am suggesting here is that composition courses as I imagine them—courses in which reading and writing are at the center of concern—might find value not only in imitation or in learning certain rhetorical moves but in helping students gain a personal, intellectual, theoretical, and operational understanding of the ways in which binary thinking can become a barrier in achieving those "peculiar ways of knowing" that lead to complicated and compelling prose—the kind of writing we hope to write and teach students to compose as well. Moving out beyond the scope of reading and writing practices, I do think that a push on binary thinking is also to move toward multiplicity. And to move toward multiplicity is to live in a world with more possibility, which "is not a luxury; it is as crucial as bread" (Butler, *Undoing* 29).

Eve Kosofsky Sedgwick explains that "that's one of the things that 'queer' can refer to: the open mesh of possibilities, gaps, overlaps, dissonances and resonances, lapses and excesses of meaning where the constituent elements of anyone's gender, of anyone's sexuality aren't made (or *can't be* made) to signify monolithically" (*Tendencies* 8). I am interested in teaching, assignments, and writing that can't be made to "signify monolithically." In other words, the assignments don't *mean* in one way, don't signify singularly. Amanda Cardo's essay is interesting to me in this way; her essay does not "signify monolithically." It instead tries to contend with its multiple significations through a study of language. Cardo focuses, and her sentences reflect, the "lapses and excesses of meaning" that are part of queering. Queer theory, for me, is a useful way of getting to the "lapses and excesses of meaning" to which queer can refer.

The girls' locker room is not safe place for a "girl" like me. And there were only so many times I could cut gym or head off to the Gifted and Talented Reading Group in place of gym. The gym part was humiliating enough, watching the boy students throw baseballs smacking into gloves while the girls' half of the room was lined with step-aerobic boxes. Up and down on the box. The embarrassing music, ending with the locker room, where several of the girls had developed their own language; this enabled them to talk about me at full volume while I pulled the wet shirts from my androgynous body. *Iway earsway e'sshay away uygay* and *Eshay ouldshay otallytay otnay angechay inway erehay*. I later found out this was pig latin. Translations: *I swear she's a guy* and *She should totally not change in here*.

Writing and Consciousness

Teaching is the collective version of meditation. Rare. Occurs in a kind of stillness that moves. Nietzsche's notion of planetary motion: "The wisest man would be the one richest in contradictions, who has, as it were, antennae for all types of men—as well as his great moments of grand harmony—a rare accident even in us! A sort of planetary motion—." How planets spin or even orbit, but are in themselves whole; they give off the appearance of being still. Being awake requires that we detect even the most subtle, the most nuanced movements; it requires that we hold (in our bodies and our minds) open spaces for contradiction, which may, in the end, turn out to be the only truth there is; it requires us to sense that the earth is spinning despite its appearing still.

Students already know what consciousness is or have thought about what it is. I found this out in the first few days of my composition seminar when I asked the question, *What is consciousness?* I was trying to help students understand and read the values in the course description and in my instructor's statement, trying to think with them about definition and possibility. I recorded the following off the board after class. This list was composed entirely by my students:

awareness
lack of ignorance
openness
being ready and alert

actually thinking about what you are doing
receptive
awake
thinking clearly
mobile
living in the moment
fully experiencing
a state of mind where you can join pieces of information and make connections
the ability to respond
educated
a state where the body can respond to stimuli
ability to reflect

We can see, most obviously, from this list that students do equate the notion of consciousness with notions of wakefulness, movement, education, and clear vision—even that some of them associate consciousness with the body response or with reflection. I am very interested, also, in one student's claim about consciousness having something to do with "living in the moment." A kind of historical approach, or ahistorical, depending on how we interpret this response. I understood this student to mean something about being present in the current moment, perhaps even related to what another student said about "fully experiencing." The current moment itself is dissolving, is already fluid. Gadamer writes, "It seems, rather, to be generally characteristic of the emergence of the 'hermeneutical' problem that something *distant* has to be brought close, a certain strangeness overcome, a bridge built between the once and the now" (*Philosophical* 22). I take Gadamer's description of the "hermeneutical problem" to mean that to be in the act of becoming a reader or writer, one must build a bridge between the past and this moment, one must understand oneself as connected to and situated within their histories, bringing that "something distant" (history, their respective selves) closer. I am thinking here about students reading essays on male privilege in 2015 and thinking about the ways in which they see male privilege in 2015 as distinctly different from or separated out from the ways in which male privilege may have functioned in 1915 or 1950. We all read, at times, with historical amnesia. This often prevents the kind of consciousness I hope to achieve when I read, as well as when I guide my students through reading and writing. Cultivating this consciousness is the path through which writers can become aware of their interpretative limits in order to turn them to water. The current moment, of course, is always inextricably linked to the moments that preceded it and the moments that follow. So I try to unpack this notion of "living in the moment" with my students. I ask them if "living in the moment" means being connected to the past or "forgetting the past" in order to be present. We spend a few classes considering this. Something "distant," as Gadamer suggests, needs to be "brought close." History needs to be brought close. The history of gender brought close to the history of our "personal" genders. The linking of a historical and political institution with a life lived.

Many students began to become more versed in ways of discussing gender that were less shaped by the mythologies of binaries. Several students showed up in class with their psychology textbooks from another common introductory course. One of my students, Danielle, made me a photocopy from the chapter titled "The Self." Iggy joked from the back as I looked at it. *If the guys who wrote that textbook were in this class, they'd have called that chapter* "The Selves." We all laugh. As my students became more playful and fluid with their understandings of gender and identity, I wanted to write an assignment that asked students to engage with the limitations of binary thinking by writing about something other than gender and sexuality—not because their writing about these issues was less important but because I had the hunch (or hope) that the work we did together, especially on the holy and sacred gender binary, would be useful in thinking about how to encourage students to, in Bartholomae's words, "try on the peculiar ways of knowing, selecting, evaluating, reporting, concluding, and arguing that define the discourse of our community"—in this case, we might define "community" as a discourse of queer theory, or queer thinking. However, these "peculiar ways of knowing" may or may not become ways of writing. In fact, my students and I struggled with thinking about this distinction between nonbinary thinking and nonbinary writing.

One student, Marie, visited my office hours part way through the semester. She has a question about a comment I made in the margins of her last paper. I had written, rather *unconsciously* perhaps, "So, what's your argument about this?" She wants to know what I mean. She says, sort of frantically, "I thought we weren't supposed to pick one or the other position." It struck me right then that there were so many other words (like *argument*) that, for my students, had binaries built into them. For Marie, to make an argument is to "pick" from two ways to think about, or interpret, what she reads—perhaps to, as she later elaborated, "agree" or "disagree" with an author. I tell Marie the next class will perhaps help her understand my comment. I begin class with the following question: *What is an argument?* Their first responses make me feel guilty for setting the trap. Laura says, *You mean like a fight between two people?* I respond, *Why two?* The class laughs. Jenn tries to re-approach an answer: *It's when you don't agree with something or someone, then you have an argument.* I write *agree* and *fight* on the board. Danielle asks me, *Wait, are you talking about an argument paper?* I ask, *What's an argument paper?* Tearsa says, *Yeah, like before I took this class, I wrote argument papers. But they don't like those in the psychology department either.* The students laugh again. Many of them have their psychology class in common as well. Johnnie kids, *Our high school money is no good here at the college bank.* We all laugh. I ask them whether Kate Bornstein or Michael Warner could be seen as writing long argument papers in the form of books. And they're somewhat stumped at first. *It's hard to know,* says Iggy. *These books are kind of circular, but I guess Michael Warner is arguing things or trying to say certain things.* I ask them, *Do you think it will help to look at a place where Warner* (we had this book with us) *discusses someone else's work to see if he has an argument in the way we're talking about?* They agree and we go searching. We look closely at a place where Warner is quoting from Gayle Rubin's "Thinking Sex." We read it twice. *He's using her,* Johnnie says. A few giggles from the back row. *For what?* I ask. *Like she's some kind of magnifying glass,* he says. The class sighs a sort of amused sigh. They have learned to expect and decode Johnnie's use of metaphor. I do, however, think the idea of the lens is useful and one we would return to. We look for more. We find a number of ways, far more than two, that Warner engages with others' work. We think together about how to imagine these ways as kinds of "argument"—just not the kind where one agrees or disagrees with, say, Gayle Rubin. After all, part of the "peculiar ways of knowing" Bartholomae discusses in "Inventing the University," at least in composition, might mean learning how to move around, fluidly, among other voices, how to make arguments that do something more nuanced, more complicated than agreement or disagreement, how to "try on a variety of voices and interpretive schemes" (Bartholomae 60)—maybe even in the same essay. Some students were already doing this. Some struggled to see it not in Warner but in themselves.

The first time I thought that fluidity in gender might be somehow inextricably linked to fluidity in writing was while reading *A Room of One's Own*, when Virginia Woolf writes that "the androgynous mind is resonant and porous; that it is incandescent and undivided" (98). While it was, I think, part of Woolf's project to position women writers as having nothing to do with womanhood at all in order for these writers to be read and heard *as* writers, there is also more to be done, more to be understood about what her assertion might offer our understanding of what it means to teach writing. But I also hear Woolf saying that the androgynous mind is not a middle point between male and female, or between masculine and feminine, but rather a disruptive and perpetually shifting perspective from which writing (and I would also say teaching) takes place. This perspective exists not between the binary poles of gender but lacks relation to them at all. This refusal is not a reductive humanism; it is, in fact, the enactment of a consciousness in flux, a pedagogy that cannot remain still long enough to be named or fixed. The androgynous mind then is a mind in flux, a mind always at risk of losing itself, remaking itself, a mind seeking to say the unsayable. I am aware of the various ways my own body is implicated in this particular theorizing about the teaching of writing.

In asking students to approach their next essay with a kind of queer sensibility in mind, I tried to be careful in the language of the assignment not to merely ask students to "apply" what they had learned. I tried to communicate the assignment as a kind of moving, or translation, of the course from its context to others—a version of Johnnie Hart's "watery thinking." My students' responses to this assignment seemed to echo and try to grapple with that first discussion of binaries, as well as the coursework that followed, in interesting and generative ways. I am interested in working with the following student excerpts not as models of excellent papers, not as the thoughts of straight students, gay students, and so forth, and not as moments when I can politically critique or expose my students' lack of consciousness. I am interested in working with these excerpts as possibilities for queer pedagogies and as generative moves toward positioning these students' work within the larger context of the project of the course itself. In reading student writing, I often take from Lad Tobin that "[f]rom the moment I started reading drafts for potential rather than for assessment, my relationship to my students and my sense of myself as a writing teacher changed in fundamental and exhilarating ways" (*Reading* 11).

I ask myself, What kind of writing is here? How is the student engaging with the work of the course, with binary thinking, with interrogation of the kind Sedgwick describes above? I begin with a student who struggled in the course overall. An inquisitive student—one who had a difficult time breaking through some of the hollowness, a kind of lack of substance—composed an interesting essay in which she recognizes a moment of schooling that could have helped shape the hollowness I describe. The following is the introduction to her essay, entitled "Binary Blindfold":

> "What side are you on? It's got to be one or the other," my high school government teacher said during a debate on the death penalty. "I'm not sure, somewhere in the middle?" "That just means you don't know what you believe," a helpful classmate told me. Why was it that I had to choose one of these two positions? Does picking one side of an issue mean that you understand it more? Those staunchly for one side of an issue don't necessarily comprehend what they believe. After making a choice as to what they believe, they are relieved of thinking about it. Beliefs can act kind of like a blindfold; you can only know about what you have already seen, so adamant people will just blindly follow what they already chose to believe. Complicated questions never have an easy answer. It's either a woman's right or a baby killing scheme. It's either kill those who kill or side with them. Republican or Democrat. And on and on. (Anonymous Student A 1)

It is not hard to hear the echo of our earlier conversation about Bornstein in class when reading this student's introduction. But she has done far more than repeat that conversation. She has recognized herself in it. She remembers a moment in her education in which binary thinking was being constructed and encouraged. She recalls the power in it—that her classmate points out that to not engage with binary thinking is *not to know* what you believe. Here, it might be useful to think back to Bryson and de Castell's notion that a queer pedagogy means, partly, "*to intervene in the production of so-called normalcy in schooled subjects*" (284, original emphasis). A queer pedagogy, of course, values this classmate's *not to know* as another way of knowing altogether, a way that may not end up meaning *not to know* at all, a failure to know. The student uses this moment in her education to bring her reader to an important moment in her essay. She asks, "Does picking one side of an issue mean that you understand it more?" She engages, here, with a crucial epistemological and hermeneutical question, the question of whether understanding is connected with falling on one or another side of a binary. For example, some students, in their first reading of Bornstein's *Gender Outlaw*, proposed that Bornstein was "just confused" about whether she was a man or a woman. The student quoted here was among those students. But as the context has changed, as she discusses this memory from high school, some new way of knowing, and of writing, seems to emerge. She says those who choose one side or another of an issue then become "relieved of thinking about it." I am interested here in the student's notion that a binary "relieves" us of *thinking*. She proposes here just the opposite *argument* of her classmates' statements of "just confused," because to be relieved of thinking seems, for the student, to end up in *not to know*, the very place she was accused of being in her government class. Only now she begins to imagine the "not to know" as not a lack or deficiency but as a site for productive thinking—as opposed to the solid binary position where others are "relieved of thinking." This, I do think, is a significant shift in epistemology. And for this student, it was also her first time writing an introduction that was striking and fluid in its form *and* content. She is able to consider fluid ideas while composing more fluid prose. Finally, she makes two more quite interesting moves. The first, quite possibly connected to our class interest in and amusement with Johnnie Hart's constant turn to metaphor, is when she writes, "Beliefs can act like a kind of blindfold." She then moves back to refer to the list that she later informed me she had taped to the side of her computer monitor. I sat a long time with this statement about beliefs—partly because it was so interesting to me and partly because the language of "belief" had not directly come up in class. We had spoken of arguments, of opinions, even. But I was struck by what might be implied in "belief" and in how the student might connect it to binary thinking. It seemed she had arrived at the conclusion that to think in a binary way was not to *think* at all, but to *believe*, perhaps in the way we think of religion or morality as "belief." The paper that evolves from this introduction struggles; the writing slips in and out of binary thinking; it, at times, moves seamlessly and, at other times, seems to get stuck.

It's 1984. My father is a Republican and likes to watch Meet the Press *in his blue button pajamas most Sunday mornings. I am seven years old. And every Sunday he asks (as if it were actually possible) which man I will vote for (in this case Walter Mondale or Ronald Reagan). And each week he is more frustrated with my refusal to say. After all, what a parent wants to know is whether you will repeat or resist their compositions of the world. They want to know, early on, what kind of reader and writer you might be. "You have to choose before the country's election day, you know?" he says. What I have been doing, pushing my spoon in and under my Lucky Charms and milk, is an endless wavering. At this age, I hadn't yet pushed on the assumption that I had only two choices, but I did sense that deciding was a kind of mythology, that what we deem "indecisive" is not weakness. I didn't think of myself as weak.*

Later in the paper the student writes, "I question binaries and 'facts' that people 'know.' Just being able to see the binary doesn't always help me avoid slipping into that kind of thinking" (Anonymous Student A 6). This student acknowledges first the difficulty of "slipping into that kind [binary] of thinking" even though she is aware of it; she is able to see herself as moving in and out of binary thinking. I encourage her in my comments to notice which moments she seems most attached or most likely to "slip" into this binary thinking. I ask her to think about the metaphor of "slipping." What is she slipping on? What happens when we slip? Is it connected to balance? What do those connections tell her about writing? She ends the paper by saying, "As to talking with my friends about this, I just recommend that they take this class to see what it is about. 'But is it a good class or bad class?' they might want to know" (6). Not only do I appreciate this student's sense of playfulness and humor at the close of her essay, I also value how she has, through the image of telling others about our class, captured the very problem itself—the problem of slippage. In this sense, all of us can tend to slip on the very fluidity we are trying to value.

I think about my father, there in the living room, a stone of interpretation. He nods when Reagan speaks. He says, "What a wussy," referring to Mondale, who wears blue suits, which my father sees as, and I quote, "pretty boy" and "fashion queen." What would it have taken to ask this father to lift out from his body, from his suburban house and color television, in order to be able to see himself not reading, not risking? What is at stake for him? What is at stake for all of us? We live in a culture that sees wavering as weakness. You need only to look at the current discourse around election season to see this—who is a flip-flopper, who is worse than a flip-flopper. There was even a website during the 2008 election, "bothwaysbarack.com," whereupon visiting you could read that it is impossible to hold two positions at once, that both at once-ness (a kind of androgyny of its own) is a betrayal of strength and decisiveness.

Another student tries to engage this assignment in another way. Her essay entitled "Did I Say That?" functions as a kind of retrospective about her writing thus far in the course. The object this student understood as "outside the study of sexuality and gender" was her own writing in the course. So, this paper, while it quoted from several of her own writings *about* gender and sexuality, was about her former papers. She begins her essay with a discussion she borrows from her psychology class about "parapraxis," which she defines as "errors in speech due to the unconscious mind" (Anonymous Student B 1). She writes, "We try to hide some feelings and opinions, but if we feel strongly about them and are not carefully monitoring what we are saying or writing, they can be revealed" (1). The student moves forward to examine closely one moment in her own writing and then one moment of interaction with a friend. While the student seems to still be moving through what "parapraxis" means or what moments might count as such a thing, she makes a compelling, and self-implicating, interrogation of something she had written during the very first in-class writing prompt in September. She writes,

> My sentence said something along the lines of, "When my mother uses the word queer to describe me, I do not believe she is *accusing* me of being a lesbian." If I had considered this sentence more carefully, I probably would have revised it or taken it out of my paper. I don't consider myself homophobic, or anything, but I think this revealed my feelings that being a lesbian would be something to be accused of. Normally we get accused of crimes: things that are wrong. (2)

First, this student is engaged with the binary in a very different sense, and certainly less direct sense, than the prior student. The spaces she is moving between, the binary she is trying to move around inside, is a binary of the self. The excerpt above, in a sense, is the student wondering about, moving around in whether she is homophobic or not. She is aware that thinking of lesbianism as something to be *accused* of is something that she might have wanted to "take out" of the paper she had written. But she is also aware that she doesn't "consider [herself] homophobic." Of course, for her or for me to solidly answer this question would be to go against the very request of the assignment and would be more in line with the "subverting homophobia" kinds of goals outlined by Harriet Malinowitz in the 1990s. I am aware, as I am writing this, that her comment about not being homophobic can be read as that cliché, "I'm not homophobic but . . . I am about to say something homophobic" (a way of reading in line with the Bryson and de Castell reading of their students at the start of this paper). But I want to offer this student far more credit than that. She uses the assignment as a pathway through which she interrogates the self. This is no small task, and it comes with potentially great risks for her. She is aware of her instructor's queerness, of the two self-identified queer students in the class; she is aware that a homophobic viewpoint would probably not be of value in class, but she still makes an effort to understand her own homophobia—to understand that she could both not consider herself homophobic and yet speak in the language of someone who is; this person is, of course, also herself. Binary thinking could never arrive here at this paper. It could never produce a contradictory self. This paper does. She writes later in the paper, "When we accidentally let one of our hidden opinions come out in our writing or speech, we have made a mistake in revealing it but not in thinking it" (5). I sat quite some time with this sentence, feeling at first a kind of resistance to it. Of course, it's a mistake to think of lesbianism as something to be accused of. But as I read it again, it occurs to me how complicated the statement is in the sense that *thinking* cannot be a mistake in the same way that *revealing* our thoughts through speech or writing can. The thinking is more automatic, less deliberate, not always of our own control. In a sense it does seem from our work in this course that queer pedagogies may construct the spaces through which *thinking* can become less automatic, spaces where students can intervene in their own thinking, spaces without which alternative ways of knowing cannot develop or emerge.

It is useful here to consider a student who struggled with the course because the nonbinary thinking was not something that intrigued her but rather something that repelled her in a sense. Her thinking, to use Johnnie Hart's term, was resistant to becoming "watery." It remained a kind of stone. She writes, "Nothing really happens to me when I read Bornstein. Her or his ideas are too far out to do anything to me" (Anonymous Student B 2). Of course, the text has already "done" something to this student. We can notice first that when referring to Bornstein she uses the possessive pronoun "her or his"—knowing that the writer formerly named Al has transitioned to Kate and that the class had settled on calling Bornstein by the pronoun the author suggests she prefers at this time: *she*. The text has caused the student to become stone, to become the reader who cannot be moved or repositioned. This student's response is brief and continues in much the same way throughout. I could, of course, situate the student as not having completed the assignment by claiming that "nothing happens" (something that students might see as not a "valid" answer in the course), but in a sense, "nothing" is something that happens. The question this student never gets to hear herself ask (at least in this piece) is, Why is nothing happening? She puts this "nothing" on Bornstein, citing her ideas as "too far out to do anything" to her. In the endnote, I write,

> I agree with you that Bornstein's ideas seem very far out in terms of what we are all used to with regard to gender. I am less interested in the "far out-ness" of Bornstein's ideas and more interested in the "nothing" that is happening to you. For me, when someone is saying something that seems far-fetched or over the top, I do feel things and think things that aren't nothing. Is that true for you? Can you try to further investigate this stance you are taking?

Is this the part where I tell you that next week this student says, "Oh yes, I see what I am doing now. I am attached to my binary thinking"? Instead, she focuses her final course reflection on neutrality. She explains, "I have been mostly neutral about gender. While other students spend a lot of time arguing, I think it's best to stay neutral." And something startles me about this language of neutrality and about how a student could walk out the doors of this particular course feeling neutral; after all, I had tried to disrupt them, to provide a safe classroom for discomfort. Then she says, in her final sentence, "This class certainly makes you think about what's out there and how there's always more than you think and how scared people are of whatever it is. Terrible things happen when people are scared." I notice something I noticed in that "nothing is happening" response—the metaphor of distance. Everything is "far out" or "out there." There is nothing "right here" for the student to touch; yet, still she gestures at understanding. She mentions the "terrible things" she has learned can happen in the name of binary thinking. She does not, however, imagine human beings or specific identities or ideas "out there." She only imagines "whatever it is." I am interested in this student's writing not at all as a failure of queer pedagogy, of course, but as an instance of gesturing toward the possible, even as she resists it; the student knows there are possibilities. She does not, however, go on to articulate them. Because she does not articulate them, she is not writing the un-writable, or imagining (at least not in her writing) what these possibilities might mean for her or for others. She is not yet entirely aware of how "what's out there" might enable further possibilities for her thinking, her reading or writing. When the exercise of nonbinary and complicated thinking is still "far out" and "out there," it is difficult to imagine, or even frightening to imagine. So we look at it only a few steps from where we began. And sometimes that's as "far" as we are able to go. From that distance, we can only hear so much.

I never did decide between Mondale and Reagan. I never did finish interpreting Meet the Press, *though I am sure I might be ready now. At my father's funeral, all his friends say how sturdy he was, how predictable and sound. It would be a lot to ask anyone to risk this—to make his being vulnerable, to leave it out overnight in winter to see if it will freeze, or crack. In this way, the risk is terrifying because always lurking behind the act is the possibility that what we know about ourselves, about the world, is fragile, fragmented, or not made of dualisms. And we do not always know what will happen then unless we can manage to do it once, and then recover, rebuild, and re-imagine.*

I am acutely aware, as I try to understand the work of this course and the specific mergings of queer theory and composition in the classroom, of the difficulties of the project I have undertaken. So often, after reading texts on critical, feminist, and some other radical pedagogies, I find myself not only looking for the student writing in those texts but also looking for its specific connections to the teaching of composition. And primarily, I continue to look to my students for these answers. Binary thinking is built into not only our thinking about gender but, as I learned from my students, also into our thinking about *thinking* and about writing. My students repeatedly reminded me that their binary understandings of gender were "actual and present," but they were endlessly willing, in their writing and thinking, to move into that "realm of possibility," to develop new ways of thinking about gender. And for the students to be able to imagine their identities, and others', as more fluid, more like water than they might have thought, made it all that much easier to imagine writing this way as well.

A queer pedagogy for composition cannot necessarily be understood as or developed by "applying" queer theory to the composition classroom; it seems more than those connections arise out of the practice. My students are still telling me, each time I move through the course documents, transcripts, and discussion boards, what queer pedagogies allow, what writing might turn to water in my hands. In returning both to the epigraph and to the metaphor my student, Johnnie Hart, offers in his response to the course, I hope to highlight the ways in which we all need a kind of striving to "be like water," or, as Hart puts it, our thinking might "become watery." It is not something to be achieved or arrived at but a way of moving toward a kind of moving, a becoming.

CHAPTER FIVE

QUEER (RE)VISIONS OF COMPOSITION

Queerness is not yet here. Queerness is an ideality. Put another way, we are not yet queer. We may never touch queerness, but we can feel it as the warm illumination of a horizon imbued with potentiality. We have never been queer, yet queerness exists for us as an ideality that can be distilled from the past and used to imagine a future. The future is queerness's domain. Queerness is a structuring and educated mode of desiring that allows us to see and feel beyond the quagmire of the present.

José Esteban Muñoz, *Cruising Utopia: The Then and There of Queer Futurity*

Whereas the critic would strive to sort art works into genres and periods, the remixer would seek to creatively recombine disparate materials—to make a new composition by juxtaposing samples from radically disparate artistic traditions and periods.

Jason Palmeri, *Remixing Composition: A History of Multimodal Writing Pedagogy*

The Problem of Structure

In third grade, I had a teacher named Mr. Schellhorn. I distrusted him, my first male teacher—his dark mustache, his hard full chest and thick-rimmed glasses. I never raised my hand to lead the class during the singing of "John Brown Jalopy." I didn't raise my hand to turn the pages of afternoon stories. No matter how hard the other children laughed at his character voices, no matter how many times he praised my drawings and even my terrible handwriting, I would not budge. I would not, as it were, love him. Then the science fair. And I hate the other students—their maps of constellations lighting up on cardboard, their mud mound volcanoes erupting over desktops. I don't want to make anything. I don't want anything to explode or light up. I don't want the bad-smelling oak tag, the construction paper dry against my fingers. I would rather make up math problems while sitting on the radiator. For a few days, Mr. Schellhorn leaves me there. He doesn't ask what my project will be. But by the time the light-up planets begin to show he's back there with black construction paper and a handful of orange tissue paper. He folds the black paper in half and cuts for what feels like a half hour, moving the big "teacher scissors" in curves and inside-out holes. And when he opens the paper, it's wings. He glues the orange tissue paper behind them. "It's a monarch butterfly," he says. "They are perfectly symmetrical. Do you know what symmetrical means?" I'm still not budging. "I don't care," I answer, directing my stare through the back window toward the school lot, where the cars are lined up in a green blur. I do care. I want to know what symmetry means. I like the sound of it, how his teeth joined at the s, his lips touching at the m and curling together to end on the -try of the word. I do love him, you understand. I make five more butterflies when he goes. As for symmetry, the dictionary said, "match exactly."

In some ways, the title of this chapter is a contradiction. By definition, the moment I say what it might mean to "write like a queer" or "write in a queer way," the terms and definitions would shift. "Queer" works like a sheet of ice—whatever we put there slips and slides and becomes impossible to pin down for more than a temporary moment. I hope my own meditations on teaching and writing to be one of those temporary moments, a moment when, while the ice remains ice, we might slow down the slippage enough to look closely at what it makes possible for the teaching of writing. Amy E. Winans contends, "Crafting a queer pedagogy entails disrupting binary models of sexuality [and gender] in ways that engage with power, rather than obscuring such models within a language of tolerance with which we might seek to 'cure' homophobic students" (106). I think that one aspect of pedagogies that might call themselves "queer" is to disrupt these models of power, in particular those models of gender and sexuality that confine our identities and our abilities to see more complex webs of possibilities as thinkers. However, one thing that can get left out, or at times tagged onto the end of discussions of queer pedagogies, is the connection to our primary project as teachers of composition—that project being to teach students to write. I am perpetually interested in the question, What might the concerns of queer theory bring to the surface for students in terms of writing itself?

Or, put another way, What might queer pedagogies make visible or possible in the teaching of writing as an art form, skill, process, and way of thinking? I use all of these descriptors to characterize writing because I believe writing *is* all of these things at the same time, or can be.

I did try to be a real girl. In the eighth grade I swore, to my father's new wife, that I would give up my brother's old jeans, that I would stop swearing, that I would blow dry my hair in the mornings and stop tucking it back underneath what she and my father called a "ball cap." I couldn't bear it very many days. The kids at school were not so willing to let me change identities before their eyes. "You look weird," Greg Blackstein said. "Where's your Yankees hat?" Jodie Lipkin asked. They wanted to know where I had gone. They wanted the rules of my old identity, one I didn't so much shed as I left back at the house, tucked away, where it was safe.

To think about these questions again, in another way, I want to offer an account of two class meetings. The students, at this point in the course, were reading Michael Warner's *The Trouble with Normal: Sex, Politics, and the Ethics of Queer Life*, a book that attempts to trouble all forms of normativity and includes Warner's opposition to gay marriage, discussions of Bill Clinton's sex scandal and New York City's zoning laws with regard to sex toy shops, and an in-depth analysis of how sexual shame operates. As someone concerned with queer pedagogies, I am interested in my students considering Warner's ideas about normativity and queer thinking. However, I am also deeply invested in what my students can learn about writing as they consider the relation of normativity to writing itself *and* the relation of Warner's ideas to his writing style. On this particular day, during this class meeting, I began casually, not really even imagining that class had begun, just by asking them what they thought of Warner's book.

As she sits down in the front row, Laura says, *This book drives me a little crazy, he talks in circles.* "That's an interesting analysis of Warner," I say. "What makes you say 'circles'?" It appears that Laura is still relaxed. She usually doesn't talk much in class, but possibly because it seems like class hasn't officially started yet, she offers an explanation: "He just keeps looping back to the same stuff over and over and then changing it. I get all confused a lot. I mean, essays are supposed to have structure, at least that's what I learned." By this time, if I remember right, most of the students have arrived. I say, "Laura and I have just been talking about writing structure." They all sigh a bit, as would I if a teacher had said that to me. Who wants to talk about structure? It's all so boring and rule driven and formulaic. At least that's what I thought in my own high school and early college years. I ask them, "Who knows something about structuring an essay?" Johnnie raises his hand. "I don't know if I know anything," he says, "but I can tell you what I've been told." "Yes, tell me," I say. "Tell me everything you have been told." Johnnie says, "An essay's gotta be organized, and this guy isn't really organized as far as I can tell. I mean, that's why Laura said he . . . what'd you say? . . . he talks around stuff over and over." Tearsa raises her hand and asks, "Shouldn't books just be a longer version of essays? If Michael Warner took the state test on writing I took, he'd get a big fat zero." They all laugh a bit. "How do you get a high score on one of those tests?" I ask. Kelsey says, "You follow the five-paragraph flowchart." "What's that?" I ask. "Is it an actual chart? Can you draw it for me?" I hand Kelsey the chalk. She goes to the board and draws five boxes, each connected by a line, and numbers them.

Figure 5.1. Numbered boxes

Danielle chimes it, "I thought it was supposed to be the funnel method." I ask Danielle if she can draw that model. She goes to the board and draws a funnel, wide on the top and skinny on the bottom.

Figure 5.2. The funnel method #1

Johnnie adds, "I think it's supposed to get wide again at the end. I prompt him to the board, and he draws another upside down funnel next to Danielle's. We all pause a moment, looking at the two drawings—one a series of boxes connected by "think" lines, the other an image of two funnels pressed together at their tips.

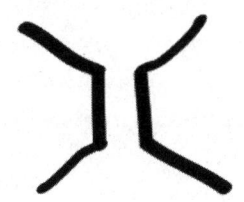

FIGURE 5.3. The funnel method #2

"Okay," I said, "if you had to draw a model of Warner's or Butler's writing, what kind of model would you draw?" (Butler was someone who, they said, also seemed to talk "in circles.") "Iggy, you draw it. What do you think it looks like?" Iggy walks slowly to the board, probably because I have just put him on the spot to do something that seems impossible to do. Iggy draws a sort of looping pattern on the board, circles crossing over and into one another.

FIGURE 5.4. Looping pattern

Kelsey says, "That's not really that different from the flowchart. Those lines are meant to connect the paragraphs just like those overlaps are supposed to." I am fascinated by what's on the board and by the possibilities it begins to offer in talking with students about structure, about how an essay is "structured." I respond, "You say it's not *that* different; does that mean it is slightly different?" "Well, yeah," she says. "How?" I ask. Johnnie offers that *lines are different kinds of connectors than overlaps*. "Different how?" I ask. *Well, lines are,* he laughs, *linear, you know, like straight thin things, like in a line.* "And . . . ," I push him a bit further. *And overlaps are,* he laughs again, *overlaps.* I am compassionate and, of course, amused by this struggle—not because I am above my students' struggle to name what we are seeing here, but because my students and I, at this moment, are having the same struggle—the same difficulty in articulating what a writer *does* (performance) rather than what a writer *says* (content). We go on, in our discussion, trying to describe the differences in these models. Students notice that, in what they started calling the "Warner Model" of loops and overlaps, it seems like the writing begins anywhere, at a sort of arbitrary point. Then Johnnie says, "It's arbitrary, but not." Tearsa says at one point, trying to illuminate how the overlaps are different from lines, "Warner's model is like a revise-as-you-go kinda thing."

We spend this class meeting and the next trying to describe Warner's model, to articulate his structure. The students also describe the five-paragraph flowchart, noting its thin linear connections, its "boxed-in" content. We talk about what it might mean for the "funnel" method to "boil a subject down" and then broaden it out again. We were, in some ways, talking about form and containment. And to write like a queer, at this moment, temporarily and problematically, meant to write like Warner or Butler, to write like a queer theorist, to write in a series of loops and overlaps that begin and end in a seemingly "arbitrary, but not" place. Students noted Warner's movement in terms of how his books move, how his chapters move, and also (more locally) how his paragraphs move. This particular paragraph from the opening pages of Warner's book became a dynamic part of their discussions:

> It might as well be admitted that sex is a disgrace. We like to say nicer things about it: that it is an expression of a love, or a noble endowment from the Creator, or liberatory pleasure. But the possibility of abject shame is never entirely out of the picture. If the camera doesn't cut away at the right moment, or if the door is thrown open unwontedly, or the walls turn out to be too thin, all the fine dress of propriety and pride will be found tangled around one's ankles. In the fourth century B.C., the Athenian philosopher Diogenes thought that the sense of shame was hypocrisy, a denial of our appetitive nature, and he found a simple way to dramatize the problem: he masturbated in the marketplace. Many centuries of civilization have passed since then, but this example is not yet widely followed. (2)

What someone might notice first about this passage is the "scandalous" nature of Warner's content, and students certainly pointed out their surprise at the "he masturbated in the marketplace" line, and a few students even suggested that perhaps an academic "shouldn't talk like this." But I tried to steer the conversation to form and movement, asking students to consider *how* Warner moves and not just *what* he says. It's at this point that the idea students called "arbitrary but not" came more directly into play. I asked my students to generate with me a list of subjects and objects, in order, that appear in this passage. As a class, we formed a list of Warner's subjects and objects in order in this passage, and the final list on the board was as follows:

Sex
Love, God, pleasure
Shame, camera, door, walls
Pants around your ankles
Fourth-century [BCE] philosopher
Human nature, masturbation
All of civilization

Students noted that the list itself was surprising, that some of the things on this list seemed connected already, and that some of the objects and subjects were more unpredictable. For example, the camera, door, and walls, and a fourth-century BCE philosopher were subjects and objects students said they "did not associate" with sex. Johnnie says, "Yeah, that's exactly what I meant by 'arbitrary but not.'" Danielle replies, "It's sort of like creative writing, like you have things in there to make the ideas like things you can see, because you can't see ideas, so the pants around the ankles thing really gives you the feeling of being 'caught with your pants down' instead of just saying it's embarrassing." Johnnie notes, "Some philosophers and stuff could stand to do that more—when it's all ideas you get all floaty and lost."

Even the bones in the human body are made primarily of water.

In the class meeting that followed, I told students to compose their next essay assignment using Warner's model as the structure or "formula." Marie asks as we are ending class, "So we write our own way, but we write within a model?" *Yes,* I said, as though I were some mysterious Zen master who puts his shoes on his head and walks out of the room. I must admit to not liking myself when I do this. It's a cop-out. It's because writing is impossible and possible to teach. It's because I both can and cannot teach them to do it. It's because I both know and do not know how to write myself. These contradictions are another reason I find queer theory and queer methodologies to be so compatible with writing and the teaching of writing: queer theory is always in the business of contradictions and paradoxes. Paradox and contradiction are the conditions under which writing is structured. It is our burden to find a way to teach students to write under these conditions whereby both their agency *and* their writing is, to return to Judith Butler's language, "riven with paradox."

Moving Like a Queer

Before students took on this difficult challenge of structuring their essays in the "Warner Model," I wanted to spend more time in class discussion considering with them the moves Warner makes as a writer more broadly. I asked them to pay attention to his moves, to try to mimic or imitate them in their own writing. This is a similar project to the one Mariolina Salvatori describes when she writes, "I try to teach readers to become conscious of their mental moves, to see what such moves produce, and to learn to revise or to complicate those moves as they return to them in light of their newly constructed awareness of what those moves did or did not make possible" ("Conversations" 447). Salvatori connects this awareness of reading to the work of writing, contending that the more aware a *reader* becomes of these "mental moves," the more aware this reader becomes of her moves *as a writer*. In class, we generated a list of things Warner does as a reader of texts in his writing—his mental moves, so to speak. Here is a partial sample of the students' list:

- Qualifies like crazy
- Lots of dashes and commas
- Uses humor, or sarcasm
- Mixes personal private matters with public ones
- Uses "I"
- Circles back to the same stuff
- Quotes all kinds of sources, not just academic ones

This list became the list of moves they were to imitate in their writing for the next essay assignment. I have included below the essay assignment corresponding to this challenge to structure their essays using the "Warner Model":

> Michael Warner tells us that a "statistical norm has no moral value" (70). He spends several pages (53–60) interrogating the use of statistics as a pathway to normalcy and shame. He proposes his own theory about the way sexual statistics work. Re-read these pages in Warner, marking up the places you find most interesting or provocative. Type out all these places on a sheet of paper—places where Warner calls your attention to something specific (maybe something you had never thought of) about statistics. Try to get a list of 8–12 quotes. Print them out. Then maybe eat a sandwich. Then take the sheet with you to a computer and do some research. Start looking up any statistics you can find about sex, gender, or sexual behavior, etc. As you look at the statistics you find, think about how those statistics reflect or seem to be in conversation with Warner. Choose one set of statistics. Provide me with the link to the website where the statistics can be found. Then answer the following: What do the statistics want you to believe? How can you tell? What kind of language is used to talk about the statistics? How do you put these statistics into conversation with Warner? (In other words, use the quotes from Warner and close-read the quotes *and* the statistics in your paper.) Finally, has Warner changed the ways you imagine what statistics do, or what they are?

I want to turn now to a piece of writing that came out of this essay assignment using the "Warner Model" and using some of Warner's moves. The day students turned in these papers, I asked them to answer three questions and to write their answers on the back of their papers. My questions were written using language from our discussion, language the students themselves had generated to describe the structure of Warner's writing. My questions were the following: (1) *At what point did you begin "arbitrarily, but not"?* (2) *What do you loop back to and change (or revise) each time you looped back?* (3) *At what point did you end arbitrarily, but not?* One of my students, Jessica Poli, whose paper I have excerpted below and whose permission I have to share both her name and work, gave the following answers: (1) Began with being a virgin. (2) Looped back again and again to statistics. (3) Ended with not buying sunscreen. Her answers seem an unlikely trio, a set of disconnected subjects, but it is fascinating to watch Poli enact her version of Warner's structure, making this unlikely trio a structural delight—arbitrary, but not. Below are excerpts from the beginning, middle, and end of her essay, "Sex in Numbers":

> I've never had sex, and apparently I'm a part of a whopping 20% of girls who haven't before they turned 19. Since we've all mastered at least our high school Integrated Algebra class, we know this means that 80% of girls are sexually active before 19. In Michael Warner's *The Trouble with Normal*, he writes in reference to statistics, "People have come to rely on these numbers in evaluating the validity of their own sex lives" (54). Oh no, it's happening. I'm reevaluating my entire lack of a sexual life. Someone get me a big slice of hunky boy love because I can't go on, I NEED SEX NOW! This thinking is part of a theory Warner invites us to explore with him—that statistics are often mistaken for standards, and that we wrongly use these statistics to form judgments on our own behaviors.
>
> The National Coalition for the Protection of Children and Families is an organization whose goal is to educate others about their code of sexual ethics based on the Bible. They are against premarital sex, pornography, gay marriage, and unmarried couples cohabitating. Even without knowing the organization's purpose or values, however, you could probably get the gist of their attitude just by reading the set of statistics they put together for their website, www.nationalcoalition.org. Here are some of the examples of statistics they offer, all of which support a part of their values they try to place in their message. "Married people are healthier than other adults." So, get hitched as soon as possible or you might catch a cold—an interesting spin on encouraging people to get married. "For every ten men in church, five are struggling with pornography." I now have this very unfortunate mental image of five men sitting in church pews with *Playboy* tucked inside their Bibles . . . *struggling*. Because pornography is obviously some deathly affliction that we have to ward off. "Cohabitating couples have twice the break up rate of married couples." Why buy the cow when the milk is free? The statistic clearly shows that the Coalition is against cohabitating couples. "Up to 20% of couples now report that they have sex no more than ten times a year, qualifying them for what experts call a 'sexless marriage.'" Who are these experts, and what exactly is their expertise? Do they sit in an armchair with a pen and paper in a married couple's bed-

room, waiting anxiously to see if they have sex? This statistic shows that the Coalition is actually all for sex—as long as it's not outside of marriage.

The language used in these statistics feeds into an attitude the Coalition conveys. Men are "struggling" with pornography, as if it's an addiction they're sent to rehab to beat. Speaking of addictions, another statistic claims, "One out of every six women grapples with addiction to pornography." The word "grapple" is used the same way "struggle" was, to make it seem as if watching pornography is something that must be overcome. I'm also curious as to what they would say an addiction was—do these addicted men and women watch porn once a day, twice a day, three times a day? How much does it interfere with their lives? Do they forget to feed their children because they're so busy watching *Naughty Nurses VII*? Pornography is often treated as if it were an unhealthy habit that needs to be stopped. In the case of the Coalition, they treat it this way because they believe it violates their morals. I've seen a couple naughty nurses videos, and I don't think I'm going to Hell, but the Coalition might have a different opinion.

Poli's essay continues and closes with the following:

What the Coalition is doing with their statistics is very interesting when thinking about Warner's position. They are using statistics to back up their morals, to raise awareness of their message. The statistic itself, however, does no work in creating or supporting morals—it is only a measurement of what *some* people *say* they do. Warner is a pretty clever guy. To me, "Statistics" was a boring high school math class, statistics were fun facts that I could sometimes use in a speech to prove a point. But if I listen to Warner, I'm now skeptical, not necessarily of statistics themselves, but of how people use them, why they're using them, and what they're trying to make me think by using them. The idea of blindly following statistical standards as a way of attaining normalcy is new to me. When I've looked at statistics in the past, I must admit I've done a fair bit of comparison between the numbers and myself, and questioned, to some extent, how normal I was based on those numbers. I'm not so sure I'll do that again. Is every statistic just a pathway to the golden gates of Normalville, where houses line the streets in identical rows, all the grass is half an inch high and the sun shines all day? I think so, and I am definitely not rushing off to buy any sunscreen.

What I find interesting about Poli's essay is the compelling voice and surprising movements Warner's "structure" seemed to allow or encourage in her writing. She experiments with humor and sarcasm, mixes the personal and the public, deploys a narrative "I," and uses dashes, circling back. In contrast, I have described her prior papers as stiffer, more "structured" even, more contained. Working in a new structure, a new set of possibilities with a new name, Poli is able to disrupt some of her normative conceptions of essays, to write not inside a container, but beside a non-normative model that queer theory brings into view.

Revision is not easy—revision of the self, revision of writing. When I reread the stories of my past through the eyes of my sixteen-year-old self writing in a notebook, working through the revision of the self in writing, I was the tourist in a gendered village. I left these notebooks out around the house for anyone to see. If one of my parents or siblings ever read a single word, they never said so.

After reading many of the students' papers that attempted to "follow" the "Warner Model," I began to think differently myself about structures, recalling something Judith Butler writes about in *Undoing Gender*: norms themselves don't do violence. In fact, she says, we need norms to live and live well. But what we *do* with norms—how we form and enforce their power—is the important question. Jessica Poli's essay calls this question to my attention when she writes about the problematic use of statistics and their troubling relationship to normativity. She writes that it's not the statistics themselves but *how people use them, why they're using them, and what they're trying to make me think by using them.* Likewise, I wonder if the funnel method and the five-paragraph essay, as norms themselves, are not responsible for the possible reductions that seem connected to their containment. Perhaps it is my own thinking about these structures—how I imagine what they are doing and why or how I enforce their authority as a teacher—that's causing the forms to *appear* to fail or to seem like formal failures.

Mr. Schellhorn shows me an anatomical diagram of dolphin. I remember its heart, and I remember him leaning in and saying, "They don't breathe automatically. They have to remember to do it. Imagine if you could forget to breathe." It stays with me for months. And that afternoon I feel short of breath, overly attuned to the movement of my lungs, unable to stop my mind from focusing on my breathing—suddenly perpetually aware of the nuances of my breath, its complicated rise and fall.

As a writing teacher, I am responsible for teaching my students about structure, about the shapes composition can take. And perhaps one of the things writing in queer theory offers to student writers and to writing teachers is the opportunity to imagine, describe, and invent alternative structures—ones that encourage and evoke (for me and for my students) movement rather than containment, ones that value shapes that are not necessarily linear, ones that are messier perhaps, ones that are "arbitrary, but not." Structure is not, as it turns out, the enemy, but what I do with structure as a teacher of writing is what matters. How might we rethink or revolutionize structure? How might we build new systems of organization guided by queerer, more fluid and flexible principles? Karen Kopelson asserts, "A queer . . . pedagogy often strives to confuse, as it strives to push thought beyond circumscribed divisions—strives to push thought beyond what can be thought" ("Dis/Integrating" 20). In my class, what we called the "Warner Model" temporarily caused confusion and then "[pushed] our thoughts beyond what could be thought" by opening up the possibility of new structures for thinking and writing. Writing queer might mean thinking of structure as thin, wet, queer ice, temporary and unstable. It means, as Jessica Poli writes, to begin with virginity, to loop around to statistics over and over, and to end by not buying the sunscreen.

Confusion and disorientation are not strangers to some compositionists, as I have discussed in earlier chapters. I want to highlight here how confusion is already a part of our thinking about teaching writing and how queer theory and queer methodologies might offer a particular kind of confusion—one that can be embodied and practiced by students and teachers alike. For example, James Slevin reminds us in *Introducing English*, "Allowing ourselves as teachers to become confused in the face of students' questions and needs is perhaps the best thing we can do to become their teachers. Embracing this kind of disorientation seemed then, and still seems today, at the heart of composition's work, especially as it makes possible the critical examination of any discipline's intellectual 'canon of methods'" (32).

Slevin takes his term "canon of methods" from Robert Scholes's *The Rise and Fall of English*, and in some ways this book pushes on the boundaries of the "canon of methods" used to teach, describe, and evaluate writing. And while Slevin refers to the "canon of methods" teachers of writing have used in composition, I think this critical examination applies to any teacher's individual "canon of methods" as well. For me, queer pedagogies are about a constant experimenting with and reinventing the "canon of methods" I have used as a teacher. Both my students and I needed to examine and reconsider our "canon of methods," even as their canon and mine might, at times, be of different sorts.

Certainly imitation is part of a long tradition of methods used by writers and writing teachers. But I think it is worth considering who and what are students imitating and why. Confusion and disorientation as concepts are not the property of queer theory or queer pedagogies. Slevin is not a queer theorist but a scholar and teacher of composition I have long admired. Kopelson's notion of confusion is informed primarily by queer theory, offering us a lens through which to radicalize confusion, to face its danger, its risk, and its undeniable connection to embodied writers and lived experience. I teach in the spirit of disorientation; I write in that same spirit. I agree wholeheartedly, but queerly, with Slevin, that I need to "become confused" in order to be a good teacher. In the same way, I am asking students to "become confused" to be "better" writers. Jacqueline Rhodes reminds us, in her video essay, that "[q]ueer teaching involves deliberately courting paradox and discomfort, for your students and for yourself."

In any one body, there are two types of muscle: voluntary skeletal muscles and involuntary smooth muscles. In this sense, only some movement is about choice.

Scavenger Writer

Mr. Schellhorn had a habit of taking me (or any other kid exhibiting behaviors that indicated a rough patch) for walks, leaving the teacher's aide to manage the classroom. When one of the "real girls" in the classroom exclaims loudly that I have hair on my neck, Mr. Schellhorn redirects her to practicing her times tables. Let's take a walk, champ! he says, patting my back. I follow him to the courtyard. We walk together along the chain-link fence, looking into the backyards of houses that lined the grounds of the school. Let's collect things, he says. And we pick up oak leaves, twigs, wrappers tossed along the path. I gather some pebbles in the front pocket of my hooded sweatshirt. We bring the collection back, leaving the items on the activity tables. We'll use these, he says.

When Halberstam describes queer methodology as "attempts to combine methods that are often cast as being at odds with each other," we are asked to consider the possibility that we might write in ways that go against each other, write in ways that purposefully create tension and friction, write in ways that "refuse the academic compulsion toward disciplinary coherence" (*Female* 13). On some level, many of us in composition already encourage this kind of writing when we ask students, for example, to try writing essays *outside* their five-paragraph training, or when we try to complicate our students' writing rules (rules like *don't shift tenses* or *never use the first person in a critical essay*). We know when we trouble these writing rules, students can feel off balance or hesitant about how to approach their writing if these kinds of structures are removed or not needed. So we can likely all imagine what might happen if we asked students to (on purpose) draw from sources that *don't* fit together, to write in multiple modes in the same piece of writing, to switch tenses on purpose, to "creatively recombine disparate materials" (Palmeri 13), to, essentially, disrupt every basic assumption about writing they (and many writers) have. Here, I am reminded again of Halberstam, in the introduction to *Female Masculinity*: a "queer methodology is . . . a scavenger methodology, that uses different methods to collect and produce information" (13). I deploy this quote in the introduction to this book in thinking through my own writing, but I also became interested, through my work in queer pedagogy, in discovering how I might engage my students with a scavenger approach.

I know, in composition studies, we have used many terms to think about the act of blurring genres: collage, hybrid text, mixed genre. We have deployed many interesting and generative terms to describe multimodal writing, like Palmeri's "remixing." We have ignited terms with which to imagine our field and our work within it—like Shari Stenberg's "repurposing" or Geoffrey Sirc's "happening." In current queer theory, we might understand overlaps and intersections as taking on new meaning with work like Jasbir K. Puar's—work that would offer the term "assemblage" as a way of thinking through methodological approaches to the complex matrixes of identity. Recently, in composition, we find Patricia Suzanne Sullivan's *Experimental Writing in Composition: Aesthetics and Pedagogies* (2012), which offers both theoretical and historical views of composition's relationship to experimentation with writing. Sullivan's book and so much of the work above *are*, indeed, ways of thinking about what I describe, though the scope of these projects does not intend to think through queer politics and queer theory as having a bearing on how we think about forms of writing.

At a young age, I was always looking for alternative forms. It was hard to find models, to find adults who I wished to be, to imagine myself growing up into anything besides beaten into submission. But I never stopped looking, and I did find models—UPS women, softball coaches, rule breakers. One has to know where to look to find oneself.

The reason I choose, in the end, to engage Halberstam's term "scavenger methodology" is twofold. First, the scavenger method implies there *is* a scavenger, an agent who looks, seeks, and writes. Even the "scavenger hunt," which is the most familiar way that many of us imagine the term, has agents who participate. And, second, the scavenger hunt is a kind of game, which doesn't mean it has no meaning but *does* mean it is something we *play*, something that has its own set of guidelines, but we may or may not take the confines of a "game" very seriously. Getting students to take writing *less* seriously, I believe, means getting them to mess with the forms and formula, to question the accepted knowledge about writing and about themselves. As Steve Ramsay puts it, "I don't know what I'm looking for, really. I just have a bundle of 'interests' and proclivities. I'm really just screwing around" (117).

In the opening pages of his book *Composition as a Happening*, Geoffrey Sirc suggests a "return to that point of disenchantment with established spaces and the desire for new forms" (12). For me, engagement with writing that embraces a scavenger methodology, as Halberstam describes, is part of a "desire for new forms." To think about the notion of the writer as scavenger and about scavenger methodologies, I want to consider, as an example, another student essay from a first-year writing course. In response to an assignment (given after a reading from Judith Butler's *Undoing Gender*) that asked students to explore the ways that others' expectations about their identities influenced or affected them powerfully, a student wrote a paper about his father expecting him to become a doctor (his father and grandfather were both surgeons). The essay is a really powerful piece of writing that evolved in my course, and I want to draw from relevant excerpts to discuss the ways his process and his openness to a "scavenger" approach to his writing disrupted usual ways of thinking and significantly enriched the complexity of his essay.

The first draft of the student's paper began with a general-to-specific introduction about expectations as he proceeded to tell the story of how he had been pressured since grade school to be a premed major in college. It's a solid narrative with a linear argument that could be summed up in a kind of "parents shouldn't pressure their kids into doing stuff" kind of way. The student even quoted the Butler essay we had read and included two quotes from a psychologist about parenting and the impact pressure has on high-achieving students. It is a tidy and logical essay, maybe even an A essay in many contexts. In our conference, he and I talked about the essay being, well, boring, full of stuff we (the members of his writing community in class) have heard repeated for years: that parents should let their kids be who they want, that perfectionism is no good, that kids shouldn't have to be who their parents believe they should be. I talked about the piece as having a conventional approach, which then also meant it was only able to say conventional things, to repeat dominant clichés about life.

So what should I write? he asked. *Just do the whole paper over?*

The move I take from Halberstam here is how I can teach this student to be a scavenger, to draw from more surprising places, to disrupt himself and his usual ways of "knowing" how to write a "paper," to bring things together that may not, at first, seem to belong together. In one sense, this isn't queer at all. Creative writers have been saying this for years—that you need to surprise a reader, take turns they can't predict. And feminist compositionists have told us many complicated things about the use of narrative, about self-implication, about how the personal narrative can interrupt or disrupt conventional knowledge. So how is the scavenger methodology different, or how could it be different?

I told this student to go collect some scraps. I talk to my students a lot about scraps—little pieces of the world you pick up as you move through. If Halberstam is right, that a queer methodology is a scavenger methodology, then it might indeed be useful to think about scavenger hunts whereby we look for certain categories of objects to bring together. I asked my student a two-part question: If you were on a scavenger hunt for certain categories of things to bring into this essay, what kinds of things would they be? What would you tell yourself to go find? This, of course, was a puzzling question (it's a puzzling question to me, too), but because this student is a generous spirit and a thoughtful person, he tries it out. *I'd tell myself to find something that goes against what it's supposed to be?* "Okay, write that down," I said. "Keep going." He ended up with a list of three tasks for his scavenger hunt. His list read, (1) *find something that goes against what it's supposed to be*, (2) *find something that puts pressure on something else*, and (3) *find something disappointing*. I told him to go find these things and to find a way to bring them into the essay. And so he did. And the second draft was a glorious mess and wonderfully strange. Here's a piece of it:

> My Dad's a doctor. My grandfather's a doctor. And I was supposed to be one too by now. When my father and grandfather look at me, they see a doctor. And it's pretty weird how whenever we look at something, we see what we want to see. I guess I do it, too. Today when I was walking trying to find the things for this weird scavenger hunt, I noticed myself thinking about this girl I like in my bio lab and how she laughs at my jokes a lot. And I was thinking about how it's probably because she likes me too, and I thought about this paper and how this could be part of my scavenger hunt for related stuff. I am seeing what I want to see, too. But my dad being a doctor doesn't mean I am a doctor, and laughing at someone's jokes doesn't mean you want to hook up.
>
> Down the street at the capital [sic] building, some men are arguing about the Keystone pipeline, a bunch of them putting pressure on the other ones to get them to do what they want. Does this count as something putting pressure on something else? (Anonymous Student G, Untitled writing)

I love this writing, and perhaps many writing teachers wouldn't (though I think any teacher with a feminist or queer investment should be delighted to receive such a piece of writing from any student). But that's not the important part; the important part is what this writer said about the draft in his author's note, which, in part, reads, "I tried to do what you said, but honestly my first paper seems a lot more responsible. This one feels like just random stuff. So I'm really sorry if I mistook what you said." I am focused on his term "responsible," particularly when, in the first draft, he critiqued his family for thinking being a doctor was more "responsible" than liking history courses. He apologizes; he seems to feel his second draft is a disappointment, something to be ashamed of. And, well, that's how doing something queer, something that moves against what seems evident, "natural" even, feels inside a dominant culture.

The final draft brought the brief mentions he makes above together quite interestingly in an essay that ends up being about power—about the power of influence, and because of the girl in his bio lab, it also becomes about gender—and not because I told him to get some gender politics in his work but because he found a way to look around, to scavenge, and to worry about coherence later, or maybe not at all. More composition could happen this way because it is deeply political indeed to be able to see the connections between things—connections that maybe no one wants you to see. As this writer said, we see what we want to see—that is, until something else is brought into view.

I was a senior in college when I heard the news from my father that Mr. Schellhorn had died. In fact, I was in the middle of writing my undergraduate honors thesis—a collection of disobedient poems that took biblical figures and rewrote their narratives from queer and feminist perspectives. Early that afternoon, before my father called, I had been looking up the word anachronistic *in, of all things, a dictionary. I was looking it up because one of the professors on my thesis committee, a professor of religious studies, had given me feedback on my poems and said they were "going overboard with the anachronism" in the passages of poems in which Noah was shopping at Wal-Mart before heading to the ark and in poems with Ruth stealing rape kits from the local precinct. Looking back, the irony does hit me—that I am now a writing teacher, often writing about the ways writers might gather seemingly contradictory, impossible combinations to make new knowledge, or to make new pathways to knowing.*

Contradiction, Confusion, Cohesion

In "Confronting the 'Essential' Problem: Reconnecting Feminist Theory and Pedagogy," Joy Ritchie argues that courses that "allowed ideas to be held up to reexamination, to contradiction, and to the multiple stories of women's lives hold at least some promise to counter the absolutist forms of thinking that prevail in our society and to allow more students to remake their view of the world" (101). Ritchie points to patterns of thought, to "forms of thinking." And if we think in forms, and write in forms, why not change the forms in order to arrive at different content? We can change the content, yes. We can ask students to write *about* more civically engaged or politically conscious positions. But will that change *the form of the thinking*? Will it change how we come to know in the first place?

In "Queer Pedagogy and Its Strange Techniques," Deborah Britzman asks, "What if one thought about reading practices [and perhaps writing practices as well] as problems of opening identifications, of working the capacity to imagine oneself differently precisely with respect to how one encounters another, and in how one encounters the self? What if how one reads the world turned upon the interest in thinking against one's thoughts, of creating a queer space where one's old certainties made no sense?" (55). The scavenger methodology I explore with my students is very invested in the idea of "thinking against one's thoughts" and embracing (rather than avoiding) contradictions. I am sure all writers can remember a time when a teacher indicated they were "contradicting themselves." And this indication meant, of course, that contradiction was *not* something that was supposed to happen in an essay—that an essay was something that made *consistent* and *linear* points that did not go against one another. From the perspective of queer theory particularly, I want to argue that going "against one's thoughts" and becoming curious and writing *into* our contradictions is both what we want to do as scholars and what we want to teach our students to do. We are living in a political moment of "either/or"—either we can carry guns in Taco Bell or we cannot bear arms, we either socialize medicine or privatize it, and so on. The last thing I want to teach my students is to write an essay that fits itself into one of these either/or boxes. Rather, I want my students to notice the contradictory nature of the issues themselves. Just as queer theory tries to honor the complex and often contradictory nature of identity, so composition must do the same, even when it is uncomfortable to do so.

When I ask students to make essays from scavenged parts, from seemingly unrelated fields, styles, areas of their lives, voices, and so on, I am inviting their contradictions *into* their essays, rather than creating assignments that help students keep their contradictory selves at bay. And I try, in the scholarship I generate, to honor that work—bringing in the aspects of self and story that shape the pedagogies I advocate, disrupting and interrupting myself. Working as a queer person on the subject of queer pedagogies, I have been asked many times some version of the question, *Are you just interested in queer pedagogies because you're queer?* I get asked this as a kind of "gotcha moment." But the answer is what the answer could only be: yes, absolutely. I advocate for queer methodologies because I am queer, because queer teenagers all over the world are killing themselves at horrifying rates, because if oppression is really going to change, it's our civic duty to think in queerer ways, to come up with queer kinds of knowledge-making so that we might know truths that are non-normative, and contradictory, and strange.

I have already discussed one interesting moment of contradiction in this student's writing—the conflict between his essay (where he critiques the notion of what is "responsible" in the eyes of others) and his author's note (where he feels guilt that his essay is less "responsible" than perhaps others he has written—others that were likely more tidy, more cohesive than the essay I have urged him to compose). In his subsequent revisions, I asked him to push more into this contradiction, to think more about why it's a contradiction in the first place, and perhaps even about why it might always remain a contradiction. The temptation with contradictions is to *resolve* them. But in writing, as in life, some tensions are not resolvable. And sometimes that impossible resolution is perfectly productive. The student writes, "The term responsibility is thrown around alot for manipulation. Who doesn't want to be responsible? When you tell someone what the responsible thing to do is, you are basically telling them there is no other option. Responsibility is a weapon our parents use against us so that we then learn to use it against ourselves and people we interact with in our lives." This passage reflects a commitment to pressing into the contradiction, to thinking closely and carefully about the concept of *responsibility* as it works on, against, for, and in us. To accept *responsibility* as good, as right, is the most normative move we can make in our minds. To question that which seems obvious, to, as Britzman says, "think against our thoughts" is to do the real work of composition.

I got mostly As in elementary school, but I didn't think of myself as a smart kid. I always gave the second answer I thought of, because I thought of my first answer (my instincts) as weird or inappropriate. I learned this from Mrs. Walsh in second grade. I remember being so excited when Charlotte wrote nice things in her web in order to save Wilbur from being slaughtered. I remember that feeling that writing could save me, too. So when Mrs. Walsh asked a question on the quiz about what saved Wilbur, I was supposed to write "Charlotte," but I wrote "writ-

ing" instead. She marked it wrong. When I tried to protest, it was of no use. "You have to be more specific," she said. I remember she said my answer was "kind of out there."

Re-Vision the Future

Imagining a future, for me, has always been about imagining other worlds, other ways of being outside the ones I had always known. I remember, in 1986, when Halley's Comet was about to rise over Long Island sometime around three in the morning. I was nine years old, and my mother (against my father's wishes) snuck me out of bed. It was March, so not quite cold but not quite warm. And my mother watches from the window, dozes off from time to time as I lay on the cool blacktop of the driveway and wait with my cheap grade-school telescope, to see something fleeting, unknowable, and beautiful—to see something that I knew I might see only once. I never did find the comet that night. But it mattered less that I saw it and more that I imagined doing so. It mattered more that I was up past my bedtime, looking out at a world I knew was beyond my understanding or grasp, wondering about what might be possible.

Most scholars in English are likely familiar with Adrienne Rich's assertion that "[r]e-vision—the act of looking back, of seeing with fresh eyes, of entering an old text from a new critical direction—is for women more than a chapter in cultural history: it is an act of survival" (339). As I understand Rich, re-vision is "the act of looking back," but it is also the act of acknowledging the present and the act of looking forward simultaneously. And that "contradiction" is not only possible but also imperative for the field of composition. It truly matters *how* we look and from what "critical direction," as Rich calls it. For example, in "Composing a Rhetorical Education for the 21st Century," Jessica Enoch invites us to reconsider the angle from which we look; she calls us to search outside traditional educational contexts, especially to activist communities, in order to "energize our understanding of rhetorical education" (167). Similarly, but with a very different focus, Halberstam argues in the book *In a Queer Time and Place: Transgender Bodies, Subcultural Lives*, that "part of what has made queerness compelling as a form of self-description in the past decade or so has to do with the way it has the potential to open up new life narratives and alternative relations to time and space" (2). To me, this opening up of "new life narratives and alternative relations" makes queerness integral to composition. There is something queer about writing—something indescribable, something contradictory, something at times, dare I say, impossible to "teach" in the traditional ways. So if we think of our scholarship (and our students' writing) as having "alternative relations to time and space," the scavenger methodology is just one way of making those alternative relations visible. And if we take Enoch seriously and understand that, as compositionists, we need to look to our activist communities to illuminate what might be possible in our classroom communities, then the activism of our queer communities should also inform our teaching. This inevitably means we will need to misbehave, to disobey our own disciplinary rules, to push the boundaries of what we think we already know about teaching and writing, to take on the work of teaching students "sexual literacy," as Jonathan Alexander calls it.

Those of us who work in composition and rhetoric know that the field has a deep anxiety about its "home." Some writing programs have broken off from their English departments, some compositionists are less respected in their more conventional English departments, and yet the imperative that students must "learn to write" remains explicitly on the shoulders of our field. In thinking about the possible connections between work in queer theory and work in composition, I cannot help but think of Halberstam's "Reflections on Queer Studies and Queer Pedagogy": "The liability of not having an institutional home, of course, is that the study of sexuality is central to no single discipline or program and in fact may be taught everywhere and nowhere simultaneously. However, the advantage of the stealth approach to the study of sexuality is that it remains multidisciplinary, a promiscuous rogue in a field of focused monogamists" (362). One can hear the same said of composition—that it is "central to no single discipline or program" and that it "may be taught everywhere and nowhere simultaneously." After all, to whom does the teaching of writing *belong*? What fields are *not* the site of composition? In the spirit of queering composition and pedagogy, it is my hope that we truly embrace our multidisciplinarity, that we more fully become this "promiscuous rogue in a field of focused monogamists." The scavenger, after all, is promiscuous, licentious, and perhaps even, in the best ways, irresponsible.

Perhaps it's naïve to think that changing our patterns of thought can change the world, but, well, I think it can. When Audre Lorde explains, in several of her essays and speeches in *Sister Outsider*, that there is a distinct difference between "revolution" and "reform," I think of changing our methods, our approaches, our ways of knowing as part of the revolution—and as the only way to catalyze changes in consciousness. I've never talked to my student quoted here about queer theory explicitly, though he read some essays that might be counted as such for class. I never asked him to write a paper on gay marriage, or abortion, or gun violence. But I do believe that the processes he practiced in my course could *not* lead him to any of the same old binary positions on these matters. I believe he'd have something very complicated to say, maybe even something contradictory. In his final reflective essay for my course, a response to my request that students discuss what they've learned about writing, he responds, "Maybe it seems odd, but I think the thing that's improved my writing the most is learning that the first thing I think of is probably not the most well thought out thing I've ever said. In addition, I learned that in some cases outlining an essay before I write it is like a prison and I need to leave myself room for unexpected ideas" (Anonymous Student G, Reflection assignment).

It's fascinating to me that as a child I thought of my first answer, my "queer" answer, as the real answer I should not share, and that this student sees his first answer as the normative or obvious answer. His reflection suggests a way to understand what the scavenger methodology can teach writers. His idea that "the first thing" he thinks of is "not the most well thought out thing" is another way of expressing what it means to think beyond whatever our current patterns and systems of thought allow, or beyond whatever prescriptions might have been constructed for us as we learned to think and write critically. His recognition that an outline has the potential to become "a prison" and that he needs to create the space "for unexpected ideas" signals a dramatic shift in his approach, a shift that means neither his essay nor his thoughts have to obey the logics set before him or conform to predetermined structures or clusters of belonging. In *Borderlands/La Frontera*, Gloria Anzaldúa writes, "The act of composition, whether you are composing a work of fiction or your life, or whether you are composing reality, always means pulling off fragmented pieces and putting them together" (238).

Mr. Schellhorn took us on frequent field trips. And there are some parts of field trips I hate: the bus rides, the lining up, the public bathrooms of visitors' centers and rest stops. For one trip, we visit the Long Island Central Pine Barrens. I'm fascinated by the nearly hundred thousand acres of plant life said to be growing on "infertile" soil. I'm obsessed with telling my parents, after the trip, "The pine barrens need to burn in brushfires to survive." The idea that sometimes something needs to burn in order to live really appeals to me. Mr. Schellhorn walks me through the woods, along the Peconic River. He tells me this is really the last part of Long Island that is truly wilderness. Everything else is kept in order by landscapers, he says. What I remember perhaps most vividly about third grade was leaving Mr. Schellhorn's classroom on the last day of school, turning to look at the room as I made my way down the hall. The place was a mess. Unsafe even. Scissors everywhere, dead insects scattered around the microscope, wet paintings hanging in the coat closet. By some measure, he was a terrible teacher—disorganized, partial to particular kinds of misfit students, prone to letting the room "get out of control," as I heard my father put it. But it was in that room I learned that the weird stuff I wrote counted for something and that writing did save Wilbur, even if it can't save all of us. We can, at least, still teach it like it could.

Teaching the Impossible

I am pretty sure I was the only third grader who tried to cut gym. When it was time to change clothes, I'd sneak down to the library to see if I could get Mrs. Sullivan to talk to me about books long enough to miss gym class and give me a pass. It worked the first couple of times. And I felt relieved of the responsibility of taking off my clothes in the girls' locker room. Instead, I talked incessantly about Jupiter Jones, the star character in the Three Investigators series I was reading that year. But eventually my absences were noticed by the gym teacher, who called my mother. *You love sports,* my mother said. Why would you cut gym class?

In *Sexuality and the Politics of Ethos in the Writing Classroom*, Zan Meyer Gonçalves asks, "If we believe, as many do, that paying attention to identity issues and social forces facilitates rhetorical growth for all our students, then how exactly do we incorporate these elements into our writing classrooms?" (27). In many ways, this experiment, this book, these pedagogies try to respond to this question and to the question of the ultimate impossibility of how to do queer work in the classroom and in the world. To return to an essay that I engage at the start of this book, "Queer: An Impossible Subject for Composition," we might again consider Jonathan Alexander and Jacqueline Rhodes's remark that they "have now come to believe that queerness is not simply one of composition's difficult subjects" but that "queerness is one of composition's impossible subjects" (179). In many ways, I would tend to agree for some of the same reasons they offer: that sex and schooling are perhaps an impossible pair, that being "composed" is not queer, that "queerness is essentially about impossibility and excess . . . queerness is the gesture of the unrepresentable, the call for a space of impossibility, the insistence that not everything be composed" (180). But I might also suggest that if queerness is an impossible subject for composition, does that make it an impossible method? And for what discipline, or for what purpose, would queerness *not* be impossible? If "a space of impossibility" is how we imagine a queer space, then how might we create spaces of impossibility within the confines of some not very queer institutional contexts or educational standards? To revisit their remarks on where we are now: "Now it seems more important to see how queerness challenges the very subject of composition, of what it means to compose, of what it means to *be composed*" (182). And perhaps this is one of the questions of this book. If one of the incompatibilities between queerness and composition is that "excess, often characterized as the extraneous, the 'off topic,' must be trimmed to produce shapely texts" (194), then perhaps composition might come to mean something else, might come to mean producing unshapely, uncomposed, queerer texts. Perhaps the work in both queer and digital spaces in the field is addressing precisely this call to action from Alexander and Rhodes. Queer pedagogy, then, is impossible. Queer composure, also impossible. But this does not mean that methodologies that embrace the impossible, that engage the queer, are not worth our failing grasp. What is writing, after all, if it is not imagining the world as other than it is, thinking imaginatively to make seemingly impossible connections, and even perhaps imagining ourselves other than we are?

In her book *Touching Feeling: Affect, Pedagogy, Performativity*, Eve Kosofsky Sedgwick writes,

> Simply to be with this teaching makes far more difference than would either believing or disbelieving it. Take, for example, the game or meditation—so likely to arise with the teaching of rebirth—of picturing your life, even your character, otherwise than it is. So many questions emerge. Yet their emergence is not into a context of blame or self-blame, nor of will or resolve. The space is more like—what? Wish? Somewhere, at least, liberated by both possibility and impossibility, and especially by the untetheredness to self. (179)

Joey Lavarco was a troublemaker, didn't wash his beautiful red hair very much at all, and had a lisp. Sometimes it was hard to tell whether he was left back because he had failed third grade or because he wouldn't survive without Mr. Schellhorn, the generous king of all us weird kids. My parents divorced that year. And I had decided not to talk at school. I don't remember why. But I made exceptions to talk to Joey, who stole erasers from the other kids' desks and wandered off to look at insects during recess. Nothing made sense about Joey, and I loved him with my whole queer heart.

WORKS CITED

Ahmed, Sara. *Queer Phenomenology: Orientations, Objects, Others*. Duke UP, 2006.
Alexander, Jonathan. *Literacy, Sexuality, Pedagogy: Theory and Practice for Composition Studies*. Utah State UP, 2008.
Alexander, Jonathan. "A 'Sisterly Camaraderie' and Other Queer Friendships: A Gay Teacher Interacting with Straight Students." *The Teacher's Body: Embodiment, Authority, and Identity in the Academy*, edited by Diane Freedman and Martha Stoddard Holmes, State U of New York P, 2003, pp. 161–78.
Alexander, Jonathan, and Michelle Gibson. "Queer Composition(s): Queer Theory in the Writing Classroom." *JAC*, vol. 24, no. 1, 2004, pp. 1–21.
Alexander, Jonathan, and Jacqueline Rhodes. "Flattening Effects: Composition's Multicultural Imperative and the Problem of Narrative Coherence." *College Composition and Communication*, vol. 65, no. 3, 2014, pp. 430–54.
Alexander, Jonathan, and Jacqueline Rhodes. "Queer: An Impossible Subject for Composition." *JAC*, vol. 31, no. 1, 2011, pp. 177–206.
Alexander, Jonathan, and David Wallace. "The Queer Turn in Composition Studies." *College Composition and Communication*, vol. 61, no. 1, 2009, pp. 300–320.
Anonymous Student A. "Binary Blindfold." Unpublished essay, U of Pittsburgh, 2007
Anonymous Student B. "Did I Say That?" Unpublished essay, U of Pittsburgh, 2007.
Anonymous Student C. Untitled writing, U of Pittsburgh, 2007.
Anonymous Student D. Untitled writing, U of Pittsburgh, 2007.
Anonymous Student E. Untitled writing, U of Pittsburgh, 2007.
Anonymous Student F. "Let Them Drink Beer." U of Nebraska, 2013.
Anonymous Student G. Reflection assignment, U of Nebraska, 2013.

Anonymous Student G. Untitled writing, U of Nebraska, 2013.
Anzaldúa, Gloria. *Borderlands/La Frontera: The New Mestiza*. 2nd ed., Aunt Lute Books, 1999.
Bartholomae, David. *Writing on the Margins: Essays on Composition and Teaching*. Palgrave Macmillan, 2005.
Bartholomae, David, and Anthony Petrosky. *Ways of Reading: An Anthology for Writers*. 6th ed., Bedford/St. Martin's, 2002.
Benson, Thomas, and Michael Prosser. *Readings in Classical Rhetoric*. Routledge, 1995.
Bergman, Hannah. Unpublished essay, U of Pittsburgh, 2006.
Berthoff, Ann E. *The Making of Meaning: Metaphors, Models, and Maxims for Writing Teachers*. Boynton/Cook Publishers, 1981.
Berthoff, Ann E. "Reclaiming the Active Mind." *College English*, vol. 61, no. 6, 1999, pp. 671–80.
Birkenstein, Cathy. "We Got the Wrong Gal: Rethinking the 'Bad' Academic Writing of Judith Butler." *College English*, vol. 72, no. 3, 2010, pp. 269–83.
Boone, Joseph Allen. *Libidinal Currents: Sexuality and the Shaping of Modernism*. U of Chicago P, 1998.
Bornstein, Kate. *Gender Outlaw: On Men, Women, and the Rest of Us*. Vintage Books, 1994.
Bornstein, Kate. *Hello, Cruel World: 101 Alternatives to Suicide for Teens, Freaks, and Other Outlaws*. Seven Stories Press, 2006.
Bourdieu, Pierre. *Distinction: A Social Critique of the Judgement of Taste*. Translated by Richard Nice, Harvard UP, 1984.
Bourdieu, Pierre. *Masculine Domination*. Translated by Richard Nice, Stanford UP, 1998.
Bracken, Jennifer. "There Are No Stupid Questions." U of Pittsburgh, 2007.
Britzman, Deborah P. "Is There a Queer Pedagogy? Or, Stop Reading Straight." *Educational Theory*, vol. 45, no. 2, 1995, pp. 151–65.
Britzman, Deborah P. "Queer Pedagogy and Its Strange Techniques." *Inside the Academy and Out: Lesbian/Gay/Queer Studies and Social Action*, edited by Janice L. Ristock and Catherine G. Taylor, U of Toronto P, 1998, pp. 49–71.
Brookfield, Stephen D., and Stephen Preskill. *Discussion as a Way of Teaching: Tools and Techniques for Democratic Classrooms*. Jossey-Bass, 1999.
Bryson, Mary, and Suzanne de Castell. "Queer Pedagogy?! Practice Makes Im/Perfect." *Radical In<ter>ventions: Identity, Politics, and Differences in Educational Praxis*, edited by Suzanne de Castell and Mary Bryson, State U of New York P, 1997, pp. 269–94.
Bullen, Kyle. Unpublished essay, U of Pittsburgh, 2006.
Burke, Kenneth. *Rhetoric of Religion: Studies in Logology*. U of California P, 1970.
Butler, Judith. *Bodies That Matter: On the Discursive Limits of "Sex."* Routledge, 1993.

Butler, Judith. *Gender Trouble: Feminism and the Subversion of Identity*. Routledge, 1990.
Butler, Judith. "Melancholy Gender/Refused Identification." *Constructing Masculinity*, edited by Maurice Berger, Brian Wallis, and Simon Watson, Routledge, 1995, pp. 21–37.
Butler, Judith. *Undoing Gender*. Routledge, 2004.
Cardo, Amanda. "All About Them Words." U of Pittsburgh, 2007.
Cardo, Amanda. Reflection assignment, U of Pittsburgh, 2007.
Coles, William E. *The Plural I: The Teaching of Writing*. Boynton/Cook Publishers, 1988.
Collins, Patricia Hill. *Black Feminist Thought: Knowledge, Consciousness, and the Politics of Empowerment*. Rev. 10th anniversary ed., Routledge, 2000.
Condon, Frankie. *I Hope I Join the Band: Narrative, Affiliation, and Antiracist Rhetoric*. Utah State UP, 2012.
Connell, R. W. *Masculinities*. U of California P, 2005.
Dejka, Andrew. "Stupid Is as Stupid Does." Unpublished essay, U of Nebraska, 2011.
Edelman, Lee. *No Future: Queer Theory and the Death Drive*. Duke UP, 2004.
Enoch, Jessica. "Composing a Rhetorical Education for the 21st Century: TakingITGlobal as Pedagogical Heuristic." *Rhetoric Review*, vol. 29, no. 2, 2010, pp. 165–85.
Fagan, Kelsey. Unpublished essay, U of Pittsburgh, 2007.
Faigley, Lester, and Jack Selzer. *Good Reasons: Designing and Writing Effective Arguments*. Pearson Education, 2006.
Finders, Margaret. *Just Girls: Hidden Literacies and Life in Junior High*. Teachers College Press, 1997.
Foucault, Michel. *The Archaeology of Knowledge and the Discourse on Language*. Pantheon Books, 1972.
Foucault, Michel. *History of Sexuality*. Translated by Robert Hurley, vol. 1, Random House, 1978.
Gadamer, Hans-Georg. *Philosophical Hermeneutics*. Translated by David E. Linge, U of California P, 1976.
Gadamer, Hans-Georg. *The Relevance of the Beautiful and Other Essays*. Translated by Nicholas Walker, Cambridge UP, 1986.
Galarte, Francisco J. "Pedagogy." *Transgender Studies Quarterly*, vol. 1, no. 2, 2014, pp. 146–48.
Garber, Linda. *Tilting the Tower: Lesbians Teaching Queer Subjects*. Routledge, 1994.
Gibson, Michelle, Martha Marinara, and Deborah Meem. "Bi, Butch, and Bar Dyke: Pedagogical Performances of Class, Gender and Sexuality." *College Composition and Communication*, vol. 52, no. 1, 2000, pp. 69–95.

Glenn, Cheryl. *Unspoken: A Rhetoric of Silence.* Southern Illinois UP, 2004.

Gonçalves, Zan Meyer. *Sexuality and the Politics of Ethos in the Writing Classroom.* Southern Illinois UP, 2005.

Graff, Gerald. *Clueless in Academe: How Schooling Obscures the Life of the Mind.* Yale UP, 2003.

Graff, Gerald, and Cathy Birkenstein, editors. *They Say/I Say: The Moves That Matter in Persuasive Writing.* Norton, 2007.

Greene, Maxine. *Releasing the Imagination: Essays on Education, the Arts and Social Change.* Jossey-Bass, 1995.

Griffin, Susan. *A Chorus of Stones.* First Anchor Books, 1992.

Haggerty, George E., and Bonnie Zimmerman. *Professions of Desire: Lesbian and Gay Studies in Literature.* MLA, 1995.

Halberstam, J. Jack [Judith]. *Female Masculinity.* Duke UP, 1998.

Halberstam, J. Jack [Judith]. *In a Queer Time and Place: Transgender Bodies, Subcultural Lives.* New York UP, 2005.

Halberstam, J. Jack [Judith]. *The Queer Art of Failure.* Duke UP, 2011.

Halberstam, J. Jack [Judith]. "Reflections on Queer Studies and Queer Pedagogy." *Journal of Homosexuality,* vol. 45, no. 2, 2003, pp. 361–64.

Halperin, David. *Saint Foucault: Towards a Gay Hagiography.* Oxford UP, 1997.

Halperin, David. *What Do Gay Men Want? An Essay on Sex, Risk, and Subjectivity.* U of Michigan P, 2007.

Hart, Johnnie. Unpublished essay, U of Pittsburgh, 2007.

Hayles, N. Katherine. *How We Became Posthuman: Virtual Bodies in Cybernetics, Literature, and Informatics.* U of Chicago P, 1999.

Hugo, Richard. *Triggering Town: Lectures and Essays on Poetry and Writing.* Norton, 1979.

Jones, Raymond C. "The 'Why' of Class Participation: A Question Worth Asking." *College Teaching,* vol. 56, no. 1, 2008, pp. 59–63.

Kameen, Paul. *Writing/Teaching: Essays toward a Rhetoric of Pedagogy.* U of Pittsburgh P, 2000.

Kelly, Andrew Ignatius "Iggy." Unpublished essay, U of Pittsburgh, 2007.

Kennedy, George A., translator. *Aristotle: On Rhetoric.* Oxford UP, 2007.

Kennedy, X. J., Dorothy M. Kennedy, Ellen Kuhl Repetto, and Jane E. Aaron. *The Bedford Reader.* Bedford/St. Martin's, 2013.

Kopelson, Karen. "Dis/Integrating the Gay/Queer Binary: 'Reconstructed Identity Politics' for a Performative Pedagogy." *College English,* vol. 65, no. 1, 2002, pp. 17–35.

Kopelson, Karen. "Of Ambiguity and Erasure: The Perils of Performative Pedagogy." *Relations, Locations, and Positions: Composition Theory for Writing Teachers,* edited by Peter Vandenberg, Jennifer Clary-Lemon, and Sue Hum, NCTE, 2006, pp. 563–71.

Kristeva, Julia. *Powers of Horror: An Essay on Abjection*. Translated by Leon S. Roudiez, Columbia UP, 1982.

Lloyd, Moya. *Judith Butler: From Norms to Politics*. Polity, 2007.

Lorde, Audre. *Sister Outsider: Essays and Speeches*. Crossing Press, 1984.

Luhmann, Susanne. "Queering/Querying Pedagogy? Or, Queer Pedagogy Is a Pretty Queer Thing." *Queer Theory in Education*, edited by William F. Pinar, Lawrence Erlbaum Associates, 1998, pp. 120–32.

Malinowitz, Harriet. *Textual Orientations: Lesbian and Gay Students and the Making of Discourse Communities*. Boynton/Cook Publishers, 1995.

Mayberry, Katherine J. *Teaching What You're Not: Identity Politics in Higher Education*. New York UP, 1996.

McIntosh, Peggy. "White Privilege: Unpacking the Invisible Knapsack." *Peace and Freedom: The Bi-monthly Journal of the Women's International League for Peace and Freedom*, vol. 49, no. 3, 1989, pp. 1–5.

McKerrow, Ray. *Explorations in Rhetoric: Studies in Honor of Douglas Ehninger*. Scott, Foresman, 1982.

Micciche, Laura R. *Doing Emotion: Rhetoric, Writing, Teaching*. Boynton/Cook Publishers, 2007.

Miller, Nancy K. *Getting Personal: Feminist Occasions and Other Autobiographical Acts*. Routledge, 1991.

Miller, Richard. *Writing at the End of the World*. U of Pittsburgh P, 2005.

Moltner, Krystin. Unpublished essay, U of Pittsburgh, 2007.

Monson, Connie, and Jacqueline Rhodes. "Risking Queer: Pedagogy, Performativity, and Desire in Writing Classrooms." *JAC*, vol. 24, no. 1, 2004, pp. 79–91.

Morris, Marla. "Unresting the Curriculum: Queer Projects, Queer Imaginings." *Queer Theory in Education*, edited by William F. Pinar, Lawrence Erlbaum Associates, 1998, pp. 227–36.

Muñoz, José Esteban. *Cruising Utopia: The Then and There of Queer Futurity*. New York UP, 2009.

Muñoz, Vic, and Ednie Kaeh Garrison. "Transpedagogies." *Women's Studies Quarterly*, vol. 36, no. 4, 2008, pp. 288–308.

Olson, Gary A., and Lynn Worsham, editors. *Critical Intellectuals on Writing*. State U of New York P, 2003.

Palmer, Richard E. *Hermeneutics: Interpretation Theory in Schleiermacher, Dilthey, Heidegger, and Gadamer*. Northwestern UP, 1969.

Palmeri, Jason. *Remixing Composition: A History of Multimodal Writing Pedagogy*. Southern Illinois UP, 2012.

Pinar, William. Foreword. *Thinking Queer: Sexuality, Culture, and Education*, by Susan Talburt and Shirley R. Steinberg, Peter Lang, 2000.

Pinar, William, editor. *Queer Theory in Education*. Lawrence Erlbaum Associates, 1998.
Poli, Jessica. "Sex in Numbers." U of Pittsburgh, 2007.
Puar, Jasbir K. *Terrorist Assemblages: Homonationalism in Queer Times*. Duke UP, 2007.
Ramsay, Steve. "The Hermeneutics of Screwing Around; or, What You Do with a Million Books." *Pastplay: Teaching and Learning History with Technology*, edited by Kevin Kee, U of Michigan P, 2014, pp. 111–20, doi: dx.doi.org/10.3998/dh.12544152.0001.001.
Reda, Mary M. *Between Speaking and Silence: A Study of Quiet Students*. State U of New York P, 2009.
Rhodes, Jacqueline. "The Failure of Queer Pedagogy [video]." *Queer and Now*, special issue of *The Writing Instructor*, March 2015, www.writinginstructor.org/rhodes-2015-03.
Rhodes, Jacqueline. "Homo Origo: The Queertext Manifesto." *Computers and Composition*, vol. 21, no. 3, 2004, pp. 385–88.
Rhodes, Jacqueline, and Jonathan Alexander. *Techne: Queer Meditations on Writing the Self*. Computers and Composition Digital Press/Utah State UP, 2015.
Ritchie, Joy S. "Confronting the 'Essential' Problem: Reconnecting Feminist Theory and Pedagogy." *Feminism and Composition: A Critical Sourcebook*, edited by Gesa E. Kirsch, Faye Spencer Maor, Lance Massey, Lee Nickoson-Massey, and Mary P. Sheridan-Rabideau, Bedford/St. Martin's, 2003.
Rich, Adrienne. "When We Dead Awake: Writing as Re-Vision." *Adrienne Rich's Poetry and Prose: Poems, Prose, Reviews, and Criticism*, edited by Barbara Charlesworth Gelpi and Albert and Gelpi, Norton, 1993.
Ritchie, Joy S., and David E. Wilson. *Teacher Narrative as Critical Inquiry: Rewriting the Script*. Teachers College Press, 2000.
Rose, Mike. *The Mind at Work: Valuing the Intelligence of the American Worker*. Penguin, 2005.
Rosenwasser, David, and Jill Stephen. *Writing Analytically*. 5th ed., Thomson Wadsworth, 2009.
Rothenberg, David. *Blue Cliff Record: A Poetic Echo*. Codhill Press, 2001.
Salvatori, Mariolina. "Conversations with Texts: Reading in the Teaching of Composition." *College English*, vol. 58, no. 4, 1996, pp. 440–54.
Salvatori, Mariolina Rizzi, editor. *Pedagogy: Disturbing History, 1819–1929*. U of Pittsburgh P, 1996.
Salvatori, Mariolina Rizzi, and Patricia Donahue. *The Elements (and Pleasures) of Difficulty*. Pearson Longman, 2005.
Sedgwick, Eve Kosofsky. *Epistemology of the Closet*. U of California P, 1990.
Sedgwick, Eve Kosofsky. *Tendencies*. Duke UP, 2006.

Sedgwick, Eve Kosofsky. *Touching Feeling: Affect, Pedagogy, Performativity*. Duke UP, 2003.
Seitz, James E. *Motives for Metaphor: Literacy, Curriculum Reform, and the Teaching of English*. U of Pittsburgh P, 1999.
Shaughnessy, Mina P. *Errors and Expectations: A Guide for the Teacher of Basic Writing*. Oxford UP, 1977.
Sirc, Geoffrey. *English Composition as a Happening*. Utah State UP, 2002.
Slevin, James. *Introducing English: Essays in the Intellectual Work of Composition*. U of Pittsburgh P, 2001.
Spurlin, William J. *Lesbian and Gay Studies and the Teaching of English: Positions, Pedagogies, and Cultural Politics*. NCTE, 2000.
Stenberg, Shari J. "Cultivating Listening: Teaching from a Restored Logos." *Silence and Listening as Rhetorical Arts*, edited by Cheryl Glenn and Krista Ratcliffe, Southern Illinois UP, 2011, pp. 250–63.
Stenberg, Shari J. "Making Room for New Subjects: Feminist Interruptions of Critical Pedagogy Rhetorics." *Teaching Rhetorica: Theory, Pedagogy, Practice*, edited by Kate Ronald and Joy S. Ritchie, Boynton/Cook Publishers, 2006, pp. 131–46.
Stenberg, Shari J. *Repurposing Composition: Feminist Interventions for a Neoliberal Age*. Utah State UP, 2015.
Stockton, Kathryn Bond. *The Queer Child, or Growing Sideways in the Twentieth Century*. Duke UP, 2009.
Sullivan, Patricia. "Feminism and Methodology in Composition Studies." *Methods and Methodology in Composition Research*, edited by Patricia A. Sullivan and Gesa E. Kirsch, Southern Illinois UP, 1992, pp. 37–61.
Sullivan, Patricia Suzanne. *Experimental Writing in Composition: Aesthetics and Pedagogies*. U of Pittsburgh P, 2012.
Talburt, Susan, and Shirley R. Steinberg. *Thinking Queer: Sexuality, Culture, and Education*. Peter Lang, 2000.
Tobin, Lad. "Car Wrecks, Baseball Caps, and Man-to-Man Defense: The Personal Narratives of Adolescent Males." *College English*, vol. 58, no. 2, 1996, pp. 158–75.
Tobin, Lad. *Reading Student Writing*. Boynton/Cook Publishers, 2004.
Wallace-Sanders, Kimberly. "A Vessel of Possibilities: Teaching through the Expectant Body." *The Teacher's Body: Embodiment, Authority, and Identity in the Academy*, edited by Diane Freedman and Martha Stoddard Holmes, State U of New York P, 2003, pp. 187–98.
Warner, Michael. *The Trouble with Normal: Sex, Politics, and the Ethics of Queer Life*. Harvard UP, 1999.

Winans, Amy E. "Queering Pedagogy in the English Classroom: Engaging with the Places Where Thinking Stops." *Pedagogy*, vol. 6, no. 1, 2006, pp. 103–22.

Woolf, Virginia. *A Room of One's Own*. 1929. Harcourt Brace, 1981.

Young, Vershawn Ashanti. *Your Average Nigga: Performing Race, Literacy, and Masculinity*. Wayne State UP, 2007.

INDEX

abjection, 40, 43–46, 48, 199
agency, 27, 101, 102, 118–19, 136, 174
androgyny, 17
Anzaldua, Gloria, x, 33, 102, 190, 196
autodidact, 32, 28

Bartholomae, David, ii, x, 103, 106, 108, 109, 112, 141, 148–50, 156–58, 196
becoming, vii, viii, 23, 25, 27–55, 64, 84, 95, 101, 104, 106–15, 117–21, 126–66, 186
Berthoff, Ann, 118, 119, 123, 124, 196
binary, 18, 101, 146–48, 151–53, 156, 158–66, 168, 190, 195, 198
Birkenstein, Cathy, 151–53, 196, 198
body of knowledge, 18–20, 22, 23, 32, 48, 50, 54, 67, 68, 103, 143
Bornstein, Kate, x, 33, 37–39, 51–53, 61, 67, 98, 99, 102, 110, 113, 114, 126, 128, 134–37, 145–47, 157, 160, 164, 196
Bourdieu, Pierre, 30, 32, 33, 43, 196
Bracken, Jennifer, 59, 64, 65, 109, 196

Britzman, Deborah, 4, 107, 141, 142, 186, 187, 196
Bryson, Mary, 159, 163, 196
butch/butchness, 12, 17, 32, 37, 42, 48, 50, 80, 197
Butler, Judith, 8–14, 27, 34–36, 40, 46, 47, 54, 80, 87, 102, 112, 113, 118, 122, 131, 149, 152, 153, 171, 172, 174, 178, 182, 196, 197, 199

Cardo, Amanda, 130, 131–34, 136–42, 153, 197
Condon, Frankie, x, 16, 197
class participation, 24, 57, 72–75, 78, 83, 84, 198
cliché, 62, 72, 108, 109, 163, 183
close-read, 114, 118, 119, 121, 128, 175
comet(s), 8, 188
composure, 6, 192
consciousness, 79, 94, 96, 128, 144, 154–56, 158, 190, 197
contradiction, 17, 36, 46, 53, 57, 58, 62, 65, 68, 77, 100, 113, 118, 119, 123, 127, 139, 140, 152, 154, 168, 174, 185–88

course description, 24, 94, 95, 96, 97, 100, 154
critical pedagogy, 10, 97, 201

Danielle (student), 11, 14, 62, 114, 122, 146, 156, 157, 170, 171, 173
Dejka, Andrew, 72, 73, 76–79, 81, 82, 84, 197
decentering, 66, 84, 142, 143
desire, 4, 22, 35, 42, 43, 46, 51, 52, 54, 57, 63, 65, 82, 86, 94, 96, 119, 122, 139, 182, 198, 199
dolphin, 8, 25, 89, 90, 93, 95, 95, 98, 100, 101, 103, 112, 122, 178

embodiment, 18, 19, 23, 35, 36, 65, 66, 100, 195, 201
Enoch, Jessica, x, 188, 189, 197
epistemology, 9, 10, 128, 129, 132, 136, 160

Fagan, Kelsey, 20, 21, 120, 197
failure, vii, 6, 23, 24, 37, 48, 56–86, 104, 127, 148, 160, 165, 178, 198, 200
feminism/feminist, 4, 10, 15, 33, 50, 52, 53, 68, 112, 147, 165, 183, 184, 185, 197, 199, 200, 201
feminist pedagogy, 165, 185
Foucault, Michel, 9, 46, 80, 102, 197, 198

Gadamer, Hans-Georg, 134, 135, 142, 155, 156, 197, 199
Garber, Linda, 4, 5, 197
gaze, 27, 31, 42, 76, 120
gender terrorist, 37, 38
genderqueer, 43, 61, 83, 108
Gibson, Michelle, 42, 67, 143, 195, 197

Graff, Gerald, 150, 151, 198
Griffin, Susan, x, 56, 198

habits of mind, 89–94, 98–100, 102–4, 109, 113, 119–21, 143
Halberstam, Jack, 7, 8, 25, 33, 57, 58, 77, 82, 142, 181–83, 188, 189, 198
Halperin, David, 44–46, 198
Hart, Johnnie, 9, 11–14, 25, 62, 114, 145, 146, 157, 158, 160, 164, 170–73, 198
Hayles, N. Katherine, 35, 36, 198
horror, 31, 38, 39, 44, 49, 199

inquiry, 5, 7, 10, 14–16, 25, 43, 48, 56, 67, 83, 88, 101, 106, 119, 126, 139, 200
instructor's statement, 24, 94, 97, 98, 100, 154
interpretation, viii, 9, 20, 25, 53, 80, 89, 99, 105, 123, 125, 127, 130, 131, 133, 132, 136, 140, 141, 144, 145, 148, 161, 199
interrogation, 9, 10, 162
intersex, 44, 73, 80

Jones, Raymond, 75, 125, 191, 198

Kameen, Paul, x, 16, 198
Kopelson, Karen, 5, 40, 48, 80, 132, 179, 180, 198
Kristeva, Julia, 40, 42–44, 46, 199

labor, 104
legibility, 131
LGBTQ, 5, 58, 99, 101
liquid, viii, 9, 25, 125–66
Lloyd, Moya, 112, 113, 198
loon, vii, 3, 8, 17, 23, 24, 27–55, 62

Lorde, Audre, 77, 78, 102, 104, 108, 110, 189, 199
Luhmann, Susanne, 86, 115, 116, 199

Malinowitz, Harriet, 4, 61, 163, 199
masculinity/masculine, 7, 17, 25, 27, 28, 29, 30–34, 38, 40–44, 48, 54, 57, 108, 138, 158, 181, 196, 198, 202
McIntosh, Peggy, 47, 102, 104, 108–10, 128, 199
melancholy, 31, 46–48, 197
Miller, Richard, x, 16, 199
monarch butterfly, 8, 168
movement, 15, 17, 19, 25, 46, 58, 62, 93, 101, 108, 111–13, 122, 123, 126, 129, 134, 136, 143, 152, 154, 155, 172, 173, 178–80
multidisciplinarity, 189
multimodal, 167, 199
muscle, 30, 58, 62, 63, 65, 68, 180

names/naming, 9, 17, 25, 54, 58, 60–63, 66, 67, 92, 100, 118, 128, 153
narrative(s), 8, 9, 11–16, 48, 55, 56, 68, 83, 178, 183, 185, 188, 195, 197, 200, 201
noise, 36, 85
normativity, 6, 34, 77, 80, 108, 120, 121, 132, 169, 178

ontology, 29, 115
orientation, vii, 4, 24, 86–124, 179, 180, 195, 199

Palmeri, Jason, 167, 181, 199
passing, 3, 20, 39, 93
performative, 5, 23, 31, 40, 48, 54, 80, 109

Poli, Jessica, 175–79, 200
possibility, 6, 11–13, 24, 25, 37, 38, 41, 45, 47, 52, 63, 71–73, 81, 84, 95, 96, 102, 105, 118, 131–33, 137, 140, 153, 154, 165, 166, 172, 179, 181, 191, 192
power, 4, 10, 12, 14, 33, 36, 42, 44, 45, 56, 73–75, 77, 78, 80, 91, 97, 98, 102, 119, 124, 136, 147, 159, 168, 178, 182, 185, 199

queer composition, 25, 57, 101, 165–93, 195
queer literacy, 25, 132, 137, 141,
queer methodologies, 7, 23, 101, 122, 123, 174, 179, 187
queer pedagogy, 4–7, 10, 14, 15, 36, 40, 16, 56, 57, 66, 86, 87, 93, 97, 106, 107, 115, 122, 134, 140, 141, 142, 147, 160, 165, 166, 168, 179, 181, 186, 192, 196, 199, 200, 202
queer studies, 4, 9, 83, 87, 100, 196, 198
queer texts, 3, 5, 6, 11, 14, 99, 101, 192,
queer theory, 5, 6, 7, 12–15, 22, 36, 40, 58, 66, 67, 80, 83, 87, 100–103, 107, 115, 118, 123, 124, 127, 130, 132, 134, 139, 143, 144, 150, 152, 153, 165, 166, 168, 174, 178–80, 182, 186, 189, 190, 195, 197, 199, 200

reading, 5, 9, 11, 14, 17, 10, 21, 30, 33, 38, 41, 45, 48, 50–54, 57, 78, 81, 82, 88, 89, 94, 95, 96, 99, 100, 101, 103–16, 118–21, 123–31, 133, 135, 140, 141, 143–46, 149–56, 158–60, 162,

163, 165, 169, 174, 176, 178, 182, 186, 191, 196, 200, 201
representation, 7, 13, 19, 44, 67, 120, 143
revision, 64, 65, 103, 114, 116, 122, 143, 178, 187
Rhodes, Jacqueline, 3, 6, 7, 56, 57, 68, 86, 87, 143, 144, 180, 191, 192, 195, 199, 200
risk, x, 5, 14, 15, 30, 44, 47–49, 56, 78, 81, 91, 98, 135, 136, 158, 162, 163, 165, 180, 198, 199
Ritchie, Joy S., 56, 83, 185, 200, 201
Rose, Mike, x, 143, 200

Salvatori, Mariolina Rizzi, x, 29, 30, 86, 111, 114, 119, 145, 174, 200
scavenger, 7, 8, 180, 181–84, 186, 189, 190
Schellhorn, Mr. (teacher), 167, 168, 178, 180, 185, 190, 191, 193
Sedgwick, Eve Kosofsky, 9, 10, 80, 102, 111, 112, 153, 159, 192, 200, 201
Semenya, Caster, 44
silence, 24, 41, 56, 63, 73–82, 113, 198, 200, 201
Sirc, Geoffrey 181, 182, 201
Slevin, James, 144, 145, 179, 180, 201
s/m, 98
spectacle, 15, 16, 24
Stenberg, Shari J., ix, 68, 79, 80, 181, 201

structure, 10, 14, 24, 37, 87, 89, 94, 151, 167, 169–76, 178, 179, 181, 190
Sullivan, Mrs. (teacher), 11, 26, 191
syllabus, 36, 49, 73–75, 87, 92, 94, 97, 98, 100, 110

tai chi 19, 25, 126, 129, 131, 137, 148, 150
Talburt, Susan, 123, 199, 201
teaching queer, i, iii, 1, 4, 6–8, 23, 24, 56
thesis, 58, 60–63, 65, 185
Tobin, Lad, 70, 159, 201
transgender, 22, 44, 66, 112, 137, 188, 197, 198

values, 23, 67, 86, 88, 89, 97, 98, 104, 132, 148, 152, 154, 160, 176

Warner, Michael, 33, 102, 157, 158, 169–79, 201
water/watery, 9, 17, 25, 27, 30, 39, 50, 53, 55, 60, 95, 125, 131, 133, 156, 164, 166, 173
Winans, Amy E., 66, 106, 107, 168, 202
writing queer, 6, 8, 9, 24

Young, Vershawn Ashanti, x, 8, 33, 202

Zuccaro, Ms. (teacher), 96